Praise for *The Rite*

'Truth is stranger than fiction . . . and far more terrifying. Forget what Hollywood tells you about demonic possession and exorcism, *The Rite* will open your eyes to the awesome truth. I've been investigating paranormal events for some time, but this book taught me much that I didn't know about the timeless battle for the human soul waged between the forces of good and evil. Fascinating, inspiring and scary, a great read' John Kachuba, author of *Ghosthunters: On the Trail of Mediums, Dowsers, Spirit Seekers and Other Investigators of America's Paranormal World*

'Matt Baglio's book is a wake-up call. It smashes the many myths created by Hollywood movies and other amateurs on the subject about exorcism and the role of the exorcist in the Catholic Church' Fr. Basil Cole, OP, professor of moral and spiritual theology of the Pontifical Faculty at the Dominican House of Studies, Washington DC

'*The Rite* is in my opinion one of the best books ever written on the topic of exorcism. I have read very few books that give a description as appropriate, as precise or as detailed, and the author's deep knowledge of the subject makes it a true instrument of knowledge – useful for many people' Fr. José Antonio Fortea, author of *Interview with an Exorcist: An Insider's Look at the Devil, Demonic Possession and the Path to Deliverance*

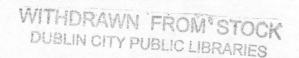

THE RITE

THE MAKING OF A MODERN EXORCIST

MATT BAGLIO

SIMON &
SCHUSTER

London · New York · Sydney · Toronto

A CBS COMPANY

First published in Great Britain by Simon & Schuster UK Ltd, 2009
A CBS COMPANY

1 3 5 7 9 10 8 6 4 2

Simon & Schuster UK Ltd
1st Floor
222 Gray's Inn Road
London
WC1X 8HB

www.simonandschuster.co.uk

Simon & Schuster Australia
Sydney

A CIP catalogue for this book
is available from the British Library.

ISBN: 978-1-84737-331-1

Typeset by M Rules
Printed in the UK by CPI Mackays, Chatham ME5 8TD

For Sara and Noah

CONTENTS

PROLOGUE

And war broke out in heaven; Michael and his angels fought against the dragon. The dragon and his angels fought back, but they were defeated, and there was no longer any place for them in heaven. The great dragon was thrown down, that ancient serpent, who is called the Devil and Satan, the deceiver of the whole world – he was thrown down to the earth, and his angels were thrown out with him.

Revelations 12: 7–9

The 35-year-old woman lay on a padded folding massage table, her arms and legs held by two men.[1] She wore a black Puma sweat suit and her dark brown hair was pulled back tightly into a ponytail. While not heavy, she was a little on the stocky side and, as she grunted and struggled, the men fought to hold on. Nearby, another man and woman hovered ready to intervene. The exorcist stood a few feet away, a small crucifix in one hand and a silver canister filled with holy water in the other. Surveying the scene, he had a decision to make. The exorcism had been going on for the better part of an hour and the strain was beginning to show on everyone. Should he continue?

Suddenly the woman's head turned, her eyes fixating on a spot near the far wall. 'No!' the demon said in a deep guttural voice coming from deep within her. 'The one in black is here, the jinx!'

The exorcist felt a momentary ray of hope, knowing from past exorcisms that this was the demon's code to describe Saint Gemma Galgani.[2]

'And the little white one from Albania!' the demon roared.

'Mother Teresa of Calcutta?' the exorcist asked.

The demon let fly a string of blasphemies in a rage, then his voice took on a mocking childlike tone. 'Oh look at them! They are hugging and greeting each other!' Then, back to a deep guttural rasp, 'Disgusting! Disgusting!'

To the woman lying on the table, the two figures appeared as if in a dream. Saint Gemma was dressed in her traditional black, and looked very much as she had in her twenties. Oddly, Mother Teresa also looked very young – perhaps only twenty-five.

The exorcist glanced over his shoulder to where the woman was staring and saw nothing but the blank wall. 'Let us thank Saint Gemma Galgani and Mother Teresa for being here with us today,' he said.

'No, him too. Send him away, send him away!' the demon wailed.

Unsure of who had just arrived, the exorcist added, 'I say thank you that he is here.'

Then suddenly the woman sat bolt upright, her arms extended in front of her as if she had been yanked up by some unseen force. 'Leave me alone!' the demon screamed even as the woman flailed to break free from the invisible grasp. The two men went to pull her back down but the exorcist motioned for them to stop. 'Let's see who just came. In the name of Jesus and the Immaculate Virgin, who is this person?'

'Nooooooo!' the guttural, ferocious voice growled. 'Totus tuu-uuuus!'

The exorcist smiled inwardly, recognizing the Latin motto. 'Thank you, Holy Father John Paul II, for coming to help our sister,' he said.

'No, no!' the demon shrieked. 'Damn you! Get away from me!'

Again, in her dream-like state, the woman watched Pope John Paul II, who seemed no older than thirty and was dressed all in white, bless her forehead three times.

Wanting to take advantage of the apparent reinforcements, the exorcist pressed on. 'Repeat after me: Eternal Father, you are my Creator and I adore you,' he said to the demon.

'Up yours!' the voice responded.

'Eternal Father, you are my Creator and I adore you,' the exorcist insisted.

'A bomb is going to explode if I say it!' the demon shouted.

'I order you, in the name of the Immaculate Virgin Mary and in the name of Jesus Christ, to repeat those words,' the priest commanded again.

All at once, the woman felt awash in an incredible feeling of love as the veiled figure of Mary appeared before her, wrapped in a gold and white veil that covered half her face. Watching in amazement as the figure approached, the woman was even more surprised to see that Mary was gazing at her tearfully.

As the exorcist watched, the demon once again went into a fit. 'No, no, no, don't cry!' he screamed, and the woman's body convulsed.

Then for an instant the woman snapped out of the trance, saying, 'A tear from Mary is all it took,' before falling back into the state.

The exorcist was elated to know that Mary was present and helping. He instantly launched into a Hail Mary. Everyone in the room joined in, even the woman on the table. Yet somehow the exorcist knew it wasn't over. The demon must be hiding to allow her to recite the prayer, he thought. 'Say after me: Eternal Father, you are my Creator and I adore you,' he said to the demon.

The woman thrashed and screamed. 'No!' the demon barked. 'I'm not going to say it! I must not say it! I can't. It is against everything.'

The exorcist could feel that the demon was weakening. He

asked everyone in the room to kneel. 'Eternal Father, you are my Creator and I adore you,' he intoned, while everyone repeated.

The woman, sensing the torment of the demon, saw all the saints in the room respond as well.

'No, no, even those other ones kneeled down – the white one, the black one, and the little white one,' the demon said. Then the exorcist noticed that the demon's voice changed slightly to a tone of forced reverence when he added, 'Her, her [Mary] – she kneeled down as well.'

'This must be it,' the exorcist thought. The demon is going to break. 'In the name of Jesus Christ I order you to repeat the phrase.'

The woman struggled, but slowly a croaking noise came from her throat. 'Eee . . t . . er . . nal . . . Fa . . . ther . . . I must a . . . dd . . . ooo . . r . . . yo . . u.'

Ecstatic, but realizing it still was not over yet, the exorcist made the demon repeat the phrase two more times. When the demon had finished, the exorcist recited the conclusion of the Eucharistic prayer: 'Through him, with him, in him, in the unity of the Holy Spirit, all glory and honor is yours, Almighty Father, for ever and ever.'

'This humiliation was given for the glory of God not because you commanded it but because God commanded it. You are damned,' the demon said, addressing the exorcist.

The exorcist did not falter. 'Che Dio sia benedetto [God be praised],' he continued.

'I go away but you are going to be damned for life,' the demon sneered. 'You and your companions, you are going to be perse-cuted for life!'

INTRODUCTION

Among her sacramentals, the Catholic Church, in obedience to the Lord's Prayer, already in ancient times mercifully provided that through pious prayers her people may ask God to liberate the faithful from all dangers and especially from the snares of the Devil. In a truly unique way, exorcists were established in the Church who, in imitation of Christ, could cure those obsessed by the Evil One, even by commanding demons in the name of God, so that they might depart, lest for whatever reason they do further harm to human creatures.

Decree from the Congregation for Divine Worship
of the Faith, 22 November 1998

When people hear the word exorcism, many think of images made popular by Hollywood films – girls writhing in torment, their bodies contorting in impossible ways as they launch a continuous stream of pea-soup-green projectile vomit. In truth, such theatrics, as well as those in the woman's exorcism that took place in January 2007, in Rome, Italy, are quite rare. Instead, exorcisms can be rather mundane, almost like going to the dentist – complete with a stint in the waiting room and a card to remind the recipient of his or her next appointment. The reality is that few people realize what goes on during an exorcism, and that is true for Catholic priests as well, many of whom would just as soon forget that exorcism exists at all.

The word exorcism itself is an ecclesiastical term that comes from the Greek *exorkizo*, meaning 'to bind with an oath', or to demand insistently. During an exorcism, a demon is commanded in the name of God to stop his activity within a particular person or place. As understood by the Catholic Church, an exorcism is an official rite carried out by a priest who has been authorized to do so by his bishop. In ancient times, exorcism was an important way for early Christians to win converts and prove the veracity of the faith. The power itself comes from Jesus, who performed numerous exorcisms, as detailed in the New Testament, later instructing his disciples to do the same.

In light of the tremendous advances in modern medicine – including a more sophisticated understanding of neurological and psychological illnesses, the advent of psychoanalysis, and similar advantages – the rite of exorcism has become an embarrassment to many within the Church, who see it as a superstitious relic from the days when illnesses like epilepsy and schizophrenia were considered 'devils' to be cast out.

Much of this misunderstanding comes from the nature of exorcism itself, as well as from the Devil's attributes that have more foundation in folklore than in theology. A beast with horns and half a goat's body ravaging innocent virgins in the dead of night? Soul-leaching shape-shifting she-demons on the prowl for their next victim? Without any courses on demonology to educate seminarians, it's no mystery as to why priests have turned away from exorcism in large numbers.

At the core of the issue lies the problem of evil. Is it a physical reality, a fallen angel called Satan (as says the *Catechism of the Catholic Church*, a small but dense book of about 900 pages),[1] or is it a lack of good in something, an inability to live up to the designs of the benevolent Creator?

Many priests, not wanting to turn their backs on the rich history associated with their faith, while at the same time wanting to embrace the modern view of reality in which the Devil is seen as a metaphor, would like to have it both ways. Others believe in the traditional teachings, but prefer not to talk about it. On the extreme end, some priests simply deny the Devil's existence.

Ironically, while many priests and bishops seemed bent on scepticism, the general public has become enamoured with the occult, gravitating to new religions such as Wicca. According to an American Religious Identity Survey, Wicca grew in America from 8,000 members in 1990 to over 134,000 in 2001 (by 2006 that number was said to have risen to 800,000).[2] The sales of occult and New Age books have skyrocketed,[3] as has the number of people who believe in angels and demons (according to a 2004 Gallup poll more than 70 per cent of Americans said they believe in the Devil). All this coincides with an explosion in the numbers of people who say they are afflicted by evil spirits. According to the Association of Catholic Psychiatrists and Psychologists,[4] in Italy alone more than 500,000 people see an exorcist annually.

For many years, a small but vocal group of overworked exorcists in Italy, led by Father Gabriele Amorth, has tried to get the Church to take more seriously the increasing numbers of people who claim to be possessed. First, they said, more exorcists need to be appointed. However, the Church would have to ensure that any new exorcists be properly trained. Advocates such as Father Amorth assert that, in the past, too many exorcists were appointed in name only. In addition, some of these 'untrained' exorcists gave the rite of exorcism a bad name by abusing their authority. One of the most egregious took place in 2005, when a Romanian nun who'd been gagged and bound to a crucifix in a room at her convent was found dead; the priest who had been performing the exorcism was charged with murder.[5]

Hoping to rectify the situation, in the autumn of 2004, the Congregation for the Doctrine of the Faith sent a letter to the various Catholic dioceses around the world, starting with those in America, asking each bishop to appoint an official exorcist.

At the same time, a Vatican-affiliated university in Rome began putting together a groundbreaking course entitled

'Exorcism and the Prayer of Liberation' with the intention of educating a new cadre of exorcists about the official teachings of the Church on the Devil and exorcism.

A remarkable American priest answered this call and travelled to Rome in the summer of 2005 to be trained as an exorcist. Over the span of nine months he delved deeply into a world he never knew existed, completing the course and participating in over eighty exorcisms along with a senior Italian exorcist. As a result, his view of the world – and his place in it – changed dramatically, and he later returned to the US, determined to use his new awareness of evil and its manifest presence to help people in their everyday lives.

CHAPTER ONE

ROME

*We should try to be so closely united to our Lord that we repro-
duce his life in our own, that our thoughts and words and actions
should proclaim his teaching, so that he reigns in us, lives in us.*

Charles de Foucauld

When Father Gary Thomas stepped out on to Via delle Fornaci
at 7.45 on the morning of 13 October 2005, the road was already
clogged with traffic. A long line of cars and buses inched towards
the intersection of Via di Porta Cavalleggeri, funnelled into the
mouth of the tunnel by the canyon of four- and five-storey
buildings that run along the base of the Gianicolo, one of Rome's
many hills. A traffic policeman, festooned with epaulettes like an
airline pilot, was doing his best to maintain order, waving cars
through and screeching at the more aggressive motorists with his
whistle. When the light turned green, drivers wasted no time
laying into their horns.

On either side of the road, morning commuters hurried along
in the direction of the Vatican, the acrid smell of cigarette
smoke trailing behind them like contrails. Occasionally
commuters would duck into a bar for their morning cappuccinos,

and the roar of an espresso machine spilled out on to the sidewalk.

Standing on the corner, caught up in the chaos, Father Gary took a second to admire the scene as if it were some exotic postcard come to life. This was nothing like any rush hour he had experienced back home in San Francisco. The city, the cars, the people – all seemed to harmonize like some massive orchestra.

Even though he was wearing his black clerics, he blended in seamlessly with the crowds. Rome is, after all, full of priests. According to some estimates, the city has more than 15,000 priests walking its narrow streets, and that doesn't even include the several thousand seminarians who also wear the Roman collar and black garb.[1] In addition, with all the chapels, monasteries, convents and hundreds of churches, not to mention the Vatican itself, it was no wonder that Father Gary dubbed the city the 'aorta of Christianity'.

As if he needed an additional reminder, the massive *palazzo* that houses the Congregation for the Doctrine of the Faith, the all-important gatekeeper of Church doctrine, stood directly across the street. And beyond that, the distant sunlit cupola of St Peter's Basilica floated above the tops of the buildings like an apparition. The sight of it – Father Gary could also see it out of his bedroom window – never failed to move him. In Rome he felt he was part of something bigger than himself, bigger than just the petty day-to-day concerns that sometimes overwhelm a parish priest. 'When you are a pastor, you have to wear nine hats,' he said later, with a hint of regret. 'It's not that it's all administration, but it does tend to take you away from the things that are more important, such as focusing on people's prayer life.'

At the age of fifty-two he had recently left his post at Saint Nicholas parish in Los Altos, California, where he had served for the last fifteen years, twelve of them as pastor. While he'd enjoyed the work at Saint Nicholas immensely and had made innumerable friends, the gruelling daily grind of being pastor had taken its toll. He had not only helped completely to refurbish several buildings at the parish school; he'd also raised millions of dollars to turn the old rectory into a state-of-the-art community centre that pleased parishioners so much they had named it after him.

With his medium height and build, thinning but neatly trimmed brown hair and gold, circular wire-framed glasses, Father Gary had the unassuming appearance of a person content to put others at ease. While not physically imposing, he exuded the quiet confidence of a man who loves his job and knows he is very good at it.

Ordained in 1983, he had been a priest for twenty-two years, and over that time he had seen – and been through – a great deal. In 1997 he had nearly died in a terrible accident. While hiking with a friend in the foothills of Yosemite, he'd fallen off a sixty-foot cliff on to river rock, miraculously surviving, though during his painful two-year recovery he sometimes wished he hadn't.

Since the rules of his diocese require that priests be relocated after fifteen years of service, Father Gary took advantage of the opportunity to take a well-deserved sabbatical. Rome, with its numerous seminaries and prestigious universities, presents visiting priests with a unique opportunity. For many, studying at pontifical universities such as the Gregorian, where fourteen previous popes and twenty saints have studied, is an intensely sought-after privilege. Most of these students are full-time, either getting their licence (equivalent to a master's degree) or doctorate. A few priests, however, are sent by their diocese for some reason, or, like Father Gary, are taking a sabbatical year to do further study. One programme that catered to this latter group was the Institute for Continuing Theological Education at the North American College (NAC), the largest American seminary on foreign soil. Started in the 1970s as a way to implement some of the calls by the Second Vatican Council for priestly renewal, the institute began offering a three-month 'sabbatical' programme for priests who wanted to keep pace with current trends within the Church. At the same time, participants got a chance to enjoy Rome and to meet fellow priests from around the world.

Back in April, Father Gary had signed up to attend the continuing education programme from September to November, after which he was going to take a couple of classes on spirituality at the Angelicum, the pontifical university run by the Dominicans across town.

When he'd first arrived in the city in August 2005, he'd found Rome intimidating. Not only was there the language barrier (he didn't speak Italian), but the city, with its myriad tiny streets, proved extremely difficult to navigate. Now, after living in Rome for two months, he could laugh at himself for his early trepidation. He knew the bus system as well as any local and could go just about anywhere he wanted.

In addition to his time at the NAC and in other classes, Father Gary had another important assignment: his bishop requested that he take a specific course to become an exorcist. In fact, that morning he was on his way to the first session. Concerned about being late, he turned up Via de Gasperi and quickened his pace.

In the winter of 2005, as Father Gary was winding down his time at St Nicholas, exorcism had been the last thing on his mind. At his Jesus Caritas monthly priest support group,[2] he was surprised when his good friend Father Kevin Joyce mentioned that the Vatican had sent a letter to every diocese in the United States, asking that an exorcist be appointed, and that the bishop had pegged Father Kevin for the post.

Tall, lean, and studious-looking, Father Kevin personified the image of a thoughtful, composed priest. Yet perhaps most striking was his youth and vigour: despite being fifty-seven, he appeared easily fifteen years younger. Father Gary had known Father Kevin for nearly twenty years and with his background (he had a doctorate in religious education with a speciality in spirituality) he seemed like the perfect choice to become an exorcist. But Father Kevin explained that he intended to decline the appointment. He had recently started the diocese's spirituality centre and wouldn't have time to cope with both.

The fact that the diocese was planning to appoint an exorcist caught Father Gary off guard. The subject of evil spirits and demonic possession didn't often come up in his parish. In the previous year, he'd only spoken about the Devil twice, once prompting a parishioner to ask him not to do it again for fear of frightening his kids. It wasn't a popular topic with priests in general.

While not exactly ambivalent about the Devil, Father Gary hadn't spent that much time thinking about him either. He knew there was a big difference between talking about the concept of evil behaviour and the 'person' of evil. Sometimes good people did evil things, he was well aware; but whether or not they were caused directly by the Devil he couldn't say. In thinking back to the little he had learned about exorcism in the seminary, he remembered that the scriptural basis for demonic possession was fairly well established. Beyond that, his mind drew a blank. In all his time as a priest, he hadn't heard of a single case of demonic possession or of an exorcism being performed. Now, however, he found himself wondering about this ancient and arcane rite. If called upon, would he be willing to do something like that?

The notion of standing in a room and squaring off against the Devil didn't frighten him because he might see bizarre or offensive things. Before becoming a priest he had worked in the funeral business from the age of fourteen. In fact, he was a licensed embalmer. Over the years he had seen some pretty horrible things, including disfigured bodies, some burned beyond recognition. He knew he had the stomach for just about anything. Helping people was one of the main reasons he had decided to become a priest. And wasn't that what Jesus was doing when he cast out evil spirits and healed the sick?

After submitting his name in place of Father Kevin's, Father Gary eventually got an answer about his appointment when he ran into his bishop at a convocation of priests a month later. The bishop was delighted by the news that Father Gary was willing to assume the role. The bishop told him that in the past twenty-four years only two investigations of possible demonic possession had been conducted in the whole diocese of San Jose. Smiling, the bishop added in his Irish brogue, 'And I hope I won't have to be calling on you too much either.'

As the conversation wound down, Father Gary confessed his concern about getting some kind of formal training. Then the bishop filled him in about the exorcism course in Rome. 'It should work out perfectly with your sabbatical,' he said.

Unlike in the American Catholic Church, where exorcism is talked about only in hushed tones, exorcism is more accepted in Italy. In 1986, Pope John Paul II gave a series of talks in which he reminded the faithful not to forget about the dangers posed by the Devil, and that one of these was the real possibility of 'bodily possession'. And as recently as 14 September 2005, Pope Benedict XVI hosted a large group of exorcists at the Vatican and encouraged them to continue their work 'in the service of the Church'.

Today, Italy has gone through an exorcism boom. Not only are the numbers of officially appointed exorcists on the rise (reported to be somewhere between 350–400) but they also created their own guild-like association – the International Association of Exorcists – in 1992. In addition, thanks in large part to a recent spate of violent crimes linked to satanic cults, the police, in conjunction with the Church, created a special squad in 2006, called the *Squadra anti sette* (Anti-Sect Squad) dubbed SAS for short, tasked with investigating the phenomena.

Interest in exorcism had been steadily growing in Italy since 1998, when the exorcism ritual, originally set down in the 1614 *Roman Ritual*, was finally updated, as per the requirements of the

Second Vatican Council of 1962–5, which called for each of the Church's rituals to be updated. (Incidentally, the ritual for exorcism was the last of these.) Journalists swarmed, looking for a story, and Father Gabriele Amorth didn't disappoint. The official exorcist of Rome and best-selling author, Father Amorth was already a well-known television personality in Italy and abroad.[3] In books and interviews he condemned a wide range of things as being Satanic – including the Harry Potter books – while drawing attention to what he claimed was the growing power that the Devil wielded in a secular world, which increasingly turned to the occult for answers.[4]

Even worse, in Father Amorth's eyes, was the plight of the exorcist. In an interview published in the Catholic magazine *30 Days* in 2001, he said, 'Our brother priests who are charged with this delicate task are treated as though they are crazy, as fanatics. Generally speaking they are scarcely even tolerated by the bishops who have appointed them.' Time and time again he chastised bishops and priests alike for their ignorance. 'For three centuries, the Latin Church has almost entirely abandoned the ministry of exorcism,' he said. And while the problem might be bad in certain parts of Italy, he believed it to be downright appalling elsewhere. 'There are countries in which there is not a single exorcist, for example Germany, Switzerland, Spain and Portugal.' Other countries, such as France, he claimed, had appointed exorcists who didn't even believe in exorcism.[5]

On 18 May 2001, the Italian bishops' conference, meeting in plenary assembly in the Vatican, issued an official statement: 'We are witnessing a rebirth of divinations, fortunetelling, witchcraft and black magic, often combined with a superstitious use of religion. In certain environments, superstition and magic can coexist with scientific and technological progress, inasmuch as science and technology cannot give answers to the ultimate problems of life.'

According to the Associazione Comunità Papa Giovanni

XXIII (Pope John XXIII Community Association) about 25 per cent of Italians, or about 14 million, are involved in some way or another in the occult.[6] In the south of Italy, for instance, certain groups still believe in tarantism – that a person can be possessed by the bite of a spider – while 'card-readers' congest the late-night cable channels hawking their prophetic wares and 'lucky' amulets.[7] This is not limited to Italy. In 1996, for instance, France's version of the HM Revenue & Customs disclosed that, during the previous year, 50,000 tax-paying citizens had declared their occupation as healer, medium or other such practitioner in the occult-related trades. At the time, there were only 36,000 Catholic priests in the entire country.[8]

However, the Church was most concerned about estimates (some would say exaggerated) that as many as 8,000 satanic sects with more than 600,000 members exist within Italy.[9]

The course 'Exorcism and Prayers of Liberation' was the brain child of Doctor Giuseppe Ferrari, the National Secretary of the Gruppo di Ricerca e Informazione Socio-Religiosa (Group for Research and Socio-Religious Information, or GRIS), a Catholic organization located in Bologna, Italy, that deals with cults and other new religions.

According to Doctor Ferrari, the idea came about in 2003 when he met with a priest from the diocese of Imola who told him that a growing number of his fellow clerics were being inundated by parishioners suffering from problems related to the occult: either they wanted to quit and couldn't, or they in some way felt afflicted by demonic forces. In many cases the priests felt so inadequate they simply sent the people away.

In looking into the Church's approach to appointing and training exorcists, Doctor Ferrari saw how haphazard it was, with each exorcist left to his own devices.[10] The solution was obvious: there needed to be some kind of university-level course that would train exorcists.

Doctor Ferrari led a group of various friends and colleagues, including a few theology professors, doctors and an exorcist, who came up with a working syllabus. Students would be introduced to a wide variety of historical, theological, sociological, and medical topics, in order to go beyond the superficial and sensationalist aspect of exorcism. The aim was simple: give priests the knowledge they need to discern when and where Satan is active. And give the few who would then go on to become exorcists (such as Father Gary) the knowledge necessary to perform their ministry.

But where to teach it? It was then that Doctor Ferrari got in touch with the rector at the Ateneo Pontificio Regina Apostolorum, Father Paolo Scarafoni, and the rest of the pieces fell into place.

Inaugurated in 2000, the sleek and modern Regina Apostolorum campus, with its large glass windows and straight lines, is a huge contrast to the old-world ambience of downtown Rome. Located on a hill just outside the city, the manicured pathways and sprawling grounds could easily be confused for the headquarters of a software company in Father Gary's native Silicone Valley – if it weren't for the groups of priests walking to and fro in their black cassocks. Run by the conservative Legionaries of Christ, an organization that some have likened to Opus Dei, the university's curriculum is decidedly right of centre, following the strict teachings of the Church hierarchy on a variety of issues, including stem-cell research.[11]

The course was being taught in a large, state-of-the-art classroom. And if the modern exterior seemed an odd setting in which to study exorcism, the bright, futuristic interior felt even more bizarre. Indeed, lab-coated technicians would look more appropriate bustling about among the white-on-white walls and ceilings, and large windows and skylights, than Franciscans wearing brown robes, rope belts, and sandals.

Having opted to take a five-minute train ride from Stazione San Pietro rather than the arduous hour-long slog through

morning traffic on the bus, Father Gary made his way through
the grounds admiring the neatness and precision of the place.
Inside, his favourable impression only grew as he climbed the
marble stairs inside the brightly lit interior. By the time he
arrived for the first lecture, a large crowd had already gathered
outside the doors to the classroom, chatting amicably and looking over a stack of literature advertising the school, which had
been placed on a nearby table. It looked to him like a good
turnout, though he was surprised at the presence of the news
media. Several TV cameras had been set up at the back of the
classroom and along the far wall.

The first session of the course, launched in the winter/spring
of 2005, had created quite a stir. Captivated by the idea of a
university-sponsored course on something as arcane as exorcism
the media had showed up in force and the headlines didn't
disappoint: 'Exorcists go back to school'; 'Priests get refresher
course on exorcisms'. The publicity actually served the organizers well, getting the message out that the Church was no longer
ashamed of exorcism.

As a result of this success, the school decided to run the course
again in the autumn and winter of 2005 and 2006, with only
some minor changes. All the professors from the original course
would be back, but this time lessons would be available via video
conference to satellite locations in Bologna, Modena and a few
other cities. For the last class, several prominent exorcists were
going to be invited to share their experiences and answer questions. And this time, rather than being limited to priests, the
course had been opened to professionals such as psychologists
and doctors who might, for example, want to hear how to dis-
tinguish between mental illness and possession.

When Father Gary had heard about the course from his
bishop, he got in touch with a few Legionaries in his diocese to
ask if there was someone he could talk to about it. They in turn
gave him the name of a priest who was on the faculty at the
university. A few weeks before he left California, Father Gary

called the priest and was able to learn a little bit about what to expect.

Though the course was scheduled to run for four months, from October to February, the novice exorcists would be meeting only one day a week – on Thursday morning from 8.30 to 12.30 – for a total of ten classes. Five sessions would run from mid-October to late November, and the second half of the course from January to 9 February. Perhaps the most important thing he found out was that the course was going to be offered only in Italian. Disappointed at first, he'd been reassured that, since priests would be coming from all over the world, the school would provide him with a translator.

Now, however, when he approached a course organizer and enquired about the translator, he was told in an almost offhand way that there wasn't going to be one. Not today or, for that matter, next week either. How was he supposed to learn anything if he didn't understand the language?

Dejected, he wandered over to the rows of desks, as they were quickly filling up. The room was divided into two sections, consisting of long tables, almost like the pews of a church. At the head of a classroom stood a raised dais – the low kind you see at conferences and symposiums – with a blank screen behind it. Next to the dais was a cross, and on the back wall, a neo-realist painting of Christ crowned with thorns. The row of tinted windows running the entire length of one wall looked down on to a large circular patch of grass, in the centre of which stood a solitary olive tree.

A few minutes later, the chatter in the room died down and a line of priests and officials filed in silently behind the dais. Led by the organizer, everyone stood and recited the Lord's Prayer and then a Hail Mary in Italian. It was time for the course to begin.

The first speaker was a bishop that Father Gary didn't recognize, though many in the room clearly did. His name was Andrea Gemma, who at age seventy-four was a well-regarded exorcist and one of very few bishops who actually performed exorcisms. He had also written a well-received book, *Io, Vescovo Esorcista* (I Am a Bishop Exorcist).

As Monsignor Gemma spoke, Father Gary tried to make sense of it, but couldn't. Here and there he'd catch a word that sounded familiar; but before he could figure out what it meant, the bishop had already moved on to something else. After a while he gave up, becoming absorbed instead by the spectacle of the news media, who roamed the aisles, shoving huge TV cameras right into people's faces. At the break he was tracked down by some English-language reporters and spent the remainder of the morning fielding questions about exorcism, telling them candidly he knew nothing about it.

Afterwards, as he sat on the train heading back into Rome, he was disappointed. He hadn't learned anything, and the circus-like nature of the first day made him wonder if this whole course would be a waste of time. It was an inauspicious start to his training.

CHAPTER TWO

THE CALLING

In our Catholic understanding, priestly ordination is a radical, total reordering of a man in the eyes of God and his Church, bringing about an identity of ontological 'reconfigurement' with Christ. This priestly identity is at the very core, the essence, of a man, affecting his being and, subsequently, his actions.

Monsignor Timothy Dolan, *Priests for the Third Millennium*

Back in September, once he'd overcome the initial shock of Rome, Father Gary had settled in quite easily to life at the NAC. Originally founded in 1859, the NAC moved to its present site atop the Gianicolo in 1953. The massive six-storey building – complete with its own church, auditorium, media room, library, classrooms, and dining hall – seems like a mini-oasis in the heart of Rome, set back from the noisy streets by a large security wall and gatehouse. Big enough to house 300 seminarians, with adjacent gardens and a million-dollar view of Saint Peter's Basilica, it was no wonder that Father Gary spent a few days exploring the interior.

It was also true that the priests in the sabbatical programme kept a pretty busy schedule, waking up for morning mass at 6.30, followed by breakfast and then classes until lunch, with more classes in the afternoon, then evening prayer and dinner. Afterwards Father Gary might have just enough time to run down to the library to check the sports scores on the Internet. A rabid sports fan, he followed the San Francisco 49ers as well as the Giants.

He got along well with a majority of the priests in the programme, most of whom were around his age and hailed from different parts of the US. As usual, a few were of the more 'anti-social' type, which always puzzled Father Gary, whose own concept of 'priestly identity' could best be described as 'being present to people,' but he didn't let the aloofness of others dampen his spirits.

One of the treats of staying at the NAC was the chance to rub shoulders with the seminarians who lived there. Like the priests in the sabbatical programme, the seminarians represented a broad cross-section of cities and towns across America. Father Gary called them 'kids' since most were in their mid-twenties. These were the bright young minds of the Church, priests who might one day become respected canonical lawyers or even bishops (some have nicknamed the NAC 'the school of bishops'). Father Gary got into the habit of going out to lunch twice a month with a group of these seminarians, sharing with them some of the hard lessons he'd learned over the years.

Even at a young age, Father Gary knew he wanted to be a priest. His mother, Anna May Thomas, remembers her son at the age of eleven, pretending to say mass in the kitchen of their South San Francisco home – holding aloft the round piece of Wonder Bread, his expression fixed in reverence as he said, 'This is my body, I give it up to you . . .' Gary's younger brother, David, who was six at the time, remembers how seriously his older brother went about it. Everything had to be perfect – the kitchen table covered with a white towel representing the altar, the Bible placed in just the right position, candles arranged appropriately. Gary pressed his little brother into being the altar boy. David's most important task was to make the hosts, which he'd been told had to be flat and perfectly round. Unsure how he was going to accomplish that, Gary let him in on one of his trade secrets: 'Use a cookie cutter,' he'd said.

Gary Thomas was born on 2 November 1953, in San Francisco, California to San Francisco natives. AnnaMay, whose maiden name was Mahoney, was raised in a blue-collar Irish Catholic family in the Mission District. Raymond Thomas, the son of Croatian immigrants with Eastern European Catholic ties, grew up in what is now called Potrero Hill.

When he was four, the family moved to South San Francisco, known as South City; the same year, Gary's younger brother David was born, followed by his sister JoAnn a year after. By all accounts, Father Gary had a pretty normal all-American childhood. He played Little League, mowed lawns, and attended All Souls Catholic grammar school, where he served as an altar boy until eighth grade.

Typically Gary's family would be the last ones to leave church, something Gary's dad often ribbed his mother about. For Gary, something about priests made him feel comfortable; he felt a 'positive familiarity' when he was around them. He also had literal familiarity; an uncle on his dad's side was a priest and a cousin on his mum's side was a Jesuit.

In the fifth and sixth grade, everyone had a picture on the bulletin board of what they wanted to be when they grew up and Gary had chosen a priest. When he told his parents about this, his dad just brushed it off, thinking his son would eventually grow out of it.

When Gary turned fourteen he took a job at the local Nauman Lincoln Roos mortuary. His work there consisted of a variety of tasks: washing and waxing the cars, cutting lawns, answering the phones, arranging flowers for the ceremony, even taking people into the chapel. He found the work immediately rewarding. He appreciated the religious component of funerals (he had attended many over the years as an altar boy). Not unlike the role of a priest, the funeral director's job was to comfort people – especially in the days following the death of a loved one, when survivors needed it most.

Around the time he was warming up to a career in the funeral business, he began to notice that the priesthood might not be everything he'd originally thought. In the late 1960s and 1970s, the Catholic Church went through tremendous upheaval in the wake of the Second Vatican Council, which advocated that the Church 'open its windows to the modern world'. As a result, many priests began losing the sense of connection they'd once felt to the traditions that had attracted them to the priesthood. This had a disastrous effect. Priests began leaving the Church in large numbers. The entire order of nuns that taught at Gary's high school, Junipero Serra, disbanded. In the midst of this general confusion, Gary became disillusioned about his chosen vocation.

In 1972 he enrolled in the University of San Francisco, a Jesuit-run school in the heart of San Francisco. He and a friend, Robert Eagen, would be among the first generation of kids from South City to go to college. Thinking he might one day run his own mortuary, Gary majored in business management.

As Gary matured, his responsibilities at the mortuary also changed. When he turned eighteen, he went on his first 'removal', mortuary parlance for picking up a dead body. Surprisingly, despite all the funerals he'd attended and his time at the mortuary, he had yet actually to see an undressed corpse. This particular body belonged to a patient who'd died at San Francisco General Hospital. To this day he remembers the sight of the corpse, just lying there bare on the metallic slab down in the morgue. It made him nauseous. Eventually, he got used to that, but the experience of performing removals never became routine – especially not when he had to drive to homes and remove a body while a roomful of grieving family members watched him.

Meanwhile, in the spring semester of his final year at USF, mutual friends set Gary up on a blind date with Lori Driscoll (now Lori Armstrong), a freshman nursing student at San Francisco State. The two immediately hit it off and began dating.

In 1975, Gary graduated from USF and entered a year-long programme at the San Francisco College of Mortuary Science in order to get his embalming licence.

While attending the mortuary school Gary made friends easily, even picking up a nickname. One course he took was on funeral services as practised by different religious denominations. Because of his long exposure to Catholic tradition, Gary was asked if he'd be willing to teach it to the other students. Before long, everyone began calling him 'Father Thomas'.

During mortuary school, he had discovered a sort of marvel to the human body as a system, especially the circulatory system, which embalmers used for draining the blood and inserting the embalming fluid. And rather than being sickened by what he witnessed, if anything the constant exposure to death helped to elevate his spiritual life. Often, while inserting the eye caps – small plastic devices with edged 'teeth' that keep the eyes closed – he would find himself staring into the lifeless eyes of a person. The first time he did this, he could tell there was something odd about them; a presence was missing. To Gary, this was clear proof that there is eternal life, that the soul leaves the body at death.

After completing the programme in only nine months, Gary went to work as an apprentice for a mortuary in South City and then later in Los Altos. During his time there, a feeling he thought was long gone began to gnaw at him; he started thinking seriously about the priesthood again. Despite having a rewarding career, he felt deep down that he was destined to do something different. He began asking himself a hard question: Was the life that he had mapped out for himself as a mortician the one that God intended? Rather than just comfort people through his job as a mortician, he longed to bring them into a closer relationship with Christ.

There was also his relationship with Lori to consider. In the end he knew he couldn't be fair to her if he continued to harbour doubts. A few weeks later, one September afternoon, he and Lori drove down to Vasona Lake Park in Los Gatos for a picnic. Lori had no idea what was coming, though perhaps she should have seen the writing on the wall. For the last five months Gary had been dropping hints about his interest in joining the priesthood. Lori's mind, however, had been focused elsewhere. In fact, she had expected to get a ring for her twenty-first birthday in August. At the park, the two wandered out to a shady spot on the grass, overlooking the lake. There they sat for a few minutes, watching the water, each of them looking at a very different world. In Gary's he was alone, a priest dedicating himself to a life of celibacy and service to God. In Lori's she was a mother and the wife of a funeral director. At some point Gary turned to her and those two worlds collided.

Lori was dumbfounded but realized that she could not stand in his way.

Gary entered Saint Patrick's Seminary in August 1979. One of the things he enjoyed most while attending was the opportunity to work in a parish, which allowed him a chance to interact with people. It also gave him a taste of his future life as a priest. Unlike some seminarians who preferred losing themselves in intellectual pursuits, Gary loved the fieldwork. He was a natural communicator, thriving on human interaction.

During his third year he began working fifteen hours a week at O'Connor Hospital in San Jose. He specifically requested to be moved to the 'death ward'. He had been around death most of his life, but his experience at O'Connor was something else entirely. Ever conscious of his priestly duty to alleviate suffering, he wanted to know what to say when people were at their most vulnerable and needed comfort. Unlike the priests he would later see shy away from suffering, Gary experienced these moments as the times when a priest was needed most. In the end, the experiences taught him that death can sometimes be a lonely experience and that often it is best to say nothing at all.

Gary was finally ordained in December 1983, during one of the worst storms to hit San Jose in twenty years. Caught out on the highway, Gary's parents braved the torrential rains and hurricane-force winds, thinking that there'd be nobody at the cathedral when they finally arrived. However, they were amazed to see the place packed, even though the storm had knocked out the power (which miraculously returned ten minutes before the ceremony was to start).

Initially Gary's dad had called him 'nuts' to want to enter the priesthood at such a tumultuous time, but as he and Anna May sat through the ceremony they realized their son had made the right decision.

Before entering the seminary, Gary had heard a talk by a Marian priest that summed up for him what it meant to recognize a vocation: 'Part of it was desire, part of it was excitement for a service with people, and part of it is an inability to respond to some kind of prompting in any other way other than going with what your heart tells you.' The words had a huge impact on Gary.

In the context of the Catholic Church, the priesthood is more akin to an identity than a job. It is not something that a priest can turn his back on or take a vacation from. As Pope John Paul II wrote, '[A] priest, by virtue of the consecration [. . .] is called to love selflessly, to put the needs of his "flock" before those of his own.'

Father Gary had seemingly internalized his desire to engage with people early in life. Now that he was a priest his dedication to this concept carried new meaning. In lieu of his ordination, he had a responsibility to embrace humanity in all its beauty and ugliness. He already knew he was comfortable with death; now he looked forward to helping his parishioners confront the trials of life.

CHAPTER THREE

GOING BACK TO SCHOOL

The Devil is present everywhere that evil things happen within the normal laws of nature. In anyone who says: I don't accept love, the love of my brothers and sisters, the love of God. And in many places, in all massacres, in every murder, in physical catastrophes, in every concentration camp, in all evil. Sometimes he shows himself, strangely, but also in cases of possession. But he's much more dangerous where he doesn't let himself be seen, where he can't be done away with through exorcism.

Father Pedro Barrajon, excerpt from interview in *Die Welt*,
2 December 2005

When Father Gary first heard about the exorcism course he'd wondered how such a class might be structured. Obviously the organizers had worked this out carefully and systematically.

After Doctor Ferrari contacted Father Scarafoni about the idea, they began collaborating on the syllabus and choosing the faculty. The goal was to scrape away all the misinformation so priests could re-learn what the Church actually taught on these matters. However, beyond just a straightforward course on the theology of demons, the organizers also wanted to ensure that potential exorcists would be well rounded and so had also decided to include lectures by a psychiatrist and a criminologist. Students would attend lectures on Satanism and youth culture, on how to discern spirits, on the powers of the Devil, as well as on the Church's teachings regarding angels and demons, taught by a Legionaire of Christ theologian. In addition exorcists would be called upon to discuss their ministry and share practical tips. Unfortunately, the International Association of Exorcists had refused Father Scarafoni's request to perform an exorcism live, in front of the students.

After the first day of the course, things had improved dramatically for Father Gary. As soon as he'd returned from the Regina Apostolorum, he'd searched the NAC for a priest who might be able to translate for him. Yet after a week he was unable to find anyone. Thinking that the second day might be a waste of time like the first, he none the less took the train out on the morning of 20 October, hoping that he would be proved wrong. As it turned out, he was. In the interim, the course organizers had scrambled and found a very competent Legionaire seminarian to translate for him, communicating via a headset that he and Father Gary would wear. While not perfect (sometimes the seminarian had to abridge in order to keep pace), the system worked pretty well.

Right off the bat, Father Gary was amazed to learn that exorcism was actually central to Jesus's gospel message. In fact, in the early Church, every Christian was thought to have had the power to perform exorcisms.

Back at the NAC, as he got to know some of the priests and seminarians better, he quickly realized that he wasn't the only one to have misconceptions about the real nature of exorcism. As he shared the fact that he was a fledgling exorcist, he predictably got mixed reactions. Some complimented him.

Another group responded with 'You shouldn't have told us. We're not supposed to know'. Perplexed by this, he got in touch with his bishop and asked if his appointment was indeed some kind of 'state secret'. The bishop said this was the first he'd heard about it. True to his open nature, Father Gary thought that the priests in the diocese ought to know, so they could come to him with questions. Members in the third group responded to his revelation simply by giving him a blank look and saying flatly, 'I don't believe in that.' And while it may seem strange that a group of Catholic priests did not believe in the Devil or exorcism, to Father Gary, who was ordained in the aftermath of the Second Vatican Council, it wasn't surprising at all.

Up until the 1960s, the Church as a body was relatively unified in its belief that the Devil was an evil spirit, a fallen angel created by God and granted with certain powers and free will.

In the early Church, the Devil was seen as the leader of a vast army of demons arrayed against 'the community of the faithful' as represented by the apostles and the other followers of Christ. Later Saint Augustine would come to refer to this conflict in terms of a struggle between 'two cities', created when the angels were put to a test by God.[1] As a result, Christians had to be on constant guard against this enemy who sought mankind's ruin as a way to get even with God. In this war, the chief weapon of the Devil was temptation; however, as stated in the New Testament, in certain circumstances he could attack an individual directly, taking control of the person's body. When that happened the only remedy was an exorcism.

Since Satan is a created being, and therefore subject to the power of God, an exorcism is valid only when it is performed in the name of God and by the authority of the Church, to which Christ gave that power. 'Then Jesus summoned his twelve disciples and gave them authority over unclean spirits, to cast them out, and to cure every disease and every sickness' (Matt. 10: 1).

The New Testament is full of stories of Jesus exorcizing
demons, which not only proved his divinity but also offered tan-
gible evidence that he had come to defeat the kingdom of Satan
and usher in a new one. 'But if it is by the Spirit of God that I
cast out demons, then the kingdom of God has come to you'
(Matt. 12: 28).[2]

Perhaps the most dramatic exorcism in the Gospels is the
case of the Gerasene demoniac (Mark 5: 1–20).[3] As Jesus steps
out of a boat near a town called Gadarenes he is immediately
accosted by a man out of the tombs on the hillside. The people
of the town have tried to restrain him with 'shackles and
chains' but he has 'wrenched them apart' during his ravings. He
is always shouting and bruising himself with stones. Upon
seeing Jesus he cries out, 'What have you to do with me, Jesus,
Son of the Most High God? I adjure you by God, do not torment me.' Jesus then commands the evil spirit to leave the man
and asks his name, receiving the answer 'Legion'. The evil spirit
then begs Jesus 'not to send them out of the country' but
instead to allow him to be sent into a herd of swine feeding
near by. Jesus grants permission and the herd of swine, 'num-
bering about two thousand' then 'rushes down the steep bank
and into the sea'.

While not the only exorcist of his day,[4] it was Jesus's method
that was special. Rather than using the complex rituals and
props of his contemporaries, he simply ordered the demon to
depart, sometimes even in the first person. In fact Jesus's exorcisms were considered so radical that he was accused by his
enemies of harnessing the power of demons (Mark 3: 20–30), a
charge Jesus answered by saying simply that it was impossible for
a demon to cast out a demon.[5]

These exorcisms had a powerful effect on Jesus's followers.
The evangelist Mark thought them so spectacular that the first
miracle he reports Jesus performing is an exorcism (Mark 1:
23–7).

In the years following Jesus's death, exorcism became an

important tool for believers to win converts and spread the faith. Almost all the Apostolic Fathers (the writers who came after the apostles) wrote about it. In his *Dialogue with Trypho*, Justin Martyr, one of the earliest Christian theologians, states: 'Any demon who is commanded in the name of the Son of God . . . will be overcome and defeated.'[6]

The importance of exorcism is clear in the early ceremonies of baptism, in which candidates underwent a series of formal exorcisms over a period of days while renouncing Satan (the renouncing of Satan is still used in baptisms today).[7]

Despite this early importance, a fierce debate erupted between 'liberal' and 'conservative' theologians in the 1960s about whether the figure of the Devil was ever meant to be taken literally. Since the Church goes about defining truth through two distinct elements – divine revelation (the Bible) and tradition, which are authentically interpreted by the Church's Magisterium, or teaching authority – both sides used a mixture of historical and biblical evidence to make their case.

For liberals, it was incomprehensible that the Church would continue to believe in such things as 'unseen spirits' or that the Devil was a 'person'[8] when advances in science and human reason had clearly shown most of the foundations for these beliefs to be obsolete.[9] 'We cannot use electric light and radio, or turn to modern medicine in cases of sickness,' wrote Rudolf Bultmann in 1969, 'and at the same time believe in a spirit world and in the miracles that the New Testament presents us.'[10] Taking aim at the Bible, they analysed the passages that mentioned the Devil and pointed out their allegorical nature – a literary device used by the writers of the Gospels to underline the hold that evil had over the world. And while Jesus's actions clearly indicate that at least *He* believed in the Devil, this was debunked by critics like Herbert Haag, Bas van Iersel, and Henry Ansgar Kelly, who claimed that He was simply doing the modern PR equivalent of 'dumbing down' the message to get his point across to an uncultured society.[11]

For conservatives, not only did these interpretations misrepresent scripture, but they also completely disregarded long-standing traditions set down by the Apostolic Fathers. If the Church had never come out with a binding statement on the Devil's existence in the past that was because it had never had to; the reality of the Devil had never been doubted. To dispute these teachings, they said, would be to call into question the very credibility of the Church. As if to underscore the point, on 15 November 1972, Pope Paul VI spoke out on the matter in a general audience saying that 'evil is not merely a lack of something but an effective agent, a living spiritual being, [and that] it is contrary to the teaching of the Bible and the Church to refuse to recognize the existence of such a reality'.[12]

Both positions seemed to have their limitations. While the liberal view was in many respects a continuation of Enlightenment thinking, its labelling of Jesus's exorcisms as allegorical had disturbing ramifications for anyone claiming to be a Christian. If Jesus were indeed the Son of God, as every Christian believes, why would he misinform his followers by commanding them to cast out evil spirits if no such beings existed?[13]

Meanwhile, for conservatives, while their defence of the faith on traditional grounds did agree with the fathers of the Church, it was perceived by rank-and-file priests of the day as being medieval and out of touch with modern society.

In the end, it would be this last view that would win out, as more and more priests found themselves affected not only by a growing acceptance of a modernist worldview, but also by a kind of existential relativism that took hold as a result of the Second Vatican Council.[14] While not necessarily rejecting the official teachings of the Church, most clergymen found the concept of the Devil a sideshow that no 'serious-minded' priest would lose time considering. For all intents and purposes, it was Charles Baudelaire's well-known phrase come to life: the Devil had finally convinced the world that he no longer existed.[15]

*

At the course, Father Gary also benefited from being introduced to other novice exorcists like himself. Most were from Italy and didn't speak English. One priest, however, a Franciscan from America, proved extremely helpful.

Father Daniel, originally from the New England area, had recently been stationed at the shrines in Jerusalem.[16] His black robe bore the symbol – a red cross surrounded by four smaller ones – of his order. With his robe, close-cropped hair, and beard, he appeared to be from another era. And yet, upon closer inspection, the subtle hints of his New England background rose to the surface – a sliver of blue jeans below his robe, Birkenstock sandals, the frayed collar of a green, button-down shirt.

During one of the breaks, Father Daniel explained to Father Gary what compelled him to take the course. That summer he'd been at a shrine in Abruzzo, east of Rome, where he'd had a terrifying experience. One day, while he listened to confessions at the shrine, a woman approached him and asked if he believed in demonic possession. Despite his lack of firsthand knowledge in the matter, he told her that he did. The woman responded, 'Good, because I suffer from it and I want to confess.' Unsure what she meant, he none the less began with his blessing and continued to hear her confession. He could see immediately that something was amiss; she began to twitch and clear her throat repeatedly. Then things got worse. All of a sudden she began to grunt and the word *zitto* (shut up) escaped involuntarily from her pursed lips. Then, when it came time for him to say his final blessings and absolve her of her sins, to his utter shock, all the muscles in her face contorted to such a degree that he could no longer recognize her. Next, her jaw completely unhinged and, dropping down, shifted over to one side of her face, giving the impression that her mouth had become nine inches wide. At this point, Father Daniel nearly panicked but kept calm long enough to bless the woman in the name of Jesus Christ, after which she got up and bolted from the church.

After he had recovered and his fears had subsided, he became curious about what he had just witnessed. In order to get answers, he volunteered to help the local exorcist who worked at the shrine. It didn't take long for him to realize that he had seen only the tip of the iceberg – there was a whole world out there that he never knew existed. As a result, when he was transferred to Rome in the autumn to begin his doctoral studies, he petitioned his superior for permission to apprentice with an exorcist. Father Tommaso at the Scala Santa, a church that has been long associated with exorcism, took him on shortly thereafter.[17]

As he listened to Father Daniel, Father Gary had no reason to doubt the Franciscan's sincerity. Far from boastful, Father Daniel had been incredibly humble, even self-deprecating – almost as if even he couldn't believe what had happened. Father Daniel's story only made Father Gary realize just how little he knew about demonic possession. It was a stark reminder that before he could ever perform an exorcism himself, he would need to learn more about who or what he was going up against.

CHAPTER FOUR

KNOW YOUR ENEMY

The capacity to love has been annihilated from the psychology of a demon. A demon knows but does not love. The pleasure achieved in doing an evil act is the same as that which a human being feels when he gets revenge on an enemy – it is a pleasure filled with hate.

Father José Antonio Fortea, *Interview With an Exorcist*

The idea of the Devil is something that has evolved over time, primarily as a way to explain the existence of evil in a world created by an all-powerful and loving God.[1]

The word 'Devil' comes from the Greek *diabolos*, which means 'adversary, slanderer, opposer'. When the Hebrew Bible was translated in 200 BCE into Greek (known as the Septuagint version), the Greeks commonly used this word in place of the Hebrew word *satan*, which meant 'accuser'.

In the Old Testament, which was written between 1000 and 100 BCE, the Devil is only mentioned a few times, and even then he is far from a coherent, personified being. Some theologians, such as Thomas Aquinas, have speculated that this is because Moses was 'addressing uncultured people' and didn't want to promote any beliefs that might tempt them to worship false idols.[2] Other theologians have suggested that the lack of a coherent demonology in the Old Testament might be because the Israelites had a strict law in place that prohibited magic.[3] Satan's most prominent appearance is in the Book of Job; but as some scholars have pointed out, here his name is really just a title.[4] He still has access to the heavenly court and appears to be acting as God's agent, a kind of 'prosecuting attorney'. In this role he convinces God to give him the power to torment Job to test Job's loyalty (Job 1: 6–12).

In the New Testament, however, the Devil plays a much bigger role. At the time of Christ's coming – thanks to original sin – 'the whole world lies under the power of the Evil One' (I John 5: 19). To heal this rift, God sends his only Son. The Synoptic Gospels address this concept directly and repeatedly. 'The Son of God was revealed for this purpose, to destroy the works of the devil' (I John 3: 8).

The New Testament is full of the battles that these two sides wage. Satan tempts Christ directly in the desert (Matt. 4: 1–11; Mark 1: 13; Luke 4: 1–13) and attacks him indirectly through his followers: by temptation (Matt. 13: 19); by inflicting bodily harm (Luke 13: 11); and by possession (Mark 1: 23–8). Jesus teaches his disciples the Lord's Prayer, and confronts the Devil head on by performing exorcisms.

The belief in spirits or intermediaries between God and man exists in just about every religion. The Assyrians, for instance, had numerous books (written on clay tablets) dedicated to incantations and conjurations to ward off evil spirits.[5]

According to the Greeks, 'demons' or *daimones* were thought to be either good or evil. Socrates, for instance, famously credited a *daimon* as being the source of his inspiration.

For Catholics, the belief in angels is an article of faith, based on divine revelation and the teachings of the Church. The Apostles' Creed professes that God is 'Creator of heaven and earth'. The Nicene Creed makes it explicit that this profession includes 'all that is seen and unseen'.[6]

The creation of the angels is affirmed in numerous passages of the Bible. Saint Paul writes to the Colossians: 'For in him [Christ] all things in heaven and on earth were created, things visible and invisible, whether thrones or dominions or rulers or powers – all things have been created through him and for him' (Col. 1: 16).

The angels occupy a natural order or hierarchy of beings whose purpose is to reflect the glory of God. As thirteenth-century theologian Thomas Aquinas explains in his great treatise on angels, in *Summa Theologiae*, 'There must be some incorporeal creatures, for what is principally intended by God in creatures is good, and this consists in assimilation to God Himself [. . .] hence the perfection of the universe requires that there should be intellectual creatures.'[7]

To many theologians it seems only natural to believe in higher intelligences superior to our own, especially when one considers the ordered nature and varying degrees of intelligence that exist in the world, from single-cell organisms right up to man. 'It would be most extraordinary if (man) formed the last link,' writes Pie-Raymond Régamey, OP.[8]

The *Catechism of the Catholic Church* teaches that Satan was at first a good angel, created by God: 'The devil and the other demons were indeed created naturally good by God, but they became evil by their own doing.'[9]

As an expression of His love, God created the angels with free will so that they could love Him back and 'render [themselves] similar to God who is love' (1 John 4: 16).[10] In simple terms, according to the Christian tradition, love is a kind of metaphysical necessity for created beings since it is only through love that such beings can realize their full potential. And since love not freely given is not really love at all, this meant that the angels (along with man) needed to have the ability to choose.

However, God knew that, once he gave this freedom, it could be used either for evil or for good. 'By creating the pure spirits as free beings, God in his Providence could not but foresee also *the possibility of the angels' sin*,' said Pope John Paul II.[11]

After their creation, God tested the angels before admitting them to the beatific vision (the direct experience of God in heaven). Many angels remained faithful to God while a smaller number, led by Satan, 'rebelled', choosing to place themselves before God. Though no specific passage in the Bible dealt directly with the 'sin' of the fallen angels, various theories abounded among the early Apostolic Fathers: Justin Martyr (d. 163–76) thought the sin to be lust, while Irenaeus (d. 202) thought it was envy. Over time, the most widely accepted theory would be the one promulgated by Origen (born in 185), that the fallen angels sinned through pride. Though, as Thomas Aquinas says, this pride was less a belief that they could become God, which would be impossible, than that they wanted to be 'as God', beings who could attain ultimate happiness through their own powers.

After their sin, the angels were immediately stripped of their everlasting grace and condemned to an 'eternal punishment' (Matt. 25: 46).[12] Theologians call this punishment the 'pain of loss'.[13] The fallen angels were cut off from the only source that could have given them happiness: God. In this 'hell', the demons are forever tormented and remain obstinate in their hate, a hate that 'ascends continuously' and deforms their very nature.

According to Christian tradition, Satan was the principal fallen angel, the brightest and most perfect of all God's creations. The Bible makes it clear that he holds a higher rank than the other fallen angels: 'the Devil and his angels' (Matt. 25: 41), 'the ruler of the demons' (Luke 11: 15), 'the dragon and his angels' (Rev. 12: 7–9).

Ever since Origen attributed the fall to pride, Satan's name has been interchangeable with Lucifer. The name, taken from a verse in Isaiah, is used metaphorically to describe the king of Babylon. 'How art thou fallen from heaven, Lucifer, son of Dawn! How are you cut down to the ground, you who laid nations low! You said in your heart, "I will ascend into heaven; I will raise my throne above the stars of God"' (Isa. 14: 12–13). Some theologians have argued against this association. Indeed, some exorcists like Father Amorth say that Lucifer and Satan are two distinct demons. Despite this, however, the tradition of associating Lucifer with the Devil continues, even as the Catholic Church maintains that the name 'Lucifer' symbolizes the state from which the Devil has fallen and is not a proper name.[14]

After the angels 'fell', God created the material world, including the first humans. When this happened, Satan turned his rage on mankind, and, as described by Pope John Paul II, 'transplant[ed] into man the insubordination, rivalry and opposition to God, which had become the motivation for his existence'.[15] The Book of Genesis relates how Satan, taking the form of the serpent, tempted Adam and Eve to sin.

As a result of this sin and humanity turning its back on God, Satan has been given some degree of dominion over man. In the Bible he is called 'the ruler of this world' (John 12: 31) and 'the god of this world' (2 Cor. 4: 4).[16]

In the early days of the Church the nature of angels caused some confusion. Writing in the second century, Justin Martyr thought that fallen angels had denser bodies than the good angels, and that they actually ate a special kind of food (Ps. 78: 25; Ps. 105: 40).[17] The word angel is also deceiving. Deriving from the Hebrew *mal'ak* or the Greek *angelos*, it signifies 'messenger', or 'envoy', which indicates more of a function than a nature.

Today, the Catholic Church teaches that angels are incorporeal spiritual beings. Saint Augustine says: 'Angel is the name of their office, not of their nature. If you seek the name of their nature, it is "spirit"; if you seek the name of their office, it is "angel": from what they are, "spirit", from what they do, "angel".'[18]

There has been much speculation over the years about what might constitute the nature of a pure spirit. And while not a part of official Church doctrine, a majority of Catholic theologians follow the teachings of Thomas Aquinas, also known as the Angelic Doctor. Aquinas explains that pure spirits are not composed of matter and form, but of essence and existence, act and potentiality. Where the early Church fathers fell short, Aquinas suggests, was in not according enough importance to intelligence. Because of their wholly spiritual nature, angels are complete beings and occupy 'the first and highest place in the scale of created things', nearer to the likeness of God who is pure spirit rather than man, who is a mix of the spiritual (soul) and material (body).[19]

Every angel is a distinct being endowed with intellect and free will.[20] However, as Aquinas explains, this doesn't mean that the angels are comprised only of intellect, but rather that their knowledge is derived from the intellect, compared to a human soul that attains knowledge through both the intellect and senses.[21] As theologian A. M. Lépicier notes, 'An angel possesses such penetration that he is able, at one glance, to take in the whole field of science laying open to his perception, just as we, at a glance, can take in the entire field of vision lying exposed to our eyes.'[22]

For the ministry of an exorcist, perhaps the most important distinction that Aquinas makes is that since angels (or demons) do not occupy space, therefore, they cannot be physically present in a place like a person can. In this way, they are not anywhere. Instead, when a demon is alleged to move an object (slam a door for instance, or slide a chair across a room) the demon is *acting* on that object.[23] Their being immaterial means that angels do not move from point A to B by any kind of locomotion, but instead suddenly shift their activity from one point or place to a different one. Some theologians have likened this movement to the human mind, which can instantly transfer thoughts over long distances or on to random objects.[24]

Since the Church teaches that God never rejects his creatures, even when they use his gifts for evil means, the Devil is said to still retain his former angelic stature and powers. As St Augustine established, though, God does not give Satan a free hand, otherwise 'no man would be left alive'. Theologians stipulate that the Devil and the fallen angels are limited in their actions in two main ways: by the limits of their nature as created beings, and by the will of God.

Limits of the Devil Based on His Nature:
The Catholic Church teaches that no matter how superior he is to humans, the Devil is still a finite creature. He cannot, for example, perform true miracles because by definition a miracle is something that surpasses the power of all created nature. To perform a miracle requires 'supernatural' power, and Satan has only 'preternatural' power.[25] He can, however, create the appearance of a miracle since his powers allow him to surpass the limits of human abilities.[26]

The Devil is also limited in his ability to know the secrets of the inner heart, a field strictly open to God, who is all-knowing, say theologians. However, according to exorcists, the Devil can tell what we are thinking by using his superior powers of observation, just as a physician might glean some information about a man's health by checking his pulse.

The Devil cannot foresee the future, say exorcists. He can however fake the appearance of psychic ability by accurately 'predicting' what will happen based on his knowledge of human nature and the powers he has as a spirit.[27]

Limits of the Devil Based on God's Will:
The second limitation on the Devil's power comes from God's will. In the Christian tradition, an important distinction is made between the Devil's status as a lower being, created by God, and his false reputation as 'god of evil' (a view held by many satanic cults). As a result, the Catholic Church

emphasizes that even though the Devil, because of his angelic stature, has more power than humans, he can do nothing unless God allows it. The Book of Job attests to the fact that God can restrain the Devil: 'The Lord said to Satan, Very well, all that he has is in your power; only do not stretch out your hand against him' (Job 1: 12).

Many have asked the question: Why would God allow the Devil to harm us? While not easy to answer, Catholic theologians such as Thomas Aquinas have tried to show that, ultimately, God permits the Devil to act in order to turn evil to good.[28]

Typically, the Devil is permitted to act in ways broken down by exorcists into two categories: ordinary and extraordinary.

Ordinary Activity of the Devil:
The ordinary activity of the Devil is temptation. Temptation is essentially nothing more than an attraction to commit a sin. In order to sin, we first have to realize that whatever act we are committing is a moral evil, otherwise we would be guilty of only ignorance and not sin. Saint Paul says in a letter to the Romans: 'I do not understand my own actions. I do not do what I want, but I do the very thing I hate. Now if I do what I do not want, I agree that the law is good. But in fact it is no longer I that do it but sin that dwells within me. [. . .] I can will what is right, but I cannot do it. For I do not the good I want, but the evil I do not want is what I do' (Rom. 7: 15–20). It is in this capacity of tempting us to go against the good of our nature that the Devil is most active. However, theologians are quick to point out that it would be a mistake to assume that all temptations come from the Devil. As Thomas Aquinas says, 'The devil is not the cause of every sin: for all sins are not committed at the devil's instigation, but some are due to free-will and the corruption of the flesh.'[29] The Catholic Church teaches that overcoming temptation is a normal way for the soul to strengthen in grace and virtue.

Extraordinary Activity of the Devil:
Any demonic activity that is considered more powerful than temptation is 'extraordinary'. Over the years, numerous terms have been used in the field of exorcism and deliverance to describe the various ways in which the Devil and demons can afflict people directly. When the new rite of exorcism was promulgated in 1998, the Conference of Italian Bishops asked the International Association of Exorcists to come up with a list of terms that could be used by everybody. The Devil's extraordinary activity was lumped into four major areas: infestation, oppression, obsession, and demonic possession.[30]

Infestation:
Infestation is the presence of demonic activity in a location or object, such as a 'haunted house'.

The various kinds of phenomena that can occur in this situation are vast and include unexplained sounds or noises like mysterious footsteps, loud bangs, laughter, screams; the temperature of a room dropping or the feelings of a cold wind with no discernible source; objects disappearing suddenly and materializing in other parts of the house; strange presences felt; the presence of offensive odours; interruption of electric current or the malfunction of electronic devices; pictures that mysteriously bang or fall off the wall; doors and windows that open and close on their own; dishes or other objects levitating and flying about the room.

One exorcist described going to bless a house and seeing mysterious, blood-like spots appearing on various objects, including articles of clothing tucked away in drawers and even a set of brand-new bed sheets that were still sealed in plastic. In the same instance, a rosary that had been strung with ornate glass beads was found hanging on the back of a door with all the beads mysteriously removed. The beads were found crushed into a fine powder and placed into a neat little pile outside the house.

In another instance, a woman baked a cake and placed it on the kitchen table; but when she re-entered the room, it had been mysteriously moved to the top of a cupboard even though no one else was in the house.

Generally, say exorcists, such disturbances occur for a number of reasons, including the presence of a cursed object in the house or the house itself being cursed; use of the location for occult activities such as séances or for a criminal activity of some kind, such as prostitution or drug-dealing; performance of a Satanic ritual on the premises; or gruesome murders or suicides having taken place there. Often, say exorcists, manifestations are caused by a person being attacked by an evil presence rather than attributed to an evil spirit being attached to the house.

Typically, instead of performing an exorcism, exorcists prefer to do a simple blessing and say a mass on the premises.

Oppression:

Also called 'physical attack', oppression often takes the form of mysterious blows raining down on the individual or scratches inexplicably materializing on the body. Some people have had strange signs or even letters appear on their skin, while others claim to be pushed down stairs or out of bed by an invisible force. The Bible attests to the power of the Devil to inflict physical infirmities. In the Gospel of Luke, for example, Jesus heals a woman who has been bowed over and deformed by a 'spirit of infirmity' (Luke 13: 10–16). Typically, this kind of direct attack is aimed at people who are closest to God, such as the saints. Saint Catherine of Siena (1347–80), Saint Teresa of Avila (1515–82), Saint John Vianney (1786–1859), and Saint Gemma Galgani (1878–1903) to name a few, have all been the objects of demonic oppression at some point in their lives, as has Saint Paul, whose 'thorn in the flesh' (2 Cor. 12: 7) is generally considered to have been caused by a demon.[31]

As in the Book of Job, victims of this kind of attack may also suffer in their work, health or relationships. The purpose is to drive these people toward isolation and despair so they may turn their backs on God.

Obsession:

Obsession has also been called 'demonic temptation' and it involves an intense and persistent attack on the mind of the victim. Generally, say exorcists, these attacks include random and obsessive thoughts that, though often absurd, are so intense that the victim is unable to free him- or herself. Victims feel tormented by a fixation that completely dominates their thoughts. These thoughts can make the victim think he is going insane, which only compounds the feelings of sadness and desperation. As Italian exorcist Father Francesco Bamonte notes, 'Some are thoughts and impulses that urge people to harm others; some make people think that only a pact with Satan can get them out of their troubles or bring them success; some are thoughts to profane the Eucharist; others are thoughts to drive one to suicide.'[32] Often the obsessions affect a person's dreams and terrible nightmares are common.

Possession:

Also known as 'involuntary possession',[33] demonic possession is by far the most spectacular activity of the Devil and also the rarest. Some exorcists believe they have gone their entire lives without seeing a full demonic possession, while others encounter the phenomenon more frequently. Almost all exorcists are unanimous in their belief, however, that more people are becoming possessed today than in the recent past.[34]

In a demonic possession, the Devil takes temporary control of a person's body, speaking and acting through it without the person's knowledge. This control, however, doesn't last indefinitely, but rather occurs only during 'moments of crisis' in which the victim enters a trance state. Generally speaking, after the crisis passes, the victim will not remember what transpired (rare individuals will be conscious during the ordeal and will remember). As a result of this 'loss of control' the individual is considered blameless for whatever happens. However, having a free will, they are responsible for their actions when they are not in the trance state, and so, say theologians, demonic possession in no way exculpates them from guilt.

In between their crisis moments, it is also possible for victims to carry on as if nothing is wrong. This does not mean, however, that they are not affected by the demon. 'People who are possessed can keep undergoing influence of the demon in their mind,' says one Italian exorcist. 'As the Holy Spirit can acquaint divine things to a person such as good feelings, pleasant sensations, a state of physical wellbeing, a state of calm, of inner peace and also of intuition of things, an evil spirit through his ugliness can do the same thing though in the opposite way, like agitation, anxiety, desperation, hate, or thoughts of suicide.'[35]

During moments of crisis, the Devil can manifest in various ways: bodily contortions that defy rational explanation; unnatural strength; knowledge of hidden things; or abilities to speak or understand foreign languages. In stronger cases, the demon will speak through the person, usually in an odd or unnatural voice that is full of rage and hatred.

It is also possible for strange occurrences to happen at the homes of possessed individuals such as weird animals appearing or disappearing, say exorcists. For instance, one eighteen-year-old girl was suddenly awakened one night by a slap across her face. Looking around she saw that she was alone. However, as she searched the room, she noticed that bizarre insects (with antennae or wings missing, for example) began appearing on the walls. Frightened, she called out to her mother, who also saw the insects. The two then tried to kill them with a shoe, but they kept appearing on the walls as if out of thin air.

It is important to note that in the case of demonic possession, say exorcists, the soul of the individual is not possessed, just the body. A great debate has raged among Christians about whether a person in a state of grace could also be possessed. According to the Catholic Church, the answer is yes (the lives of the saints bear witness to this) because the soul remains in a state of grace while the body is taken over. The only exception would be when a person 'invites' a possession to take place, such as during a satanic ritual. 'In this case,' says one Italian exorcist, 'the presence in the soul is completed, which means that the will of the person completely identifies with the demon, having given himself completely to him. In that case the person becomes constantly possessed, and is like a demon walking on the earth.'[36]

CHAPTER FIVE

OPENING THE DOOR

My dear Wormwood,

  Everything is clearly going very well. I am specially glad to hear that the two new friends have now made him acquainted with their whole set. All these, as I find from the record office, are thoroughly reliable people; steady, consistent scoffers and worldings who without any spectacular crimes are progressing quietly and comfortably towards Our Father's house.

C. S. Lewis, *The Screwtape Letters*

Confound the race / Of mankind in one root, and Earth with Hell / To mingle and involve, done all to spite / The Great Creator?

John Milton, *Paradise Lost*

The image of a desecrated church with satanic graffiti – '666' and upside-down crosses – spray-painted on the walls filled the large white screen behind the dais.

'These photos were taken in the chapel of an abandoned hospital just outside Rome,' asserted the deep baritone voice of

Doctor Marco Strano, a criminologist and psychologist with the state police. A brooding, bald man with an intense gaze made more pronounced by a set of thick black eyebrows, Doctor Strano appeared right at home next to the gruesome images – elaborate Satanic tattoos, self-mutilations, shattered storefronts blocked off by yellow crime-scene tape – that paraded across the screen.

With the blinds shut and the lights turned off, Father Gary didn't bother to take too many notes, but instead just sat back and tried to digest it all.

In recent years, satanic cults had been on the rise in Italy, and several high-profile satanic murders had grabbed attention in the Italian news. In 2001, three teenage girls stabbed a nun to death in a northern Italian town as a part of a satanic ritual. In the autumn of 2005, members of a satanic rock group, the *Bestie di Satana* (Beasts of Satan) were brought to trial for the brutal murder of one band member and two female friends, one of whom was shot and buried alive. As recently as 2007, a man with amnesia wandered into a police station in a town near Milan covered with small puncture wounds and missing three litres of blood. Later, his blood was found splattered all over the walls of his apartment seventy miles away in the form of satanic writings. Police found upturned crosses and other satanic symbols there even though the man had no recollection of belonging to any cult.

Because millions of people are reportedly involved in the occult around the world and the numbers are on the rise, the exorcism course would explain the ramifications to novice exorcists.

Modern Satanism, say experts, borrows from a number of historical traditions, and its tenets are hard to pin down. There is no unified belief system, as some members of the same group may become involved for more abstract practices while others do so for carnal reasons.

The Gnostics in the mid-second century heavily promoted the notion that Satan was a god-like being with certain powers. Later condemned by the Church as heretics, the Gnostics believed that the material world was too full of evil to have been created by a good God. Therefore they proposed a dualist system whereby God was distant and unknowable while Satan was the creator of the physical world. Later, in the Middle Ages, the Cathars took up this theory once again, even going so far as to say that the Catholic Church was established by the Devil to mislead people. This emphasis on the material world being created by Satan wasn't for the purposes of worshipping him, but to more powerfully oppose him. But this view was easily perverted by certain groups putting the Devil on an equal footing with God.[1]

In the eighteenth and nineteenth centuries, on the heels of the revolutions in America and France and in the throes of the Enlightenment, Satan's desire to rebel against God was cast as a bid for freedom. The Church, seen by some as being too authoritarian, was accused of repressing man's natural carnal desires. As a result, numerous groups sprang up, including the infamous Hellfire Club led by the rake Sir Francis Dashwood, which, while not necessarily believing in the reality of a personified Satan, still espoused a hedonistic lifestyle involving supposed orgies and other debaucheries done in the Devil's name.[2]

According to Italian exorcist Father Bamonte, who also authored a book on the occult, *Cosa Fare con Questi Maghi?* (What Do We Do with These Magicians?), published in 2000, there are two currents of Satanism. In the first, known as 'personal', adepts actually believe that Satan is a physical entity, a god that can be prayed to and who will grant certain privileges, such as money and fame, if offered sacrifices. While in the second, known as 'impersonal', acolytes hold that Satan represents more of a force or energy, a part of the cosmos that can be developed and used to serve them.

In both the 'personal' and the 'impersonal' currents of

Satanism, the power of the individual is exalted above anything else, while the seven capital sins are celebrated.[3] As Father Bamonte says, 'The key to understanding them is to know their motto, "Do what you want; that is the only law."'[4] Beyond this basic view, the groups themselves can also be very diverse.

Father Aldo Buonaiuto, a member of the Pope John XXIII Community Association, has been working with ex-cult members for some time. Small in stature, Father Buonaiuto sports a collegiate handsomeness and a perpetual five-o'clock shadow. His appearance and mild demeanour seem completely out of place in the world of devil worship and murder. And yet, being the author of a book on the occult *Le mani occulte: viaggio nel mondo del satanismo* (The Hands of the Occult, a Voyage into the World of Satanism), he is considered an expert on the subject and was recently asked to collaborate with the SAS.

During the course of his work, Father Buonaiuto has come up with different designations within satanic cults. The first, which he calls 'Youth Acid', consists of mostly young people into the physical trappings of Satanism, the hedonistic lifestyle mixed with drugs, self-mutilation, paedophilia, suicide, and even murder to provide human sacrifices. The second designation, known as 'Power Satanism', is more sophisticated, he claims, and counts as its members very wealthy and influential people who are said to sell their souls to the Devil for the promise of power and riches, which are then used to ensure a perpetual state of strife – war, famine, economic instability, and such. The third designation he calls 'Apocalyptic Satanism', which, as the name suggests, has as its goal the total destruction of life as we know it (not surprisingly, he claims this is the most dangerous strain).

While there is no denying that groups like the 'Beasts of Satan' exist, and that they claim to kill in the name of the Devil, the larger question is this: are these groups part of a bigger problem, or just deeply troubled individuals?

Similar to the 'satanic panics' that gripped the United States in the 1980s and early 1990s,[5] when cases such as the McMartin preschool trial (in which a group of teachers were accused of ritually abusing the students) turned out to be false, some critics wonder whether the Church might be overreacting to a few isolated incidents.[6]

Italy has seen its fair share of scandals that, while garnering headlines, have failed to deliver. In 1996, for example, Marco Dimitri, the leader of a satanic cult called the Bambini di Satana (Children of Satan) was acquitted of raping a two-year-old boy and a teenage girl during an alleged satanic ritual. Likewise, in 2007, the town of Rignano Flaminio near Rome went through its very own McMartin-style scandal when fifteen students at a nursery school accused six individuals, including several teachers, of sexually abusing them in satanic rituals. A lengthy investigation, however, involving a number of child psychologists, failed to turn up any evidence.

Doctor Strano, for his part, doesn't believe the more sensational crimes attributed to satanic cults – such as human sacrifice, organ trafficking, and slavery – are going on to the extent that some people imagine. He thinks instead that many of these groups are just about rebellion, about young people doing drugs and perhaps becoming involved in petty crimes such as vandalism or theft. Most of them 'do not even know what they are doing', he says.

Father Buonaiuto, however, thinks differently. For the past six years, he has been running a cult hotline in Italy, counselling individuals and family members who are trying to get out. 'It's not true that they are isolated groups, that a sixteen-year-old kid suddenly wakes up and decides to start a group. There is always someone who gives them the permission, there is a territory, there is always someone who initiates the group with that doctrine,' he says. The hotline has opened Father Buonaiuto's eyes to a world that, he says, many people can't imagine exists. 'The thing that is the most shocking is the amount of joy that these young kids, some of them sixteen years old, get out of suffering and causing suffering for others. They celebrate death. If you read what some of the people from the "Beasts of Satan" said, you would not believe it. While they are hurting someone they rejoice in it.' According to Father Buonaiuto, the hotline gets around twenty calls a day, running the gamut from ex-cult members on the run to people just seeking attention. It can be hard to break away from these groups, in part because the destructive lifestyle is fuelled by addiction. 'LSD, music, sex and violence work together to form a kind of psychological dependence,' he says.

However, even while Father Buonaiuto is convinced that satanic cults pose a threat, he is quick to point out that the nefariousness associated with these groups doesn't necessarily have anything to do with the demonic. 'We have to be clear: The world of satanic cults is one thing and demonic possession another. Satanism is more about an exterior thing, a cultural movement in which people perpetrate crimes such as fraud and in extreme cases murder. Some people in these groups don't even believe in the Devil but use him as a shield to victimize impressionable people. Demonic possession, on the other hand, is an individual thing, which if it affects a person, does so on an internal, spiritual level.'

One, of course, could lead to the other, say experts like Father Bamonte. If a person were to enter such a group and perform magic or certain rituals, that could open them up to demonic attack. Or, claims Father Bamonte, the individual could sign a 'pact' with a demon and thereby open a doorway to 'direct contact' with him.

According to exorcists, a variety of factors can contribute to a person becoming possessed.[7]

The first thing to note, say theologians, is that demonic possession cannot occur unless God allows it. It may seem contradictory but, according to the Church, while God does not wish evil upon any person, He does permit it for some good purpose (similar to temptation). In the case of someone with a very advanced spiritual life, such as a saint, God allows Satan to test that person in the hope that the physical trials will give their soul sanctifying grace. According to John Chrysostom, 'Possessed persons can obtain a twofold benefit from their condition. In the first place they can become more holy and good; secondly, having paid the debt for their sins here on earth, they can present themselves pure before the Lord.'[8]

Demonic possession in and of itself is not evil; it is not considered a sin. In addition, there is apparently no physical or otherwise inherent quality in a person's nature that predisposes him or her to becoming possessed. Demonic possession is not contagious. A person cannot become possessed by sitting in a room or living with someone who is possessed. Generally speaking, say exorcists, one has to either open the door to the Devil, or be a victim of one who has opened the door. These are some ways the Church says a person can do this:

Occult ties: According to the Church, becoming involved in the occult is a form of idolatry that goes against the first commandment and is a common way to come into contact with the demonic.

In his book *Possessioni diaboliche ed esorcismo* (Demonic Possession and Exorcism), Father Bamonte lists the following occult activities that can potentially open the door to possession: participating in a séance; frequenting a medium or magician (the Church makes no distinction between 'white' or 'black' magic); using an amulet or talisman, especially if received from a magician; transcendental meditation, the use of crystals, and other such New Age practices that stress 'out of body' experiences; divination or the practice of automatic writing; practising satanic rituals, especially signing a 'blood pact' with a demon. The Bible is clear (and rather graphic) on the dangers involved in practising magic and divination: 'No one shall be found among you who makes a son or daughter pass through fire, or who practises divination, or is a soothsayer, or an augur, or a sorcerer, or one who casts spells, or who consults ghosts or spirits, or who seeks oracles from the dead. For whoever does these things is abhorrent to the Lord' (Deut. 18: 10–12).

The *Catechism* is also direct in its condemnation of the occult. 'All forms of divination are to be rejected: recourse to Satan or demons, conjuring up the dead or other practices falsely supposed to "unveil" the future . . . All practices of magic or sorcery, by which one attempts to tame occult powers, so as to place them at one's service and have a supernatural power over others even if this were for the sake of restoring their health – are gravely contrary to the virtue of religion.'[9]

As Father Bamonte explains, however, just participating in a card reading or using a ouija board does not necessarily risk possession. Yet engaging in this activity repeatedly, he says, could start people down a path that could open them up to possession either through a graver sin or through their own actions.

One American priest on the staff at the NAC related his experience helping a sixteen-year-old unbaptized girl who came to him. While playing with a ouija board, the girl had contacted a spirit named Nick, who dared her to do things that are dangerous, such as driving her car in a rainstorm without windshield wipers. But things got worse when she awoke one night with an overwhelming sensation of being surrounded by a darkness so thick it was choking the air out of her lungs. With no training in exorcism, the priest said a simple prayer of deliverance and the problem seemed to go away.

A curse: A curse causes the suffering of others through the intervention of a demon. Curses break up marriages, cause businesses to fail, induce illness, invite possession, and so on. Curses can be carried out in a variety of ways, say exorcists. Most are the result of magic formulas or rituals performed by a warlock or a witch. Sometimes a person is affected directly (by ingesting a cursed object) and sometimes indirectly (by having cursed objects).

One Italian exorcist knew a very wealthy person who had tried to sell her house for many years without success. People would come to look at the house, leave enthusiastic and ready to buy, but then mysteriously never return to close the deal. The exorcist said many masses, but still the house remained unsold. One day a charismatic nun came to visit and told the exorcist that something was hidden in a wall and that the house would be impossible to sell until the object was removed. The owner of the house then asked her ex-husband, who was an artist, if he had put anything inside a wall. Reluctant at first, he finally admitted that he had placed a painting behind a wall when the house was being built (in order to dedicate it to an evil spirit in the hopes of garnering favours). When the owner destroyed the wall in question, she found that it encased a painting that portrayed a satanic image. A week after the owner burned the painting, the exorcist claims, four different people offered to buy the house.

In all cases, say exorcists, the intent is the most critical part of a curse. The strongest curses (those causing the greatest harm) are those launched with true perfidy – when there is a familial or blood relationship between the victim and aggressor, such as a parent who curses a child.

Some signs that point to a curse, say exorcists, are chronic depression and sickness, infertility, breakdowns in the family and marriage, financial difficulty, and a family history of suicide or unnatural deaths. Exorcists are quick to point out that experiencing one or more of these conditions does not necessarily mean a person is cursed. Other criteria must be weighed in all cases to determine demonic activity.

The first people to be affected by a curse are often the ones who cast it, say exorcists.[10] A jilted lover who goes to a magician to have a curse put on the girl who spurned him will perhaps fall into a dangerous pattern of returning to the magician for other reasons, such as to obtain a lucky charm to win over a new girlfriend. According to exorcists, this could lead not only to financial ruin but, in extreme cases, also to possession.

To many people, belief in curses might seem far-fetched.

However, casting and removing spells is extremely widespread in many native cultures, including some that have embraced Christianity. Haiti, for example, is a predominantly Catholic country, yet Voodoo is popular.

Dedication to a demon: This category deals with people who belong to a satanic cult specifically to harness the power of evil by dedicating themselves or family members to a demon. In the case of a child being dedicated, as with a curse, the victim is blameless. It is said that parents or relatives sometimes offer new-born babies (or even foetuses) to Satan in black masses. Father Bamonte is quick to point out, however, that any such 'gifts' given in return by the Devil are almost always fleeting and have the affect of 'dazzling' people so that they give themselves over completely to the Devil, becoming like slaves.

A life of hardened sin: As defined by the Church, deciding to commit a sin is a free-will choice to do evil rather than good. According to the *Catechism,* 'Sin is before all else an offence against God, a rupture of communion with him.' One sinner who became possessed as a result of his actions was Judas Iscariot, whom the Bible describes as having the Devil enter him. According to theologians, however, sin in and of itself is usually not enough to cause possession. Certain sins (worshipping false idols), however, can open the door to demonic possession. Sins can also be an impediment to liberation, say exorcists. It is said that the demon can latch on to a specific sin (such as an unwillingness to forgive), accentuating it until the person is in bondage to that particular sin. Until the person renounces this sin, he will have no chance to break the bondage and become liberated. In these milder possessions, say exorcists, a sincere conversion and a good confession is usually enough to liberate the person.

Shortly after he had attended one of these lectures, Father Gary spoke with a seminarian originally from the Midwest who'd had a frightening experience before entering the seminary. The two met one afternoon at a coffee shop near the Trevi Fountain. They found a space amidst the busy afternoon lunch crowd standing around the counter enjoying a *panino* and the seminarian told Father Gary his story.

When he was a teenager, he and his friends had been bored, and so they bought a book on spells at the local bookstore and then purchased some ingredients online. First they decided to cast a spell calling forth a particular spirit. Much to their shock, as they read out the incantations (which required that they make a pact with the Devil for maximum efficacy, though they didn't do it), a flame appeared and floated in the middle of the living room before disappearing. During another incident, a huge crow appeared outside his kitchen window, even though there were no crows around the neighbourhood. Scared, they performed a different spell that made the crow disappear. According to the seminarian, however, it didn't fly away; it vanished. Realizing that he was in over his head, he'd thrown away the spell book the following day.

The story got Father Gary thinking about what might be waiting for him when he went back to San Jose. He knew from the course that the occult was rampant in Italy and growing. Perhaps even more alarming to Father Gary was that in the suburbs of a major Midwestern city, where kids were relatively wealthy and had a lot of free time, the occult was far more widespread than people realized. Had he missed the warning signs in his own parish?

To Father Gary, the most interesting aspect of the lecture on satanic cults was the list of reasons why people became attracted to such a world. While the traditional reasons had been trotted out by Dr Strano – namely rock music and the lack of a strong family unit – perhaps one most intriguing to Father Gary was new media. With the advent of the Internet, not only were more kids coming into contact with exotic groups, but, as one course speaker said, the computer itself – as a tool of empowerment – played a role.

Carlo Climati, who has written several books on Satanism and youth culture, coined the phrase 'new culture of isolation' to describe how today's young people, who often feel cut off from family, friends and society, sometimes treat their computers as 'friends', in a sense replacing the real flesh-and-blood neighbour next door with a keyboard and screen.

Such a concept, whether true or not, made Father Gary wonder about his previous parish. It was clear to him that technology brought huge advances to people's lives, but what effect did this have on a spiritual level? With almost anything one could want only a mouse-click away, it wasn't hard to see how using a computer might give a person a sense of omnipotence. Without the proper grounding, would unsuspecting kids be more tempted today than in the past to use these devices to seek occult knowledge, which might in turn open them up to the demonic?

Once he'd been called out by a parishioner who asked that he bless her house after her daughter had had a nightmare and seen a shadow on the wall of her windowless room. Of course, he had talked to the girl before performing the blessing, but had he dealt with the situation in the right way? Now he would know to ask if she might have dabbled with anything such as a ouija board or tried casting spells downloaded from a Web site.

At the same time Father Gary didn't want to make people paranoid or belittle their problems by pointing to a computer or a deck of Tarot cards and saying, 'Aha!' The key to the problem, he realized, was not the ouija board or Tarot cards *per se*, but the person's desire to seek knowledge through them. More often than not this pointed to a weak faith life. As one speaker in the course had said, 'Where faith decreases, superstition grows.' For Father Gary, that statement rang true.

In late November, after finishing the continuing education programme at the NAC, Father Gary moved to the Casa Santa Maria, a sixteenth-century convent located in the heart of downtown Rome. Sandwiched between Piazza dell'Oratorio on one side and Piazza della Pilotta on the other, the five-storey building – almost as large as half a city block – is deceptively tucked away from the noisy streets of Rome.

Father Gary made friends quickly among the seventy-five priests from all over the English-speaking world who lived at the residence and even knew a few of them from the States. Still, with everyone on tight schedules, there was little time to socialize, something that Father Gary would later lament. One of the highlights for Father Gary was presiding over mass in the Casa's small, wonderfully appointed Romanesque church. *Pranzo* or lunch was the big meal of the day. The priests dined in the large refectory under a fresco-covered ceiling, served by waiters wearing white jackets and ties. Afterwards the staff would set out trays of cookies in an adjoining tea room.

Since he was taking only two classes – in the late fall he'd began his twice-a-week course at the Angelicum on the Eastern spiritual masters – he had plenty of time to read about exorcism, which he usually did in the mornings.

There were a few religious bookshops that he would frequent along Via della Conciliazione – the wide, majestic avenue filled with Vatican offices, churches and religious-memorabilia shops that ran from the Castle of Saint Angelo to Saint Peter's Square. Many of the books were in Italian or Latin, but a few bookshops, such as the Ancora, had a decent English section tucked away in a tiny attic-like space upstairs. He soon found out that while it was easy to find a book on Thomistic philosophy, it wasn't so easy to find one on exorcism.

Instead, most of his research was done at the NAC library. Located on the second floor of the massive seminary, the library had the largest collection of English-language books in Rome (over 64,000), including huge sections on reference, theology and Church history.

Gracious and down to earth, Sister Rebecca personified the Norman Rockwell image of a librarian – conservatively dressed, short curly blondish-white hair and a pair of glasses dangling from her neck on a long brown strap. A Benedictine from a parish in Indiana, she had been serving at the NAC for eleven years when Father Gary walked through the door. Yet in all those years, she couldn't recall being asked about exorcism. 'Father Gary told me he had been nominated as an exorcist and that he didn't know anything about it,' she says. 'I thought exorcism wasn't real.'

None the less, being the accommodating soul that she was, she gladly helped him locate a few titles.

Most of the books were somewhat outdated when it came to exorcism, some written in the 1930s. Because of his sceptical nature, Father Gary preferred books by writers not inclined to see demons around every corner, or blame all the world's evils on the Devil. One book, *Diabolical Possession and Exorcism,* was by Father John Nicola, an American priest and theologian who for many years was an adviser to the American Catholic bishops on exorcism, as well as a technical adviser for the 1973 film *The Exorcist.* Father Nicola's book stood out for its measured approach, describing how science and religion must work in concert, and how an exorcism should be considered only as a last resort. Father Nicola writes: 'Whenever I express a fear and unwillingness to act as an exorcist, I get letters from people assuring me that they have successfully cast out many demons and that, as long as one relies on the power of Christ, there is no need to fear the demons. It is my conviction that they are thinking of something entirely different from what I am. Solemn public exorcisms are rarely performed in modern times in the Western world. When they are performed, they are as gruesome and ugly as anything in the world.'[11]

Such passages, when coupled with the information from the lectures he was attending, gave Father Gary an increasingly clear understanding of the scope of demonic activity in the world, at least in the abstract.

CHAPTER SIX

IN MY NAME

The Devil takes advantage of all the possibilities he has to act in the world, hoping to carry as many people as possible with him to eternal damnation. This is because of the hate he harbours for God and for mankind. He would destroy the good in the world in any possible way but we are protected by the action of God, Mary, the angels, and Saints, all of whom put limits on his actions.

Father Francesco Bamonte

Father Gabriele Nanni remembers the first time he ever saw an exorcism. It was 1997 and he had just been ordained a priest and was working in a parish near L'Aquila, a city east of Rome. A young married couple approached him to ask for help. Strange things were happening to the woman daily and her problems had worsened since they'd married. She suffered from numerous illnesses, stomach aches, headaches, and pains in her joints that would incapacitate her. No pain medication helped nor did the series of doctors who diagnosed one thing and then another. Even stranger, the objects in her house had begun moving around on their own. On one occasion the lid of a pot had levitated above the stove and then clanged to the floor. Theologically, Father Nanni believed in the reality of demonic possession, but he had no experience in the matter. He decided to take the couple to the diocesan exorcist.

Waiting outside the exorcist's office with the couple, Father Nanni remembers hearing the screams of people inside. The howling and screeching that he was hearing, he realized, was coming from a demon.

When it came time for the couple's turn, Father Nanni watched in shock as the woman's arms and legs flailed and her eyes rolled upwards into her head, revealing only the whites. Clearly, something was going on here; but he wasn't sure if he was seeing the work of a demon. After a month of weekly sessions, however, the 'voice' finally materialized as the demon cursed the exorcist with tremendous hatred. The demon also contorted the woman's body in unnatural ways, twisting her hands into knotted claws. On another occasion she threw herself on the floor and extended her body backwards, forming the letter 'O'.

These experiences had a profound effect on Father Nanni. The night after witnessing the demon for the first time, he lay awake in bed, unable to sleep. He felt 'impressed', 'awed' by what he'd seen and had a million questions. His eyes had been opened to a new reality, one that had given him a 'palpable' sense of the theology he had studied in the seminary. 'When you are outside these experiences, you only have an abstract idea of the spiritual world,' says Father Nanni. 'Many priests talk about theoretical things, they have faith but they are intellectuals. The spirit is something that exists for them but it is difficult to treat him as a person; usually they are just concepts.' According to Father Nanni, many theological discussions would have a different outcome if such things were taken into account. 'Through being an exorcist I understood that there is much more to the faith than what we think . . . there is an almost objective, almost material [level].'

Unable to shake this strong impression, he approached his bishop to ask if he could be appointed as an exorcist himself.

Tall, urbane, with fair skin and short grey hair, Father Nanni, at the age of forty-six, gives the impression of a sophisticated and learned man – perhaps a bank president or CEO were he given a suit to wear rather than the traditional black clerics. Born in 1959 in Forlì, he would eventually get a degree in philosophy at the University of Bologna and a doctorate in canon law at the Pontificia Università Lateranense, writing his thesis on the Church laws that regulate exorcism. He speaks several languages – Italian, French, and Spanish – and is the author of the book *Il dito di Dio e il potere di Satana. L'esorcismo* (The Finger of God and the Power of Satan: Exorcism), which was published by the Vatican in 2004. He is also a frequent TV commentator on the recent spate of satanic murders and has even appeared in a documentary on exorcism done by National Geographic.[1]

Patient, contemplative, and highly educated, Father Nanni is part of a new wave – which also includes Father Francesco Bamonte – that forms the perfect counterpart to the raving fundamentalists featured in the popular media whose demagoguery and fear-mongering have done so much to tarnish the image of exorcists. It was specifically for this reason that the course organizers had asked him to speak.

As always, the lecture began with the students standing and saying a Hail Mary along with the Lord's Prayer. For Father Gary and the few other priests who would go on to become exorcists, Father Nanni's lecture, as well as those given over the following weeks by other knowledgeable exorcists, such as Father Bamonte and Father François Dermine OP, would not only provide invaluable insights into the ritual, but also give the students some clues as to what it might actually be like to perform an exorcism.

The *Catechism* mentions exorcism only once, in paragraph 1673, stating, among other things, that 'when the Church asks publicly and authoritatively in the name of Jesus Christ that a person or object be protected against the power of the Evil One and withdrawn from his dominion, it is called exorcism. . . . Exorcism is directed at the expulsion of demons or to the liberation from demonic possession through the spiritual authority which Jesus entrusted to his Church.' According to the Church, exorcism is a sacramental, which by definition means it signifies effects associated with the intercession of the Church.[2]

There are only two types of recognized exorcisms: 'simple' and 'major'. As stated in the *Catechism*, 'In its simple form, exorcism is performed at the celebration of Baptism. The solemn exorcism, called "a major exorcism", can be performed only by a priest with the permission of the bishop.'[3]

Today, many people confuse the rite of exorcism with the practice of prayers of deliverance, which any Christian can recite. According to the Christian deliverance minister Francis MacNutt, *exorcism* 'is a formal ecclesiastical prayer to free a person possessed by evil spirits', while *deliverance* 'is a process, mainly through prayer, of freeing a person who is oppressed or infested by evil spirits but not possessed'.[4]

While it's technically true that any priest can perform an exorcism, not every priest should. Guideline thirteen of the *Ritual* states that the bishop can only nominate a priest who is 'distinguished in piety, learning, prudence, and integrity of life'. In addition, 'The priest [. . .] should carry out this work of charity confidently and humbly under the guidance of the Ordinary.'[5]

With all these conditions, it may seem odd that in the early days of Christianity there actually weren't any officially appointed exorcists. The thought then was that any Christian could perform an exorcism because this power was derived specifically from Christ, 'And these signs will accompany those who believe: by using my name they will cast out demons' (Mark 16: 17). Gradually, however, thanks to the expanded role that exorcism played in the rite of baptism as well as to combat perceived abuses, the order of exorcist was established. The earliest mention of the office of exorcist is perhaps in a letter written by Pope Cornelius (251–2) stating that in the Church of Rome there were fifty-two exorcists, lectors and doorkeepers.[6] Around the fourth century a series of steps were taken to give the bishops more control over the nominating process. The Council of Laodicea in the middle of the fourth century established a canon prohibiting all individuals from performing an exorcism unless appointed by their bishop.[7]

The importance of the nomination by the bishop comes from the power of the prayer being tied to the Church as well as to the obedience of the exorcist. As the current president of the International Association of Exorcists, Father Giancarlo Gramolazzo says, 'I always use this phrase: The prince of disobedience is the Devil and you beat him by being obedient not by your own personality, or charisms.'[8] According to Father Gramolazzo, if a priest were to perform an exorcism without the approval of his bishop, the prayers would still work to some extent because of the power of Jesus Christ's name, but they wouldn't have the same effect on the demon because essentially the exorcist would be praying the ritual in a state of disobedience and the demon would know it. 'Some priests have tried to perform an exorcism without the bishop's permission and the demon said to them, "You cannot do it, you are outside your diocese and you don't have permission,"' says Father Gramolazzo.

In the beginning, the actual 'rite' of exorcism was pretty simple and consisted of laying hands, the invocation of Jesus's name, the sign of the cross, and fasting. Later, in the third century, the practice of blowing on the person or 'exsufflation' was added.[9] In fact, rather than relying on a complicated formula, the Fathers of the Church stressed the need for simplicity. Athanasius, the Bishop of Alexandria (who died about 373), notes in a letter to Marcellinus that an exorcist who uses complicated or lengthy invocations runs the risk of being ridiculed by the demons.[10]

Statuta Ecclesiae Latinae, a collection of Church legislation that was issued about the year 500, contains one of the earliest official formulas for exorcism.[11] Over the years, the rite developed primarily in localized form in 'libelli' – small pamphlets each consisting of only a few pages. Finally, prompted by a combination of widespread abuses (exorcists incorporating their own gestures, incantations and even medicines into the ritual) and a growing climate of superstition during the Middle Ages,[12] the diverse formulas were compiled into the *Roman Ritual*, first published in 1614.[13]

Since then, the ritual has gone through a few adjustments, including a minor one in 1952 and a major one in 1998.[14] The 1998 *Revised Ritual*, known in Latin as *De Exorcismis et Supplicationibus Quibusdam*, begins with an introductory section followed by the guidelines, after which the exorcist is to recite the litany of the saints, a few gospel and psalm readings, and if he so chooses, a homily. At the core of the ritual lie the prayers of exorcism themselves, which are broken up into two sections, known commonly as 'deprecatory' and 'imperative'. The difference between these two is extremely important, say exorcists. In a deprecatory prayer, the exorcist entreats God to intervene on behalf of the person; the prayer begins 'Hear, Holy Father . . .' while in the imperative prayer, the exorcist himself commands the demon to depart in the name of Jesus Christ, 'I adjure you, Satan . . .' or 'I cast you out'. Since the imperative formula is not really a prayer but a command, and a highly suggestive one at that, the *Revised Ritual* stipulates that an exorcist may use it only when he is 'morally certain' that the person he is praying over is possessed.[15]

To follow the *Ritual* straight through from start to finish would probably take forty-five minutes to an hour. In truth, however, few exorcists pray it this way, often intermingling psalms of their own choosing or spontaneous exorcism prayers ('I cast you out, spirit of fakeness'), all of which is based on their experience.

'I never follow the *Ritual* exactly the way it is organized in the book,' says Canadian exorcist Father François Dermine OP. 'You can't follow the *Ritual* like that, with a reading from the Bible and then the litany. It comes as it comes, depending on the reaction of the person. I remember one time with one person, as soon as I started to pray, the person went under possession and, in that case, there is not really the time to read the Bible and stuff like that. You have to pray.'

Father Amorth believes that every exorcist must find his strengths and weaknesses and what works best for him. 'One exorcist I know who performs exorcisms down at San Giovanni Rotondo is also the postulant of the cause of beatification of a Capuchin, Father Matteo, who lived 400 years ago.[16] He prays to Father Matteo all the time, and when he invokes him during an exorcism the demons become very furious. Personally I tried several times to invoke Father Matteo but nothing happens. This means that every exorcist learns what for him is more efficient.' Also, since every demon has a different reaction, the exorcist needs to be able to find out which parts of the prayer hurt the demon the most. However, this doesn't mean that the exorcist can just do or say what he wants.

As of late, the International Association of Exorcists has been careful about reminding exorcists to stick with the *Ritual*. 'It is better for the exorcist to just pray the *Ritual* as it is,' says Father Gramolazzo.

An exorcist must remember not to pray the *Ritual* in such a way that it could be confused with a magic ceremony. The reason this is so important is that 'if an exorcist were to do so', explains Father Nanni, 'it would be like casting out a spell with another spell, or a demon by another demon'. It would negate the whole purpose of the rite, not to mention discredit the Church.[17]

There is also the danger of suggestion to consider. Many exorcists have acknowledged the suggestive nature of exorcism and prefer to use euphemistic expressions when performing the ritual. For example, instead of the word exorcism, they say 'blessing', and they never tell people they are possessed, but rather that they are suffering from some kind of 'negativity'. In addition, many exorcists prefer to pray the *Ritual* in Latin to avoid auto-suggestion. 'I think it is better if people don't understand,' says Father Dermine. 'If I pray in a way that the person can understand, sometimes you can risk stimulating certain reactions. If there is really a demon there, he will understand no matter what.'

In the end, the most essential thing, says Father Gramolazzo, is that the exorcist has faith. 'The power of the prayer is not in the formula but in the faith – my faith in the faith of the Church. I can like the prayer, it can be beautiful but the efficacy depends on the faith.'

At the beginning of an exorcism, the demon is loath to reveal himself. 'To be discovered is for him a defeat,' says Father Bamonte. If the demon is strong, then he can hide in the person for a lengthy period, even allowing participation in mass and other prayerful activities. ('Hiding' of course, doesn't mean that the spirit is holed up in some dark corner of the person's body; it simply means that he does not manifest.)

Usually, if the exorcist 'insists', as one Italian exorcist likes to say, the exorcism prayers will stimulate the demon and eventually force him out into the open. Father Nanni describes how this process works: 'It is like boxers,' he says, 'who can take a lot of punishment but stay up without falling. They are stronger because they have the capability of absorbing the blow, but they get hit anyway; and by getting hit and hit and hit, in the end their physical endurance collapses. For demons it is the same. If you keep going with perseverance, sooner or later they will start to give up and manifest.'

Throughout this whole process, the demon tries his best to thwart the exorcist. The demon will attempt to convince the victim that he or she is suffering from a psychological disorder or, if that fails, actually inhibit the person from physically reaching the exorcist. Cars mysteriously break down or phone calls cancel meetings – all without the victim's knowledge, say exorcists.

When the demon is finally forced out into the open, the person will lose consciousness and enter into a trance. At this point, all movement and speech is controlled by the demon. During these times the person's eyes will often roll up or down (the demon can't bear to look at holy objects, including the priest), the hands will usually curl into claws, and the person will be taken over by a rage directed at sacred or holy objects. Typically, the person remembers nothing upon awakening. Sometimes, however, the person may be conscious during the ritual and may remember some of what transpired but will typically feel as if something 'alien' had taken over. Some exorcists, such as Father Amorth, describe the latter as an example of demonic obsession, while a case involving a person emerging from a trance with total amnesia would be indicative of full demonic possession.[18]

According to Father Nanni, once he has begun praying the *Ritual*, there are five traps that the novice exorcist should be wary of: (1) no reaction from the demon for a long time, which is an attempt to trick the exorcist into thinking the cause isn't demonic; (2) the demon fakes that he has gone after manifesting, fooling the person into thinking he or she is now liberated (for this reason some exorcists ask for a sign of liberation); (3) the demon confuses the exorcist by creating in the possessed symptoms of mental illness; (4) the demon reveals the existence of an evil spell and the way in which the exorcist can get rid of it (the exorcist must not practise superstitious acts); and (5) the demon permits the victim to receive the Eucharist as a sign of liberation.[19]

Many people assume that during an exorcism the demon will speak through the person, but this is not always the case. According to Father Amorth, it is a misperception that demons like to speak. In fact, they will almost never do so unless ordered to by the exorcist. Some, however, do try to confuse the exorcist by talking or even threatening him during the ritual, to distract him from the prayers. Father Amorth has been threatened repeatedly: 'Tonight I will throw you out of your bed!' or 'I will eat your heart!' To which he responds, 'Come on, I have my guardian angel that protects me.'[20]

However, beyond the bravado, there is a real danger of an exorcist being attacked physically, mentally and spiritually by the demon during an exorcism, or even after.

Because of the unique role they play, exorcists are faced with a variety of moral and spiritual dilemmas that can open them up to potential attack by demonic forces. Perhaps the most obvious of these is sexual temptation. Exorcisms are highly charged encounters, often taking place in small confined spaces that involve a lot of thrashing and moaning from the victim, who is almost always a woman. There are several theories for the pre-ponderance of female victims: women are more intuitive and in touch with their spiritual side; or, similar to the story of Adam and Eve in the Bible, the Devil targets women specifically as a way to tempt men. Though, as Father Bamonte suggests, it may simply be because more women than men are willing to seek out an exorcist. In some cases, this prevalence may also be attributed to the strictures placed on marginalized individuals in certain societies. In traditional male-dominated cultures, for instance, possession might not only give women a chance to gain atten-tion, but also provide them with an active way of participating (especially true in certain religious circles that may place a kind of 'honour' on demonic possession, signifying that one has attained a level of holiness that warrants the Devil's direct attack).

Anthropologists have noted that women in native societies frequently use spirit possession as a tool of empowerment. For example, in some male-dominated societies of East Africa, women are said to be possessed by spirits who then require their husbands to provide them with gifts and other niceties.[21]

Given this gender dynamic, it is recommended that the exorcist have a 'helper' in the room who is also a woman (this is listed in the guidelines of the 1614 *Roman Ritual*). Being the cunning foe that he is, say exorcists, the demon will try anything to distract the exorcist and get him to stop praying, including sexual advances. According to Father Dermine, the exorcist must also use good sense when he touches a woman he is praying over, always keeping in mind the heightened level of sexual tension.

The exorcist can also be attacked through his pride. This sense of pride can come either from the admiration that an exorcist receives from the people he helps, or from the exorcist thinking himself superior because he has a connection to the supernatural or because he believes he has some personal 'power' that can liberate people. The exorcist should never claim to be a holy man or cultivate a cult-like following. This means he should never take money for his services, which would turn him into a kind of magician or faith healer.

On the flip side, while many exorcists may be admired by the victims, they are often ridiculed by their fellow priests.

An exorcist must be equally careful about familiarity. In many cases an exorcist is the only hope these people undergoing deep pain and suffering believe they have, and there is a real danger of them becoming too dependent on the exorcist (or vice versa). The risk is that the sufferers can become addicted and develop an exaggerated affection for the exorcist. For this reason, say exorcists, it is best to keep these people at a slight distance.

The demon will also try to dishearten the exorcist through intimidation or fear, usually carried out by displays of power. In one such instance, Father Daniel (who became an exorcist briefly in the autumn of 2006) had all his instant text messages erased from his cell phone one morning. He had recently signed up for a new plan and figured it must be a problem with the company. Later that night, however, when he was giving a blessing over the same phone (exorcists claim telephone blessings can be efficacious), the voice of the person changed and the demon came out taunting: 'Did you like the little joke I played on you this morning?' When Father Daniel expressed confusion, the gruff voice mocked, 'If you say a prayer that I give to you, then I will give you back all your instant messages.'

Another exorcist in Chicago, the day before he found out he was to be nominated by the bishop, was awakened by a terrible noise in the middle of the night, like a train wreck happening in his room. Opening his eyes, he then saw the TV at the foot of his bed levitate off the stand a few feet then crash to the floor, and the tape inside the VCR shoot out across the room. At the same time, the curtains of his room moved violently even though his windows were closed.

Sometimes the signs can be even more direct. In 2006, an exorcist from the Midwest was talking to a young man he thought might be possessed when he heard a raspy voice – as if out of nowhere – say, 'Get out!'

An Italian exorcist told of an episode involving members of a Catholic charismatic prayer group who thought they had a special 'gift' to cast out evil spirits. During the exorcism, the charismatics were laying hands and talking to the demon, ordering it to comply. Without warning, the demon turned on them saying, 'Who are you?' Then he launched a bookcase at them, sending them all to the emergency room with injuries.

Exorcists have seen things happening even outside, beyond the confines of the exorcism itself. Father Nanni reports that some exorcists have had their car headlights mysteriously turn off just as they were negotiating particularly dangerous curves on mountain roads. In his book, *An Exorcist Tells His Story*, Father Amorth recounted how one exorcist, after the demon threatened him with immolation, had his car catch fire while he was driving home.[22] Father Nanni, while performing a blessing by phone, had the light bulb in his room explode over his head.

In extreme instances, an exorcist may be severely injured, though this last point has perhaps been exaggerated, especially in the media.[23] Exorcists are rarely hurt. Father Nanni recalled one example: as an exorcist was leaving the house of a possessed person in Sicily he was shoved by an unseen force into an oncoming truck, which nearly killed him. When asked why God would allow such a thing to happen, Father Nanni seemed unfazed. 'We all have to bear our own burdens,' he said. In this case, the exorcist recovered, returned to the house and liberated the person.

Throughout all of this, the only armour the exorcist has to protect him is his faith. 'Faith is worth more than anything else,' says Father Amorth. 'The faith of the exorcist, of the person who is getting exorcized, the faith of the people who help and pray for the person, family and friends.'

'I learned more in performing exorcisms through prayer and faith than from my studies,' said Father Gramolazzo. 'The books that you read and study become something more theoretical; you don't get inside the world of faith. When you perform an exorcism, however, you have to enter into this world; you get in touch with the supernatural.'

As he walked back to the train station following class, Father Gary discussed some of the finer points of the day's lecture with Father Daniel. Perhaps as a result of his experiences as an embalmer, or the fact that he had survived a near-death hiking accident in 1997, he wasn't worried about being physically attacked by a demon. If he feared anything, it was performing an exorcism on someone who didn't need it. And while the course had taught him a lot, he realized that the only way to put his fears to rest would be to actually participate in an exorcism.

CHAPTER SEVEN

SEARCHING FOR AN EXORCIST

An exorcist works all his life between being admired and thanked by some and bitterly despised and persecuted by others . . . God desires that this ministry always be done from the cross. If a priest is not willing to bear this burden, he should not accept this ministry.

Father José Antonio Fortea, *Interview with an Exorcist*

On a typical Tuesday morning, a small crowd gathers outside the Scala Santa by 8.30, even though the large wooden doors won't open for another half an hour.[1] Most are women, ranging in age from their mid-twenties to late sixties, their outfits running the gamut from shawls and brooches to hip-hugging jeans and leather jackets. Milling around, some people pass the time chatting, others avoid eye contact. In addition to the normal purses and backpacks, several carry large plastic grocery sacks filled with various religious items, such as candles and plastic water bottles.

The Scala Santa or Church of the Holy Staircase has always

held a unique place among the churches of Rome, drawing countless pilgrims over the years to its venerated Sancta Sanctorum (Holy of Holies), the personal chapel of the popes, which the devout reach by climbing a special staircase. These are thought to be the very stairs from Pontius Pilate's palace in Jerusalem that Christ climbed on the day of his death (brought back to Rome by Helena, the mother of the Emperor Constantine in the fourth century), and pilgrims climb the twenty-eight steps on their knees, pausing at each one to say a prayer. Encased now in protective wood, the original steps can still be glimpsed through small glass windows that supposedly reveal actual drops of Christ's blood.

And yet, beyond the chapel and the stairs, among Romans, the church has a long association with exorcism. For thirty-six years, the Passionist monk Father Candido Amantini performed exorcisms there until he died in 1992. Long thought of as a holy man, even among exorcists, Father Candido had an open-door policy towards exorcism, never turning anybody away. It was rumoured that he saw around sixty people every day, and while not everybody needed an exorcism, he tried to at least give them a simple blessing or even just a reassuring pat on the shoulder.

When Father Tommaso took over, this open-door policy was maintained. Even as the church continues to be a major attraction for tourists and pilgrims, exorcisms and blessings are performed around the clock, screams and all.

For half an hour, most of the women wait patiently outside the church; as more show up, the ones closest to the door begin jockeying for position. A few minutes later, they hear the telltale jingle of keys from behind the door followed by the click of the lock, and even before the sour-faced custodian has time to swing the door all the way open, the women begin filing through. Hurrying past him, they sidestep the historic steps and proceed instead toward one of the two side staircases. Climbing, they move in a rush past the Sancta Sanctorum, through the

Saint Lawrence Chapel, until they reach the door to the sacristy where one half-expects to see a red ribbon stretched across the corridor.

Instead, everyone takes a place, as if settling into a 'favourite chair'. One woman bends on to a small wooden kneeler right outside the door while others slide into a ten-foot wooden pew that runs the length of the wall. More branch off to a nearby chapel, where they kneel in front of a life-sized representation of Christ on the cross. A few clutch rosaries, their fingers moving anxiously over the beads as their lips mouth silent prayers. Others keep their eyes down. By now around twenty people have gathered, and still more trickle in. One of these is an attractive young woman who walks past everyone to stand next to the door. A few people eye her and shift nervously, but otherwise seem not to mind that she has jumped the queue. One of the latecomers, a man in his sixties, asks the woman on the kneeler, 'Is he seeing anyone right now?' The woman shakes her head. Somebody near by pipes in, 'I just have to get a quick blessing and then I'll go.'

The woman on the kneeler flashes the speaker a dirty look and says, '*He* decides who goes in first.'

'Who gets chosen to go in?' someone else asks.

'He performs exorcisms first and then blessings afterwards,' the woman on the kneeler explains.

Someone pulls out a piece of paper and people begin writing their names down, as if waiting for a table at a restaurant. Most have places to go in the afternoon and a few sigh and cluck their tongues when they see themselves at the bottom of the list.

As if on cue, the door opens and Father Tommaso pokes his head out, his tired eyes searching. A few of the people near the door turn to him, but his presence keeps them back; it's clear that nobody wants to get on his bad side. He nods to the attractive woman who'd jumped the queue and she enters, the door shutting behind them.

In the ensuing silence, people settle back into their slumped postures. Then suddenly a sound like a wolverine on the loose knocking down all the chairs comes from the sacristy. A high-pitched scream followed by a woman's voice shouting 'Basta!' (Enough!) disrupts the silence. Then comes moaning and howling as if someone were being tortured. Some clutch their rosaries tighter. Some try to move out of earshot but, inside the cold, marble-floored sanctuary, sounds carry far.

When Father Gary asked about the possibility of finding an exorcist with whom to apprentice, Father Daniel's first thought was to ask Father Tommaso. However, the exorcist was too busy to take on another student. While Father Gary was disappointed, Father Daniel reassured him by saying, 'You won't learn much there anyway. The place is insane.'

Over the ensuing month, Father Gary continued to look for an exorcist he could apprentice to, a task that proved more daunting than he'd imagined. Even a cardinal whom he met in the halls of the NAC one day was unable to help. With his limited Italian, Father Gary needed an exorcist who spoke a little English, and according to a reply he received from the dean of the Lateran University, there weren't any.

Finally, Father Daniel contacted one of the exorcists who helped teach the course.

A few days later, he called Father Gary back with good news. Father Bamonte, who had studied under Father Amorth and who had been performing exorcisms since 2003, said that he would be willing to take on Father Gary as a last resort (he was not thrilled, largely because of the language barrier). In the meantime, Father Bamonte suggested that Father Gary contact a Capuchin by the name of Father Carmine (pronounced Car-me-nay) De Filippis, who he thought knew a little English.

As he got off the phone with Father Daniel, Father Gary was guardedly optimistic about this latest turn of events.

*

December rolled in and Rome's famous *sampietrini* cobblestones grew cold and wet. The exorcism course had shut down for the month so Father Gary took the time to enjoy the holiday season. There was a special mass and dinner held at the Casa on Christmas Eve; and then, on the following day, Father Gary was a Eucharistic minister at Saint Peter's Basilica during the midnight mass presided over by the pope. Afterwards, despite the bitterly cold wind, the square was packed with revellers. By the time he and the other priests walked back to the Casa, it was 3.30 in the morning and the streets were absolutely still.

A few days later, Father Gary and another priest from the Casa, Father Paul Hrezzo, decided to take a little side trip together, travelling to Vienna for a few days and then on to Medjugorje in Bosnia-Herzegovina for New Year's Eve. There, the two presided over mass for the English pilgrims visiting the shrine and spent five restful days meditating and praying.[2]

On 9 January, the second half of the exorcism course commenced at the Regina Apostolorum. Much like the first half, things got off to a bad start for Father Gary. His translator didn't show up and Father Gary was forced to search for a replacement, which he couldn't find. As it turned out, the lecture was on Italian law, so wasn't a huge loss.

Now that the holiday season was over and things were beginning to return to normal in Rome, he was finally able to get through to Father Carmine, the exorcist Father Bamonte had recommended. In his best Italian, Father Gary tried to explain his dilemma. Father Carmine listened patiently for a few minutes and then cut in. 'Yes, yes,' he said in Italian, 'I'd be happy to help you, but you need to check with my superior first.'

Hanging up the phone, Father Gary was relieved. 'Maybe this is just a formality that Father Carmine asks all his apprentices to go through?' he thought. When he finally got in touch with the superior two days later, however, he hit a dead-end. Not only was the man *not* Father Carmine's superior, but he'd never heard of the exorcist. Funny, though, he did speak a little English and had relatives in San Jose, so Father Gary ended up chatting with him for quite some time. In the end, Father Gary figured that Father Carmine had probably just given him the brush-off. 'He doesn't know me,' he thought, 'he probably just wants to get rid of me.'

The following Thursday at the exorcism course, he approached Father Daniel at the break and told him about what had happened. As luck would have it, Father Bamonte was lecturing that day so Father Daniel approached him to ask one last time if he would be willing to help Father Gary. After a few minutes, Father Daniel returned with a gloomy look on his face. 'I don't know why, but he won't do it,' he said.

'This is getting ridiculous,' Father Gary thought. 'I am going to go home soon and won't know the first thing about exorcism.'

'Try calling Father Carmine again,' Father Daniel said.

Back at the Casa that evening, Father Gary was on the verge of calling his bishop to tell him he would have to nominate somebody else but instead decided to go to the chapel to pray. 'God,' he said, as he sat in a wooden pew, 'if you want me to do this, you are going to have to help me.'

As he climbed the long flight of stairs back to his room, he decided to call Father Carmine one last time, almost certain that no one would pick up. To his surprise, the Capuchin answered. He explained to Father Carmine what had been going on. The other end of the line was silent for a long moment before he heard Father Carmine say, 'OK, OK, but I need to see you first.'

'I'll come and see you. Tell me when,' Father Gary responded.

'Come out Sunday morning and we'll talk.'

As he hung up, Father Gary couldn't believe Father Carmine had agreed to see him. Coming as it did on the heels of his prayer, he took it as a sign that God had to be involved.

Some exorcists are known to have a special 'gift' for healing or discernment (the ability to uncover the presence of a spirit). These gifts, called charisms, are said to be distributed by the

Holy Spirit to those who live devoted lives. One such exorcist was Father Candido Amantini. Supposedly Father Candido could diagnose demonic possession simply by looking at a person's photo. In addition, Father Gramolazzo remembers when a possessed person took a swing at Father Candido but the fist stopped only inches from his face, as if held there by an unseen force. Father Candido then blew on the raised fist and the man yanked it back quickly, as if it had been burned.

Lay people may also receive charisms, and more than a few exorcists include such individuals on their prayer teams to help with their discernment. The Second Vatican Council affirms the existence of these gifts but recommends caution: 'These charismatic gifts, whether they be the most outstanding or the more simple and widely diffused, are to be received with thanksgiving and consolation . . . Still, extraordinary gifts are not to be rashly sought after . . . In any case, judgment as to their genuineness and proper use belongs to those who preside over the Church and to whose special competence it belongs, not indeed to extinguish the Spirit, but to test all things and hold fast to that which is good.'[3]

Father Carmine, who studied under Father Candido, claimed no such 'powers'. Instead he preferred to rely on his experience.

Father Carmine was born in 1953 in Salerno in the south of Italy, but moved to Rome with his family when he was very young. Even as a boy he had a strong desire to enter the priesthood. 'It's not true that kids don't understand anything,' he says. 'They understand everything.' When he was ten years old, he knew that he wanted to completely dedicate his life to God through prayer and penitence, leading the life of a Capuchin friar. Frequenting religious services in his parish of Saint Teresa in Corso Italia, Father Carmine was always impressed by the friars, most of all by their way of praying, by their sacred liturgies. He entered the seminary in 1974 when he was just twenty-one.

His first experience with exorcism came when he was still in the seminary. One day while he in the middle of a theology lesson, another priest interrupted to say there was a disturbance in the church. An old lady had brought in a girl who was cursing and screaming and drooling in front of the tabernacle. The superior immediately left to see what was happening. Later he returned and surprised the students with the observation that he thought the woman was possessed so had taken her to see the exorcist of the diocese. As Father Carmine recalls, the classroom erupted into laughter, and he thought to himself, 'This is ridiculous, something from the Middle Ages. Nobody believes in possession any more, do they?'

A few days later, the superior approached Father Carmine and another seminarian to ask whether they would be interested in participating in the exorcism. Father Carmine agreed, and the experience changed his life. 'I saw horrible, horrible things,' he says. At one point during the exorcism, as the girl thrashed and screamed, her normally closed eyes popped open and she turned and looked at him. 'In her eyes I could see the hate, such pure hate that it hurt me very deeply.' During the exorcism, he and his fellow seminarian also felt mysterious blows on their shins, as if someone standing in front of them had kicked them, yet no one was near.

Eventually, toward the end of the exorcism, the girl began vomiting huge quantities of human sperm, accompanied by a nauseating stench that nearly forced Father Carmine out of the room. 'I was scared to death, shocked,' he says. 'I realized that demons do exist, that the Devil is not that puppet with the horns that we see in comic books and laugh about. I had to reverse all my theological concepts which up until that point were very superficial. I became aware that we are all under the threat of this enemy.'

After he was ordained in 1981, he spent some time in a mission in Bolivia before returning to Rome, where he began to study exorcism under Father Giacobbe, a disciple of Father Candido. Father Carmine remembers Father Candido's specifications for an exorcist's qualities. 'He has to try to live an evangelical, virtuous life, a life of prayer; he has to have knowledge, meaning that he has to study theology, the Bible; and thirdly he has to have experience.' Father Candido also stressed the role that an exorcist should play with respect to the ministry. 'He is exhorted to be as generous as possible in helping the poor people who suffer because this is a ministry of assistance of help for those who suffer.' Taking this advice to heart, Father Carmine began performing exorcisms in 1987.

After mass on Sunday, Father Gary stepped out of the tranquillity that was the Casa and merged with the throngs of people heading down Via Vincenzo dei Lucchesi and towards the Trevi Fountain. Sundays are busy days for foot traffic in Rome, when people who live on the periphery make their way down towards the city's more famous piazzas to join the never-ending stream of tourists. And rather than ones and twos, most travel in large clumps, creating havoc on the narrow streets amid snarling traffic, much to the consternation of taxi drivers who never hesitate to let their frustrations be known.

Moving on towards Via della Stamperia, he steeled himself against a gust of wind that funnelled down the tunnel-like street. On Via del Tritone he turned to his right and began walking up the hill in the direction of Piazza Barberini. A large group of people stood around on the sidewalk near a series of bus signs and he took his place among them. He wasn't sure how long it would take him to get out to the Basilica di San Lorenzo fuori le Mura (Saint Lawrence outside the Walls), but he'd given himself forty-five minutes just to be on the safe side.

The Basilica of San Lorenzo has a long association with death. Built on the site of Christian catacombs from the third century and adjacent to the sprawling city-like Verano Cemetery, the basilica houses the bones of three saints – Saint Lawrence, Saint Stephen, Saint Justin – as well as those of Pope Pio IX. From the outside, when compared to its siblings, such as Saint John

Lateran or Saint Paul outside the Walls, San Lorenzo has a very simple, almost mission-like quality – a red brick structure with white, column-like teeth that slopes backward into the crypts and mausoleums. The church is extremely old – one section was built by Pope Pelagius II in the sixth century; the second, including its simple porch-like façade, in the thirteenth century by Pope Honorius III. And unlike the encroaching suburbs of Rome, it appears that little about the building has changed over the years,[4] since it was surrounded by fields and vineyards, located along one of Rome's ancient roads, the Via Tiburtina, used by wealthy Romans to escape the city for their country villas.

Walking down from the bus stop, Father Gary found himself in a relatively peaceful part of town. The basilica was set back from the street a little, located across an expanse of asphalt shaded by clusters of towering cypresses and umbrella pines. Several flower stalls dotted the parking lot outside the arching gates of the cemetery, their owners sitting on cheap wooden chairs, reading newspapers. Since he was fifteen minutes early, Father Gary wandered towards the basilica.

Built on two different axes, the medieval interior of the basilica with its tiers of arches and wooden roof almost appeared to have been carved out of the earth. As he meandered up and down the nave, Father Gary found the place to be too cold and dark, the air too musty and stale for his taste.

At ten o'clock, he walked across the small courtyard that separated the basilica from the friary. He pushed the tiny buzzer next to the double doors and stood for a moment studying the two lion's head knockers that decorated the door, wondering about Father Carmine. He was grateful for being allowed the rare opportunity of seeing an exorcist in his working environment.

After a few minutes the door opened and a barrel-chested man of medium height in the traditional friar garb appeared. He wore his hair short, and his three-inch beard was streaked with grey. His blue eyes, though, were perhaps his most striking feature. Only narrow slits, they were sandwiched between a pair of ruddy cheeks and thin dark eyebrows that arched playfully near the ends, giving him a jocular, almost mischievous appearance that made him seem much younger than his fifty-three years. After scrutinizing Father Gary for a few long seconds, a light seemed to go on behind his eyes and his expression softened. 'Ahhh, Padre Gary,' he said, 'Bene, bene.' And then in heavily accented English, 'Welcome.'

Stepping through the door, Father Gary entered a small reception room full of mismatched furniture; various framed religious photographs, including those of the previous five popes; and a three-foot statue of Mary on a pedestal near the doorway to Father Carmine's office. Two windows covered by incongruous lace curtains completed the picture of a room originally used for something else. Father Carmine hadn't yet taken down his Christmas decorations. A large, intricate Nativity set, adorned with blinking lights, occupied a corner. The room's only living inhabitant was a rather large, mangy tabby cat that lay completely still, curled up on one of the chairs. 'Malato' (not well), Father Carmine said, indicating the cat. Father Gary, who wasn't a cat person, kept his distance.

'Come, come,' Father Carmine motioned, and led the way into his office, which had the same eclectic ambience. A large, cluttered wooden desk took up most of the small room, while a faded floral-print loveseat and a few worn office swivel chairs constituted the room's only other furniture. The walls were practically covered with all manner of religious items (some apparently handmade) and photos he had collected over his years as a missionary in South America.

Father Carmine took a seat behind his desk and Father Gary sat opposite. He handed the letter from his bishop to Father Carmine, who studied it, passing his right hand down his cheeks until his thumb and forefinger met at the tip of his beard. 'Bene, bene,' he said. Good, good. 'The bishops are finally starting to get it,' he said in Italian. The two talked for about half an hour, and, anxious to make a good impression, Father Gary decided to drop the matter of him having to call the superior and the perceived brush-off. Instead he told Father Carmine a little about himself. He could tell that the Capuchin did not speak much English, but would slip an English word in here or there. More importantly, though, he understood English pretty well, which meant Father Gary could at least express himself. Father Gary tried to speak some Italian, and though he often made mistakes, he'd learned enough to communicate the basics. 'Si, si, io capisco,' pronounced in halting little jumps followed by a long flourish, was a frequent crutch. Yes, yes, I understand.

Father Gary liked Father Carmine immediately and felt he was in good hands. He always looked Father Gary in the eye as he spoke, and his gaze was unwavering as if he were searching for something, testing. Later, Father Gary would learn that most exorcists study people's eyes, as they are the 'windows to the soul'. In fact, one of Father Carmine's criteria for discerning possession is when the victim is unable to look the exorcist in the eyes.

Father Carmine's description of how he performed the ritual – even and calm – also made a big impression on Father Gary.

At one point, Father Carmine pointed to a small woodpanelled room attached to his office, really no bigger than a walk-in closet. 'I perform the blessings in there,' he said. Father Gary tried to make out what he could from where he was sitting and saw a few metal chairs and nothing much else.

After he seemed satisfied, Father Carmine brought the conversation to a close. 'Va bene,' he said. 'Why don't you come back tomorrow afternoon at five and we'll get started on the hardest cases first.'

His fieldwork had begun.

CHAPTER EIGHT

THE FIRST NIGHT

Midway on our life's journey, I found myself / In dark woods, the right road lost. To tell / About those woods is hard – so tangled and rough / And savage that thinking of it now, I feel / The old fear stirring: death is hardly more bitter.

Dante, *The Inferno*

For the remainder of the afternoon, Father Gary couldn't stop wondering what he might see at San Lorenzo the following day. Because Father Carmine had given no indication of what to expect, he pictured the worst – images like Father Daniel's experience of the woman's jaw unhinging and moving over to the side of her face.

All he had to go on was an audio clip he'd listened to on Father Daniel's MP3 player, a recording of Father Daniel confronting a woman who had interrupted mass by shouting at the congregation. Thinking the woman might be possessed, he'd taken her and her companion into a side room to try to calm the woman down. At that point he turned on his recorder. To Father Gary, the voice on the audio clip sounded nothing like a woman's. Deep, raspy, guttural – a cornered animal came to mind. 'Devi dire di no!' You have to say no! the voice screamed over and over, followed by periods of wailing and moaning that didn't sound human. 'Devi dire di no!' The voice shouted again, this time followed by Father Daniel's, 'Basta! In nome di Gesù Cristo ti ordino di smettere.' In the name of Jesus Christ I order you to stop.

Recalling that voice, Father Gary imagined what it must have been like to be in that room, to realize that you are in the presence of pure evil. Father Daniel had told him how frightened he'd been at the time. He pictured himself listening to such a hateful diatribe in the room Father Carmine used, which was so small that he'd be practically on top of the person. If the person went crazy and started attacking, he'd be right in the thick of it.

That night, after his evening prayers he spent a few extra minutes asking God for the strength to overcome whatever lay ahead.

On Monday afternoon, Father Gary again stood among the crowds on Via del Tritone, waiting for a bus. He was wearing his black clerics and carried a small bag containing the purple stole he would wear during the ritual, as well as the small red *Ritual* book itself. He'd purchased it a couple of weeks before at a bookstore on Via della Conciliazione. Even though he was out of practice with his Latin, he planned to follow along anyway.

Sitting on the bus as it lurched through the narrow streets, he wondered how this experience would change him.

He arrived at San Lorenzo around five in the evening, just as the sun was starting to set. Traffic was heavy on Via Tiburtina, and all the rubber tyres traversing the cobblestones created a high-pitched whine that seemed to stalk him like a swarm of angry insects as he walked down to the basilica.

A small group of people stood outside the closed door to Father Carmine's office. They represented a broad spectrum – an older lady in her sixties, dressed conservatively; a man in his late thirties, who wore a V-necked sweater and collared shirt; two

young thirty-something women wearing brand new Nike train-
ers and fashionable clothes; and a serious-looking couple in their
fifties. Some chatted, while one man stood off on his own, his
arms crossed tightly over his chest.

As Father Gary approached, a few looked in his direction,
eyeing him suspiciously. One of the younger women, with
shoulder-length blonde hair, refused even to look at him.

Taking his place among them, he wondered who they might
be. He looked for signs of 'trauma', anything that might indicate
these people were suffering from demonic possession, but found
nothing. He knew from Father Daniel that exorcists sometimes
did simple blessings. Perhaps the more serious cases hadn't
arrived yet.

A few minutes later, the door swung inward to reveal Father
Carmine, who barely gave the group a glance before shuffling
back inside. One by one, and with an after-you attitude, the
group filed inside and took up positions around the waiting
room, unwrapping coats and scarves. The door to Father
Carmine's office was ajar so Father Gary gently pushed his way
inside, and said, 'Buona sera.' Father Carmine returned the
greeting and asked if he was ready.

'Si,' Father Gary replied.

'Good,' Father Carmine said. 'Allora, cominciamo.' OK, let's
begin.

Father Gary took off his coat, slipped on his purple stole, then
entered the small room off the office, which contained a wooden
end table near the door and four metal chairs, two against one
wall and two shoved into the corner. Thinking it would be best
to make himself as unobtrusive as possible, Father Gary took a
seat in the corner, still only a few feet from the other two chairs.
The room, which seemed even smaller from the inside, was an
odd setting for an exorcism. Like most European rooms, it had a
very high ceiling. The upper walls were crisscrossed by exposed
pipe while the lower walls were covered by a fake wood panelling about six feet high. Each wall held some kind of sacred

image – a framed picture of Padre Pio[1] along with a hand-woven rug depicting Mary and the baby Jesus on one wall, a purple stole (belonging to Father Candido) encased in glass on another wall, and a black-and-white picture of Christ crowned with thorns directly above the two empty chairs. To his immediate right, the room's only window, which he could reach if he were to stand on tiptoes, was latched shut.

From his seat, he could just make out the contents of a little wooden box resting on the end table near the door: a picture of St Francis, a rosary, various medallions, a roll of paper towels, a wooden crucifix, and a squeeze bottle of holy water – essentially, the tools of Father Carmine's trade.

As he waited, Father Gary glanced at the two empty chairs against the wall. Just above their backs, a patch of wood panelling was rubbed and scraped raw, as if someone, or something, had clawed it.

Seconds later Father Carmine, now wearing a thin, wrinkled purple stole, entered the room carrying a plastic shopping bag that he hung on the back of the door handle. Satisfied that everything was ready, he ducked out to the waiting room.

Father Gary eyed the bag, wondering why they would need it. A few seconds later, Father Carmine returned with the man in his late thirties.

Father Gary could tell the man was unnerved by his presence so he tried to put him at ease. 'Hello,' he said, holding out his hand. 'Mi chiamo don Gary Thomas. Vengo dalla California.'

The man smiled as he shook Father Gary's hand. 'Oh, California! È un piacere.' It's a pleasure to meet you.

The man sat down and Father Carmine stood directly in front of him. Father Gary, perplexed by the man's cordiality, took his seat and opened the Ritual book.

'In nómine Patris et Fílii et Spíritus Sancti [In the name of the Father, the Son and the Holy Spirit]', Father Carmine said as he blessed the man with a few drops of holy water from the squeeze bottle. Following this, he placed his hand on the man's head and immediately began praying the deprecatory prayer of the *Ritual* from memory, skipping a good chunk of the book that Father Gary had opened on his lap. 'Deus, humáni géneris cónditor atque defénsor [God, creator and defender of the human race] . . .' Father Carmine began, 'look down on this your servant, whom you formed in your own image and now call to be a partaker in your glory.' Father Carmine spoke with an even, almost soft tone, the Latin blending into a shushing sound.

Occasionally, as he prayed, he would turn to Father Gary and point to a spot in the *Ritual*. Father Gary tried his best to follow along though he was distracted by trying to gauge the man's reaction.

Initially, the man sat perfectly still, his eyes clenched tight as Father Carmine recited the prayers. After a few minutes, however, he began to cough – at first just a bit, but then the coughing got worse and worse. He began to move his head from side to side as if trying to dislodge Father Carmine's hand. Then he began trying to push Father Carmine away – not violently, but as if he were drunk and didn't have complete control of his motor skills.

Father Carmine, meanwhile, used his free hand to keep the man's flailing arms away. He continued praying the *Ritual* without skipping a beat, occasionally accentuating a word from the prayer. As he intoned 'Ipse Christus tibi ímperat [Christ commands you]', the word 'ímperat' (commands) was spoken louder, though still not shouted.

While he watched, Father Gary prayed a few 'Hail Marys' and 'Our Fathers' silently.

The man's cough continued to get worse, until he was hacking as if something was stuck in his throat.

Father Carmine then took his free hand and pushed on the man's sternum, causing him to let out a belching sound.

To Father Gary it sounded more like air escaping than a belch caused by food – 'Uhhhhhhhh. Huuuuhhhhhhh.'

The man continued belching for a few minutes then suddenly

stood up, and with tightly clenched eyes, pushed past Father Carmine towards the door.

Father Carmine immediately spun him around and expertly plopped him back down into the chair. He continued the *Ritual* for several minutes until he abruptly stopped and tapped the man's forehead with his index finger, at the same time roughing up his hair in the manner of an older brother razzing a younger sibling.

As he did this, the man stopped fidgeting and opened his eyes. He sat for a moment, rubbing his eyes, taking a few deep breaths.

'Come stai, giovanotto?' How are you, young man? Father Carmine asked him while patting his shoulders.

The man, now fully aware, looked up at him and nodded. 'Bene,' he replied.

It took a moment for Father Gary to realize that the exorcism was over. From start to finish, the whole episode had lasted about twenty minutes.

As Father Carmine led the man out into his office, Father Gary stayed behind in the room. The exorcism certainly hadn't gone as he had expected. He'd seen none of the symptoms talked about in his exorcism class nor the dramatic reactions Father Daniel had described. Instead this guy only coughed and belched. Father Gary hated to admit it, but he felt underwhelmed.

Next, the conservatively dressed woman in her fifties entered, accompanied by her husband, who wore a slightly rumpled suit. Again, Father Gary introduced himself and sat back down in the corner. Father Carmine asked the woman a few questions in Italian, and Father Gary caught something about 'not being able to receive the Eucharist'. She began to cry and Father Carmine consoled her, 'No, no, non ti devi preoccupare.' No, no, you don't have to worry.

Father Gary took note that Father Carmine blessed both the woman and her husband, a gesture he found touching. 'It's not only about the woman,' he thought, appreciating the pastoral significance of it and making a mental note to do the same when the time came for him to perform an exorcism.

As before, Father Carmine invoked the Holy Spirit by putting his hand on the woman's head and then skipped straight through the *Ritual* to the exorcism prayers. This time, the woman went completely rigid and didn't move a muscle.

Midway through the exorcism the phone rang in Father Carmine's office and, to Father Gary's surprise, Father Carmine interrupted the exorcism to walk out and answer it. As he did so, the woman remained where she was, though the rigidity seemed to leave her. She seemed unfazed that Father Carmine had taken a phone call, while Father Gary wondered whether his mentor was taking the woman's situation seriously.

After a few minutes, Father Carmine came back in, picking up where he had left off. Once he resumed the prayers, the woman immediately went rigid again. The exorcism continued for another fifteen minutes.

Afterwards, Father Carmine blessed a six-pack of bottled water that the couple had brought, waving his hand in the sign of the cross. As they walked out, Father Carmine, perhaps sensing Father Gary's confusion, felt compelled to explain: 'Lei è posseduta da un demone muto,' he said, struggling to find the right word in English. 'Cannot speak,' he said. 'A very powerful demon.'

'A mute demon?' Father Gary asked. Father Carmine nodded.

Father Gary had heard about mute demons through the course. Father Daniel had weighed in on them, too. He wondered, though, how an exorcist could tell whether a person was really possessed by such a demon. Before he had time to question Father Carmine further, the Capuchin was ushering in a couple in their forties. This time the exorcism lasted about ten minutes, and the only noticeable reaction was the man's continual yawning. As with the two previous cases, Father Carmine tapped the man's forehead with his index finger, which Father Gary took to mean that the exorcism was finished.

The fourth person was another woman in her late fifties, with short curly reddish hair that was noticeably thinning. She entered with her husband and a ten-year-old boy who appeared to be her grandson. They all sat and Father Carmine began bantering with the boy, asking about school and reminding him to behave. Father Gary could tell that Father Carmine had become almost like a parish priest, checking in with people, listening to their problems. After a few minutes, Father Carmine blessed the family, sprinkling them with holy water, and then the boy and the husband left. Alone with the woman, Father Carmine asked her how she was doing. 'The headaches,' she answered in Italian, holding her head. Her voice became choked and she dabbed at tears with a handkerchief. 'Terrible, terrible,' she said. Father Carmine nodded.

The woman sat with her head bowed and her arms in her lap as Father Carmine prayed the *Ritual* over her. Tears continued to stream down her cheeks and she grimaced occasionally, a little squeak of pain escaping from her clenched mouth as if she had stomach cramps.

After this case, Father Carmine took a ten-minute break, and he and Father Gary sat down in the office. Early on, Father Gary had decided he would not ask unnecessary questions or disturb Father Carmine's rhythm during the exorcisms. He didn't know Father Carmine all that well yet, and he wanted to make a favourable impression so he could keep coming back. Now, however, as they paused, he couldn't resist. 'How do you know these people are possessed?'

Father Carmine quickly explained his 'technique of discernment' – he notices things through little 'signs'. Most of these people, he said, had already been through several hospitals and had seen numerous doctors, none of which helped. 'This last woman,' he said, 'has terrible headaches, the kind that don't go away. They completely block her. No matter how many aspirins she takes, it doesn't help. You understand?'

'Si, si,' Father Gary agreed, but he still wasn't sure how to be absolutely certain. The course had stressed that an exorcist should be sceptical in the beginning and, while he trusted that Father Carmine knew what he was doing, it bothered Father Gary that the 'signs' weren't as apparent to him as they were to Father Carmine. Wary of being disrespectful, he held his tongue.

At 6.45 they took a short break and went to the basilica for evening prayer. Around fifteen people, including two other friars, crowded into the Cappella di San Tarcisio just off the sacristy. Among those praying, Father Gary recognized some of the people he'd seen in Father Carmine's waiting room. Apparently he would have to rethink his concept of what it meant to be possessed. Weren't demons supposed to stop people from worshipping?

They returned to Father Carmine's office and resumed the exorcisms. None of the reactions extended beyond coughing and yawning. One woman coughed so much that she brought up some foam. Father Carmine gave her one of the paper towels to wipe her mouth, then he threw it in the plastic rubbish bag he had attached to the door. At least Father Gary got an answer to the question about the bag's purpose.

Towards the end of the evening, Father Gary could see that the strain of so many exorcisms was starting to affect Father Carmine. Drenched and aching from being on his feet for hours, he shifted continuously and hooked his left hand into his rope belt behind his back while he prayed. Father Gary knew he must be exhausted.

Finally, at eight o'clock, Father Carmine turned to Father Gary and announced with a heavy voice, 'We're finished.'

He could see that Father Carmine was drained; still he couldn't resist. 'Un momento,' he said to Father Carmine. 'Una domanda?' A question.

Father Carmine turned to look at him, his eyes lidded and heavy.

'Come back tomorrow afternoon at 3.30,' he nodded. 'We can talk a little then.'

When Father Gary stepped outside, the streets around the basilica were practically deserted. A handful of antiquated streetlights cast a dull glow over him as he walked briskly to the bus stop on the opposite side of Via Tiburtina. Once on the bus, he realized that instead of providing answers, the evening had raised more doubts. The people had certainly appeared to be troubled, but whether the cause was demonic, he couldn't say. None had displayed the classic symptoms of demonic possession. He knew that Italy had socialized medicine, that its population was 83 per cent Catholic – maybe seeing a priest was easier for people than seeing a counsellor, he hypothesized. And wouldn't a priest locked in battle against a demon let the answering machine pick up the phone?

He had to trust that Father Carmine had the experience to diagnose these people; after all, he'd been an exorcist for more than eighteen years. Still, something about the experiences troubled Father Gary. He felt let down that he hadn't found the definitive proof that he sought.

CHAPTER NINE

DISCERNMENT

Every man has close by him two angels, the one an angel of holiness, the other an angel of perversion . . . And how then, O Lord, shall I recognize the workings of these two since they both dwell within me?

Hermas, *The Shepherd*

In mid-January, even before participating in his first exorcism, Father Gary had been asked by the director of pastoral formation at the NAC, 47-year-old Father Steve Bigler, to give a talk to the seminarians about discernment. While not an exorcist himself, Father Bigler had taken the exorcism course the year before and wanted his seminarians to have more practical exposure. He thought of Father Gary, whom he knew from their time together the previous fall at the NAC.

The concept that most terrified Father Gary about exorcism was discernment – the possibility that he might get it wrong. He knew that several mental illnesses could mask themselves as demonic possession. Performing exorcisms on people with severe mental disease would most likely harm them, 'fixing' them in this state. He was extremely wary of doing anything

that might add to a person's pain by making an existing condition worse.[1]

When Father Bigler contacted him, Father Gary immediately
warmed to the idea of imparting some of his knowledge to the
seminarians. In fact, early on, once he began to sink his teeth
into the course material, he'd realized that while he might never
be called upon to actually perform an exorcism, he could still be
a resource for priests in the parish who had questions. He had
seen how callous some priests could be in certain situations, such
as ignoring people who sought comfort for things like depression.

He gave his presentation on a Saturday afternoon in one of
the NAC's small gathering rooms, with the seminarians arranged
around a horseshoe-shaped table. Attending the talk had been
optional, so only eight seminarians showed up, along with two
spiritual directors and the director of spiritual formation, Father
Mike Tomaseck. All found the subject intriguing.

Father Gary's portion of the talk focused on the teachings of
the Church with respect to the Devil. To help the seminarians
with the concept of discernment, he passed around a list of questions they might ask a person who claimed to be possessed,
telling the seminarians that 'these are just food for thought'.

The questions ranged from the obvious ('Can you please
describe the experience that led you to believe that you are
being affected by a presence of evil?') to the less obvious ('How
would you describe your own personal self-discipline?'). At the
bottom of the page, Father Gary had written a small 'end note',
explaining how the questions had been derived from the course
material and how, in his opinion, 'many of the lectures that have
been presented do not only apply specifically to the demonic but
to experiences leading up to demonic possession or other kinds
of harassment and evil manifestations'.

Afterwards, despite the low turnout, he was pleased with how
his talk went. His main goal was to give the seminarians 'some
equipment in their pastoral bag' that could help them 'minister
and serve people, rather than tell them they were crazy'. From

the course he had picked up the phrase 'the exorcist must be the ultimate sceptic' and he never got tired of saying it.

In adopting this prudent approach, Father Gary was only following recognized protocol. The guidelines set forth in the *Ritual* clearly state that 'the exorcist should not proceed to celebrate the rite of exorcism unless he has discovered to his moral certainty that the one to be exorcized is in actual fact possessed by demonic power'.[2] In order to do this, the exorcist 'must above all exercise necessary and extreme circumspection and prudence . . . He must not be too ready to believe that someone beset by some illness, especially mental illness, is a victim of demonic possession [nor] should he immediately believe that possession is present as soon as someone asserts that he or she is in a special way tempted by the Devil, abandoned, or indeed tormented, for people can be deceived by their own imagination.'[3]

The discernment of spirits is far more than just an educated guess, not to be confused with 'intuition'. Instead, according to Sicilian exorcist Father Matteo La Grua, discernment is one of the gifts that God gives to the faithful. It is like a 'holy light' that comes from God and which allows those who receive it 'to see how God is present in things'.[4] The Bible lists discernment as one of the nine spiritual manifestations (or gifts of the Holy Spirit) mentioned by Paul (I Cor. 12: 8–10).[5]

The practice of discerning spirits has a long history in the Christian tradition. For the mystics, such as Saint Ignatius of Loyola, it was a way to understand the impulses of the soul, which, he claimed, were influenced by either good angels (who desired the soul to be filled with 'faith, hope, love and all interior joy that invites and attracts to what is heavenly') or by demons (who strive to impede our spiritual advancement with temptations of sin and desperation). And while it may sound simple, it's not, because, in their cunning, demons often disguise their attacks, sometimes even appearing as 'angels of light.'[6] The best way to differentiate between them, said Saint Ignatius, is to look at the end result of the action. If the message is one that will lead to selfishness, hate, violence, and such, then its origin is Satan and should be resisted; however, if the end result is for good, then the source is God.

The *Ritual* gives three signs that indicate the possible presence of a demon: abnormal strength, the ability to speak or understand a previously unknown language, and the knowledge of hidden things. Yet even when these things are present, the *Ritual* still cautions the exorcist about proceeding. 'These signs can offer some indication, but since [they] are not necessarily [caused by the Devil], attention should be paid to other factors, especially in the realm of the moral and the spiritual, which can in a different way be evidence of diabolic intrusion.'[7] The most common of these is an aversion to the sacred – for example, the inability to pray or say the name of Jesus or Mary, to go to mass, or to receive communion. And when the two are put together (the signs and the aversion to the sacred) an exorcist may start to suspect he is dealing with a possession.

People seek an exorcist for several reasons.[8] The person (or someone who knows the person) simply attributes various problems to the intervention of the Devil. 'When a person comes, there are many, many people who say, "Father, I have the demon inside me, give me an exorcism!" Usually they don't need it,' says Father Carmine. 'Generally, they are people who are a little unbalanced or maybe scared by some books or a movie. This is a very delicate issue. You have to divulge but without being judgemental.'

By far, say exorcists, the vast majority of people who come to see them fit into this category, and they spend much of their time convincing people that nothing is wrong with them. Unfortunately, this is not always easy. Many exorcists lament the damage done by well-meaning but overzealous people who convince someone that he or she is possessed when this is really not the case. One exorcist from a diocese in the Midwest was visited by a parishioner convinced that her daughter's problems were caused by an evil spirit. She'd gone to see a 'ghost whisperer' who told the woman that indeed her daughter was suffering from a curse that could be removed for $1,000. Upon hearing that there was an exorcist in the diocese, the woman took her daughter to see the priest. After an initial interview, the exorcist uncovered a history of mental illness in the family, so advised the woman to take her daughter to a psychiatrist, telling her that it was highly unlikely that her daughter was suffering from a demonic attack. The mother, however, was unconvinced and returned to the ghost whisperer and paid to have the curse removed.

Numerous mental illnesses can also be mistaken for demonic possession. For this reason, exorcists should insist on a full psychiatric evaluation before proceeding. More often than not, the person has already seen several doctors without relief. Based on this failure of medical intervention, if a demonic presence is suspected, the exorcist might believe he has grounds to proceed. Typically, though, an exorcist will have a team of individuals (a psychiatrist, psychologist and perhaps a neurologist) that he trusts to help him with discernment. Not just any psychiatrist will do, however; collaboration is possible only when the medical or psychiatric expert is open to the possibility of demonic possession or obsession. Their being Catholic (or Christian) is also a plus.

Doctor Richard Gallagher is an academic psychiatrist in the New York area who has worked with exorcists in the discernment process. A devout Catholic, Dr Gallagher believes in demonic possession, which doesn't necessarily mean that he seeks it out. 'The role of the psychiatrist is to make sure that these phenomena don't have a natural explanation before jumping to a preternatural or supernatural one. There are many individuals for one reason or another in life that become psychotic briefly; they are delusional, they may well hallucinate and they are prone to think that God, the Devil, a spirit, aliens, are communicating with them and they really believe it.'

Over the past fifteen years, Dr Gallagher has identified a handful of cases that he claims have shown clear signs of demonic possession. In one such case, he was working with a possessed person who was clairvoyant. One night while Dr Gallagher was at home with his wife, his cats suddenly went crazy and began tearing at each other. The following day, when he went to see the patient, she asked if he liked the joke she played on his cats the night before.

'I am an experienced psychiatrist,' says Dr Gallagher. 'Obviously I have seen multiple-personality disorders, but these cases never include the paranormal.' Instead, claims Dr Gallagher, instances of demonic possession are more straightforward than cases involving mental illness. For instance, a person who has a severe personality disorder and who simply thinks they have evil inside them won't typically have their voice completely change or experience total amnesia after a session, he says. 'In fact it is indicative of the full possession syndrome that the individual affected never remembers what the demon says while it is speaking during an exorcism.' And if it is just a case of overactive imagination, according to Dr Gallagher, an experienced psychiatrist should be able to tell the difference. 'If you have the paranormal there is no way you can believe that it is not coming from somewhere. Even if you don't believe in the Devil, you have to say that there is some explanation beyond the natural here.'

People also come to see an exorcist because they are thirsting for attention (the fakers), a category known as pseudo-possession. Exorcists say the difference between pseudo-possession and the real thing is fairly obvious. People who are faking generally will depict the evil spirit in the most banal and superficial of ways, while in a real possession, the evil spirit will correspond to the Devil as he is known in the New Testament, meaning the demon will manifest a deep understanding of theology and Church doctrine.[9]

Some exorcists have also devised little tricks to help them

weed out the pseudo-possessions. Exorcists will use regular water instead of holy water, or even read Latin prose out of a text instead of reciting a prayer, to see whether the person responds. Since in either case a demon should not react because the objects are not sacred, if the person does say, for example, 'That water is burning me!' then the exorcist knows the possession is fake.

Only in extremely rare instances, say exorcists, is a person indeed suffering from some form of demonic attack.

'The first thing the exorcist must do,' says Father Carmine, 'is to listen to the person.' The person almost always suffers from some degree of oppressive guilt or despair, so it's necessary 'to comfort the person and cheer him up, which you do by giving a little homily about the faith'.

During the first interview, the priest will usually ask victims about their lives and when their problems started. The exorcist may suspect possession if it emerges that the person was dabbling in the occult or had visited magicians or card-readers.

Any physical symptoms are carefully examined. 'I can draw conclusions from a certain behaviour that makes me suspicious,' explains Father Carmine. 'For instance, when someone doesn't want to enter my office, when they have a look of hate, or when they don't look at my face – little attitudes that with experience make me think, Ouch, ouch, ouch . . .'

People don't usually attribute their problems to a demon. Instead, they typically go to several doctors and come away with a number of diagnoses. Somehow, often at the prodding of a friend or loved one, they end up on the doorstep of an exorcist. 'This is one characteristic of a true possession; people seldom think they are possessed but attribute their problems to some other cause,' asserts Father Bamonte.

Two areas most commonly affected by evil influences are the head and stomach, resulting in terrible pains accompanied by the desire to vomit. Victims may also feel intense pain in other parts of their body, such as the kidneys or joints. The pain will then migrate, perhaps affecting their arm or neck the following day. Medicine has no affect whatsoever. According to Father Amorth, 'one of the determining factors in the recognition of diabolic possession is the inefficacy of medicines, while blessings prove very efficacious'.[10] The person may also experience temporary numbness, or excessive hair loss.

Beyond these physical symptoms, any manner of strange phenomena can accompany a possession. In addition to the intense aversion to the sacred, victims may have terrible nightmares, 'so terrible that they don't even want to go to sleep,' says Father Carmine. Hearing voices and seeing visions, or having urges to commit terrible acts such as murder or suicide, are common afflictions. Victims may have sudden mood changes, often feeling a deep depression. They believe they can also sense evil in people or know other people's sins.

The presence of foul odours is another indicator, including the smell of sulphur filling the room. During one exorcism while Father Carmine was still apprenticing, the stench of rotting garbage became so strong that he had to leave the room. Yet another indicator is the temperature in the room dropping.

During the interview, if the exorcist suspects something, he may conduct a simple blessing, such as 'Let's pray that the Holy Spirit can come upon us to guide us through this process'. Father Bamonte likes to ask the person to praise Jesus Christ: 'Let's get on our knees and praise the glory of Jesus Christ' or 'the Blessed Mother'. If there is a demon present, it will almost always refuse to do so, he says. An exorcist may also pray surreptitiously in his mind while he listens to the applicant's story.

In order to determine whether a girl was possessed, Father Nanni once said a prayer in his mind in French. The second he did this, even though the girl was sitting about ten feet away and with her back to him, her head spun around and her eyes rolled up, revealing the whites. Looking directly at him, she sneered in Italian, 'It is useless that you pray in that language because we know them all.'

In conjunction with the other symptoms, if the exorcist sees a negative reaction to a blessing or mental prayer during the interview process, then he usually has enough evidence to begin an exorcism.

Since some demons are stronger than others, meaning they can resist a simple prayer, some exorcists claim that the only way to unmask the demon is by performing an exorcism. Because of the suggestive nature of exorcism, however, the majority of exorcists frown upon the practice of using the rite itself as a diagnostic tool. 'That is not the purpose of the *Ritual*,' says Father Dermine. 'Most demons will manifest with a simple prayer. There is no need to pray the whole *Ritual*.'[11]

In the most difficult cases, say exorcists, the person may be suffering from both mental illness and demonic possession, or the demon may be masking his presence by creating symptoms that mimic mental illness. This is especially true in cases of obsession, in which the demon attacks the victim's mind. Father Bamonte writes, 'There are cases in which [obsession] has an exclusively pathological origin; other cases in which the origin is due to an extraordinary action of the demon and still others where the extraordinary action of the demon amplifies, in an abnormal manner, little obsessive thoughts and compulsive behaviours that can be normal when they happen only once in a while, are quick, and most of all controllable, but that become all of a sudden invasive, insistent and continuous under this action, heavily disturbing the psyche of the person.'[12]

A good rule of thumb, say exorcists, is that if the cause is natural, then the patient's condition will not improve dramatically with prayer. If the cause is demonic, however, a person's condition should improve after an exorcism. Since the difference between what is natural and what is demonic is such a delicate distinction, most exorcists continue to have the victim seek the help of a doctor even while undergoing an exorcism.

*

For a number of people, of course, there are a variety of natural ways to explain the phenomena of demonic possession. A whole host of mental illnesses as well as other psychological motivators, including 'goal-oriented behaviour', can all be used to illustrate the symptoms.

Schizophrenia, for example, is typically associated with hearing voices, sometimes accompanied by hallucinations and paranoid delusions. Sometimes people imagine their TV is speaking to them, or a UFO is transmitting signals to them. A person brought up in a strict religious environment might easily char- acterize these 'voices' as demonic.

Likewise, when suffering from *somatization disorder* (what used to be called hysteria), people will typically manifest various physical ailments – such as nausea, depression, even hearing loss – with no identifiable physical cause. The subconscious can convince the conscious brain that there is some kind of disabil- ity when there isn't.

People with *bipolar disease* can suffer from paranoid delusions or their moods can fluctuate, sometimes violently.

Those with *obsessive-compulsive disorder* (OCD) feel tor- mented by obsessive thoughts or compulsions that compel them to act in ways they know may be irrational.

Historically, *epilepsy*, which in Greek means 'to seize and carry off', has been associated with spirit possession, as has *Gilles de la Tourette's syndrome*, a disease characterized by uncontrollable tics, movements or speech.[13] We now know it to be a neurolog- ical disorder caused by abnormal electrical activity in the brain. Similarly, *migraines* are thought to be responsible for some of the visual auras and auditory hallucinations that may have caused accusations of possession or beatific visions in the past.

Disassociation is perhaps the most common way in which a person might feel 'possessed'. In simple terms, disassociation refers to a variety of behaviours that stem from 'a lack of inte- gration of psychological processes that normally should be integrated'.[14] These behaviours can run the gamut from 'zoning out' while driving the car, to feelings of being located outside the physical body, such as in out-of-body experiences.

'Basically, what it really comes down to is our conscious experiences as an act of construction,' says Dr Barry L. Beyerstein, a professor of psychology and a member of the Brain Behavior Laboratory at Simon Fraser University. 'It doesn't just happen. Our sensory processes scan the world around us and in order to make sense out of it, the brain has to assimilate it into a model of reality. And as we grow up we get so good at doing this that we don't even realize that we're constructing this, because it really is a state of the brain where we're trying to put together a feeling of being in a three-dimensional world.'

The problem emerges when this 'system' breaks down. 'Ordinarily this is all so seamless that everything jives with everything else; but every once in a while (thanks to a number of things such as weird migraine states or exhaustion or mental disorders like schizophrenia), the ability of the brain to make a coherent model of the world can be disrupted. And when that happens, people are apt to feel as if something odd is going on, i.e., some external entity must have usurped control of their thoughts or actions.' At the heart of the issue, says Dr Beyerstein, is the fact that most of us underestimate just how much of our own behaviour is dependent on these 'non-conscious mechanisms'.[15]

Originally from Vancouver, British Columbia, Dr Beyerstein received his Ph.D. in experimental and biological psychology from the University of California at Berkeley in the late 1960s.[16] 'I've yet to see anything that contradicts any well-established law of science or dents my belief that the mind is equal to a state of the brain in ways that science wouldn't be able to explain,' he says with a good-natured chuckle. However Dr Beyerstein is quick to point out that this doesn't negate the reality of these experiences. 'We're not saying that people aren't having these experiences, just that the onus of proof is on the claimant, and that they should have evidence that can't be explained by prosaic means.'

Many scientists think that dissociative identity disorder (DID) – what used to be called multiple personality disorder (MPD) – offers the best explanation for demonic possession. DID is characterized by an individual claiming to have one or more 'alters' that control behaviour, with distinct voices and different names, personality characteristics, even handwriting. Memory and other aspects of the person's consciousness are said to be split among the different personalities that occur spontaneously. However, the disease is fairly controversial and psychotherapists are divided on how to treat it.

DID can be diagnosed in one of two ways. One approach, which has come to be known as the traditional disease view, theorizes that DID 'is an etiologically distinct condition that is best conceptualized as a defensive response to childhood trauma, particularly sexual and physical abuse'.[17]

The other approach, known as the sociocognitive model 'conceptualizes DID as a syndrome that consists of rule-governed and goal-directed displays of multiple role enactments that have been created, legitimized, and maintained by societal reinforcements'.[18] In other words, people *act* as if they have different personalities in them. 'I think most cognitive scientists would tell you that people don't in fact house different personalities with separate streams of information-processing, separate memories . . .' says Dr Steven Jay Lynn, a professor of psychology at the State University of New York at Binghamton, who has done extensive work on disassociation and hypnotic states. 'Rather, people come to think of themselves in this way, oftentimes by things they've read about, learned about, or because their therapist has suggested it (either very explicitly through hypnosis or leading questions or subtly through implicit suggestions) and that the sense of oneself as being divided, is really shaped and created by these cultural forces.' According to proponents of this view, the media, and to a large extent the cultural mores of the society that the patient comes from, also play a big role in helping to perpetuate the condition. For instance, Dr Beyerstein points to books and films like *Sybil*, and *The Three Faces of Eve* (both about a person struggling with the effects of MPD) as having had a huge impact on the numbers of people who claimed to be suffering from MPD.[19]

One of the most relevant aspects of the sociocognitive view in relation to exorcism is 'role playing', in which either the exorcist or possessed person learns to play a particular role by participating in numerous rituals over time. Anthropologists have seen ample evidence of this. In Puerto Rico, for instance, *espiritistas* (spirit mediums) are chosen in childhood and often apprentice with a more experienced healer.[20] These experiences teach them the behaviours of the various possessing spirits.[21] Nicholas P. Spanos, author of *Multiple Identities and False Memories: A Sociocognitive Perspective*, offers a number of social issues that help explain why the belief in spirit possession has persisted over the years. 'The notion provided a culturally consistent explanation for various physical disorders and for otherwise inexplicable propriety norm violations. When coupled with exorcism procedures, the role provided a way to reintegrate deviants into the community, served as a device for proselytizing, and in numerous ways bolstered the religious and moral values of the community.'[22] In certain contexts, demonic possession can also provide marginalized individuals (especially women) with a way of empowering themselves. In looking at the popularity of demonic possession in late medieval and early modern Europe, Spanos notes, 'Those who became demoniacs were usually individuals with little social power or status who were hemmed in by numerous social restrictions and had few sanctioned avenues for protesting their dissatisfactions or improving their lot.'[23]

In the context of the different societies, the 'goal-directed nature' of demonic possession can also change depending on the social cues that the victim receives. According to Spanos, the Catholic exorcism, in which the demon is addressed, 'produces strongly cued demon self-enactments as a central component of the demonic role'.[24] Another example would be the person screaming that his skin is burning when the exorcist sprinkles him with holy water.

The prayer of exorcism itself is admittedly a highly suggestive one, according to Father Gramolazzo. It's not hard to see the correlation between a priest wielding a crucifix while saying 'I command you foul serpent to depart!' and an accommodating person undulating in the manner of a serpent. Numerous studies have shown that, through suggestive methods, people can be convinced that they have experienced events that never took place. In one such study conducted in Italy, people were made to believe falsely that they had witnessed a demonic possession or had somehow taken part in an exorcism.

Dr Giuliana A. L. Mazzoni is a professor of psychology at the University of Hull in the United Kingdom, who conducted the study in the late 1990s on how memory and suggestivity can play a role in shaping our beliefs, even when those beliefs are considered 'implausible'. In the experiment, performed on university students, Dr Mazzoni and her fellow researchers proposed a 'three-step model' for developing false memories: 'First, the event must be perceived as plausible. Second, individuals must acquire the autobiographical belief that it is likely to have happened to them. Third, individuals must interpret their thoughts and fantasies about the event as memories.' To do this, she and her team instructed people to read some articles about the reality of possession and how often it occurs. Then, they asked the subjects a series of questions about their fears, which the researchers purposefully 'interpreted' as evidence that the subjects had witnessed a possession. Then, in the last session, participants rated the plausibility of witnessing a possession and stated whether they had seen one themselves.

'One of the crucial aspects of the manipulation was that the people had to believe that these experiences were happening in their own culture,' says Dr Mazzoni. 'If they read reports about shamans or cases of possession in the ancient world they were less apt to believe in it. If you can interpret people's fears in terms of being due to a specific experience then you can get people to believe that they actually had that experience. Twenty-five per cent came out pretty convinced. The others also increased their beliefs.'[25]

Looking at the world of exorcism, it's not hard to see how this could also be applied to an exorcist, who might influence a person's opinions by, say, providing a book about exorcism for the person to read. As Dr Beyerstein observes, 'When people go to see an exorcist there is a role to be played and they assume the role or they don't agree to be part of it.' All of this points to the potential pitfalls of a priest, untrained in medicine and without the help of a trained professional, diagnosing whether or not a person's mental illness is caused by the presence of a demon.

While all these conditions could be mistaken for similar traits symptomatic of possession, they do not explain the more dramatic symptoms related to possession, such as the paranormal or 'poltergeist-type' manifestations. After all, it's one thing to be praying over a person who screams or claims to see visions; it's quite another to watch her levitate four feet off the ground, or be able to identify hidden objects sealed in a bag. 'These phenomena definitely create a big question mark,' says Dr Mazzoni. 'Perhaps in fifty years we'll be able to understand why these things happen, but at the moment we can't.'

CHAPTER TEN

CROSSING OVER

Hell hath no limits, nor is circumscrib'd | In one selfe place: but where we are is hell. | And where hell is there we must ever be. | And to be short, when all the world dissolves, | And every creature shall be purifi'd, | All places shall be hell that are not heaven.

Christopher Marlowe, *Doctor Faustus*

On Tuesday afternoon, Father Gary once again found himself in the small room next to Father Carmine's office. In a repeat of the previous night's events, the waiting room was overflowing with people, some even walking in off the street for impromptu blessings like those performed at the Scala Santa. 'Jesus, Mary and Joseph and good Saint Ann,' he thought, 'where do all these people come from?' He knew from the course that belief in the occult was rampant in Italy and perhaps here was the proof.

Again, he was surprised by the relative 'normalcy' of the folks as they entered the tiny room, pausing to take his hand and sometimes even offering gracious smiles as he stumbled through his greeting in Italian. None of them 'looked' possessed. Once again, physical reactions included coughing and yawning. A few people tried to push Father Carmine away while others cried when he touched them on the back of the neck or on their knees with his crucifix. A couple of times people would dry-heave or bring up some 'froth' that they, or the person with them, would wipe away with a handkerchief.

Sometimes Father Carmine would pray the whole *Ritual*, sometimes only a simple blessing, and sometimes he'd pray one of the exorcism prayers. Father Gary wondered how Father Carmine made this distinction. Were there levels of possession, or a set of criteria? Then there was his habit of tapping people on the forehead with his index finger at the end of each exorcism. Sometimes he would also push his finger into their foreheads or pat their foreheads a few times with his palm as if giving them a high-five. In each case, they would open their eyes and take a few deep breaths to collect themselves, and the exorcism would be over. Was this a signal of some kind?

After some exorcisms, the person broke down, sobbing. One woman in her sixties turned to Father Gary with a look as if to say 'it's not my fault'. After they'd seen around five people and were taking a quick break, Father Carmine explained, 'They feel somehow they brought this upon themselves. They are deeply, deeply ashamed.'

At the Casa later that night, Father Gary reflected on what he'd seen. In that cramped little room out at San Lorenzo, nothing had gone according to script. He wondered why Father Daniel seemed to be seeing more dramatic cases at the Scala Santa. Just recently the Franciscan had told him about a woman who vomited seven black two-inch-long nails – six of which had dissolved into a dark liquid but the seventh he kept. Father Gary had also expected to see longer, more drawn-out exorcisms, not fifteen minutes of a person sitting in a chair yawning. Did they send the harder cases to certain exorcists?

Father Carmine had told him to return the following afternoon, and he hoped to get answers to a few questions then.

*

By the time he arrived at San Lorenzo, as usual a small crowd had gathered outside the door. All the faces were new, however, and an image of a never-ending stream of people popped into his mind. A few turned to acknowledge him with a nod but most kept to themselves. Nobody talked. Father Gary noticed a pair of women wearing the navy-blue habits of religious sisters, with matching down jackets. One of the women was young, perhaps in her mid-twenties with short curly black hair and hard, tense features (her name would later be revealed as Sister Janica).[1] Her kind-faced companion was in her late fifties. The older sister gave him a polite smile, but Sister Janica refused to look at him. There was something about her that he couldn't put his finger on – she seemed profoundly troubled.

The group waited patiently for another ten minutes until Father Carmine opened the door at around 3.40, looking groggy, having just awoken up from his afternoon *riposo*.

As everyone filed in, Father Gary went into the office. 'Ciao, Father Carmine, come stai?' How are you?

'Bene,' Father Carmine answered, but seemed in a dark mood.

Realizing the toll of day-in-and-day-out work like this, Father Gary pulled out his carefully folded purple stole and draped it around his neck. He entered the now-familiar room, almost as if he were punching a time clock on the factory floor.

A few minutes later Father Carmine entered, followed by the two nuns. As she had outside, the older woman smiled at Father Gary when he introduced himself, while Sister Janica averted her gaze and sat down in the chair, not even bothering to take his hand.

Father Carmine, who usually chatted for a second or two with the person before beginning the ritual, wasted no time. Picking up the squeeze bottle filled with holy water, he blessed both women. The older woman made the sign of the cross, while Sister Janica grimaced, clenching her eyes tightly as the drops of water splashed over her head. So far, nobody had reacted so strongly to the holy water.

As he had done with the others, Father Carmine put his hand on top of the nun's head. He then invoked the protection of Saint Michael the Archangel, revered by Christians as the leader of God's army, which was something new. Then, without so much as a pause, he jumped right into the *Ritual*.

'Deus, humáni géneris cónditor atque defénsor, réspice super hunc fámulum tuam, quam ad tuam imáginem formásti et ad tuæ vocas glóriæ consortium [God, creator and defender of the human race, look down on this your servant, whom you formed in your own image and now call to be a partaker in your glory] . . .' he said, beginning the deprecatory prayer. 'Vetus adversárius eam dire torquet, acri ópprimit vi, sævo terróre contúrbat. Mitte super eam Spíritum Sanctum tuum, qui eam in lucta confírmet, in tribulatióne supplicáre dóceat et poténti sua protectióne múniat [The old adversary twists her torturously, oppresses her with violent force, and disturbs her with savage terror. Send upon her your Holy Spirit, who strengthens her in the struggle, who teaches her to pray in tribulation, and who fortifies her with his powerful protection].'

Within a minute, Sister Janica began to whine and shake her head. She halfheartedly tried to push Father Carmine's hand away.

To Father Gary, it seemed as if Father Carmine's hand had suddenly been plugged into an electric socket and a current was shooting through it, animating the nun.

'Exáudi, sancte Pater, gémitum supplicántis Ecclésiæ: ne síveris fíliam tuam a patre mendácii possidéri; fámulam, quam Christus suo sánguine redémit, diáboli captivitáte detinéri; templum Spíritus tui ab immúndo inhabitári spíritu [Hear, Holy Father, the groanings of your supplicant Church: do not suffer your daughter to be possessed by the father of lies; do not suffer your servant, whom Christ by his blood has redeemed, to be detained in captivity of the devil; do not suffer this temple of your Spirit to be inhabited by this unclean spirit].'

Sister Janica began banging the back of her head against the wall, gently at first but then with increasing intensity, until the picture of Christ hanging on the hook above her head began to rattle. Father Gary edged forward on his seat, worried that she might hurt herself. Her companion, however, slipped her arm behind Sister Janica's head to protect it and a struggle ensued. Father Gary wondered whether he might have to intervene, but for some reason remained riveted to his chair, looking between his copy of the *Ritual* and the strange rocking figure. He prayed silently that God could come to her aid.

As Father Carmine continued with the prayers, a low guttural growl began to emanate from Sister Janica. Father Gary studied her, trying to determine its source. The sound seemed to be coming from deep inside her, from her stomach. It sounded like the noise a dog makes when it's getting ready to bite someone. From his reading he did know that it was possible for a demon to attack an exorcist during the ritual. In once such instance a possessed person had ripped a bedspring from a bed and stabbed the exorcist with it. He had no idea what he would do if something violent like that occurred.

'Exáudi, Deus, humánæ salútis amátor, oratiónem Apostolórum tuórum Petri et Pauli et ómnium Sanctórum, qui tua grátia victóres extitérunt Malígni,' Father Carmine intoned. Hear, God, lover of human salvation, the prayer of your Apostles Peter and Paul and of all the saints, who by your grace emerged as victors over the Evil One.

All at once, Sister Janica lashed out at Father Carmine, trying to knock his hand off her. As she struggled, her companion tried her best to keep Sister Janica from hitting Father Carmine.

'No, no, NO!' Sister Janica shouted, followed by an ear-piercing 'Basta!'

Father Gary's gaze was now fixed on the nun, whose own eyes remained tightly clenched. Again he wondered whether he might have to jump in and restrain her. If things got worse, he didn't think that Father Carmine and the companion could do enough to stop her.

'Líbera hanc fámulam tuam ab omni aliéna potestáte et incólumen custódi ut tranquíllæ devotióni restitúta, te corde díligat et opéribus desérviat, te gloríficet láudibus et magníficent vita [Free this your servant, from every foreign power and keep her safe, so that restored to peaceful devotion, she may love you with her heart and may serve you zealously with her works, may glorify you with praises and may magnify you with her life].'

Sister Janica let out a low, tortuous moan. It didn't sound human.

Father Gary studied her again, aware that a change had come over her. What was it? He couldn't put his finger on it. It didn't seem like she was there any more.

Without pause, Father Carmine moved on to the imperative formula. 'Adiúro te, Satan, hostis humánæ salútis: agnósce iustí-tiam et bonitátem Dei Patris, qui supérbiam et invidíam tuam iusto iudício damnávit,' he said, accentuating the word 'Adiúro.' I adjure you, Satan, enemy of human salvation: know the justice and goodness of God the Father, who damns your pride and envy with His just judgement.

Once again Sister Janica screamed, an otherworldly tone that unnerved Father Gary. Then he heard it, a deep rasping guttural sound that made the hairs on the back of his neck stand on end. It was the 'voice'.

'Shut up, you stupid priest!' The furious voice screamed in Italian at Father Carmine. 'You dirty sack of shit!' was followed by more howling and groaning. Sister Janica was breathing heav-ily now, her face contorted into a mask of rage.

Father Carmine paid no attention to this tirade. 'Adiúro te, Satan, princeps huius mundi: agnósce poténtiam et virtútem Iesu Christi, qui te in desérto vicit, in horto superávit, spoliávit in cruce [I adjure you, Satan, prince of this world, know the power and strength of Jesus Christ, who defeated you in the desert, overcame you in the garden, vanquished you on the cross].'

Sister Janica screamed again. Her head shook violently. 'Zitto!' the gruff voice shouted over and over, trying to drown out Father

Carmine. 'Shut up! Shut up! Shut up! You have no power over meeeeeeeee!' A high-pitched wail was immediately followed by a deep bass groan. Father Gary had never heard such range in a human voice. Beyond the tone, there was also a certain quality to it: it seemed infused with a kind of superiority while at the same time caged – like a trapped animal striking out.

'Adiúro te, Satan, decéptor humáni géneris: agnósce Spíritum veritátis et grátiæ, qui tuas repéllit insídias tuáque confúndit mendácia: exi ab hoc plásmate Dei [I adjure you, Satan, deceiver of the human race, know the Spirit of truth and of grace, who drives off your snares and confounds your lies, depart from this creature of God].'

'Fuck off!' the voice shouted, followed by a string of blasphemies and more curses in Italian. Father Gary recoiled from the viciousness.

Sister Janica suddenly stood up and Father Carmine pushed her back down into the chair, never taking his hand from the top of her head. He said something to her, and she hissed and spat at him. He turned to Father Gary. 'I am trying to ask the demon his name,' he said in English.

It took a second for the words to register. Father Gary knew that the *Ritual* specifically prohibits the exorcist from talking to the demon, except in the case of trying to find out his name. It seemed to have something to do with how the person could become liberated.

'No, no, no,' the rasping, guttural voice kept repeating, followed by loud screaming. Like a doctor examining a patient, Father Carmine lifted Sister Janica's eyelid. Her eyeball had rolled completely up into her head. He then tilted her head to the side, poured a few drops of holy water into each ear and slightly pinched the lobe with his finger as if pressing the liquid into her skin.

Sister Janica immediately went into a fit, screaming and flailing so fiercely that she threw herself on to the floor, where she flopped around like a fish, grunting and growling.

Father Gary sat stunned. She hadn't fallen hard, but he was worried that she might have hurt herself. Before he had time to react, Father Carmine and Sister Janica's companion took hold of her and she sprang up off the floor almost like a bouncing ball, as if her body weighed nothing, and was placed back in the chair.

Father Carmine continued without pause. The room was extremely hot and Father Carmine's forehead was dripping with sweat. 'Recéde ergo, Satan, in nómine Patris et Fílii et Spíritus Sancti [Depart, therefore, Satan, in the name of the Father and of the Son and of the Holy Spirit].'

A loud screech pierced the room, followed again by that hideous, guttural voice as Sister Janica railed against Father Carmine, grunting and hissing at him between clenched teeth. Finally, after a particularly vicious struggle, the voice said: 'Chi é lui?! Che sta facendo qui?!'

Again Father Carmine turned to Father Gary, saying in English, 'The demon just asked me who you are and what you are doing here. I told him that you were here to learn to do what I am doing.'

Father Gary's heart jumped into his throat. He looked at Sister Janica as she writhed in agony in the chair, her eyes clenched tight. OK, he thought, why is the demon asking about me? He couldn't keep his mind from racing, wondering if somehow he'd been marked by this demon.

The exorcism continued for another thirty minutes, as Father Carmine followed the *Revised Ritual* with the older *Ritual*, and then brought back a few psalms and prayers from the *Revised Ritual*. It was the longest and most extensive exorcism that Father Gary had seen Father Carmine perform, and he could tell he was pulling out all the stops, using every tool at his disposal to try to help Sister Janica. The room had become incredibly stuffy, and Father Gary saw that both Sister Janica and Father Carmine were wrung out. Finally, when it seemed like the exorcism might go on for the whole night, Father Carmine smacked her lightly on the forehead, and after a few seconds she gradually came to, her eyes blinking open.

For a moment the room was still. Sister Janica looked as if she might fall out of the chair from fatigue; her black hair was matted with sweat and she panted like a marathon runner after a race.

Father Gary was at a loss for words. This whole evening had completely changed his understanding of what happened during an exorcism. Was it over? Had the demon been cast out?

Father Carmine broke the spell. 'I'm going to hear her confession now.'

Father Gary and Sister Janica's companion stood up and went out into the office to give them some privacy. Later, Father Gary would come to understand the significance of this gesture in the context of liberation. Now that the demon had been temporarily weakened by the exorcism, Sister Janica could truly confess her sins, something the demon would never have allowed her to do otherwise. For now, however, Father Gary saw the gesture as being more pastoral. Here again was an example of how being an exorcist meant more than just sprinkling holy water on to someone and saying a prayer. It was also about bringing the sacraments back into people's lives.

Father Gary and the older woman said nothing as they waited out in the office. He now had the proof he had been searching for – there was no doubt in his mind that what he'd witnessed was a demon. The pain she had undergone had been so intense. As if to underscore how dramatic this case was, he heard a thumping sound as Sister Janica once again started to bang her head against the wall. He turned to the older woman, who looked down at her hands in resignation.

Five minutes later, the door opened and Father Carmine and Sister Janica emerged. She was still a little dazed from her ordeal so Father Carmine had her rest on his office sofa, into which she sank gratefully.

Father Gary would have preferred to take a moment to digest what he had just seen and to ask Father Carmine a few questions, but that did not seem appropriate with the women still in the room. Besides, Father Carmine had already opened his office door and was motioning in two young women in their thirties. As they entered the small room, Father Gary followed them. It was time for the next exorcism to begin.

Father Gary realized that exorcism could indeed be a lot more explosive than the first two days had suggested. He sat more alertly as Father Carmine began the *Ritual* this time. As it turned out, the exorcism was similar to those he'd watched the other two nights. As Father Carmine prayed, he touched various parts of the woman's body with the crucifix – her knee, her elbow, her back. Here again was something that the course hadn't talked about. When he touched the back of her neck, she covered her ears and howled in pain. Father Carmine left the crucifix there for a few seconds while he kept his other hand on her forehead and prayed. The exorcism lasted the standard twenty minutes.

After they were finished, Father Carmine went into his office to see how Sister Janica was doing, while Father Gary stayed behind inside the small room. He could hear the two speaking but couldn't quite make out what they were saying. Once his Italian improved, he would realize that the conversation was quite banal – Father Carmine was scheduling her next appointment.

Father Carmine saw three more people after that: a young man dressed in painter's overalls who screamed 'Ahhhhhhhh!' loudly over and over as if his feet were being roasted over hot coals; an older woman who went completely rigid; and a housewife in her forties who groaned, whined and coughed.

Afterwards, with about fifteen minutes to kill before evening prayer, Father Gary took the opportunity to ask a few questions. Sister Janica was still very much on his mind. 'I have never seen anything so dramatic in all my life,' he said.

Father Carmine nodded, his face looking perhaps more wan than usual as he confirmed that Sister Janica was indeed a nun.

'How could a nun become possessed?' Father Gary asked.

'It is very sad,' Father Carmine sighed. 'It involves the whole family. She is from Austria and her father used to perform satanic rituals in the house. Some were performed on her when she was a child.'

Father Gary was astonished, but even more surprised when Father Carmine told him that she had been coming to see him for nine years.

'Nine years?' Father Gary repeated with incredulity.

Father Carmine nodded. 'She is incapable of functioning. It is a terrible thing.'

The streets were dark and cold when Father Gary stepped out from the basilica and headed up the driveway that bordered the cemetery. His mind was racing. What he had seen that night had completely reversed his opinion on the reality of demonic possession. It wasn't something that only happened in the history books, but was a living, breathing reality in the twenty-first century.

He couldn't get the voice of the demon out of his head, the unnatural way it sounded. He thought back to the demon's remark, questioning Father Carmine about his presence in the room. He wasn't one to be overly sensitive, but for a split second couldn't help but worry, 'Is there a demon following me home?'

He wondered if Father Carmine was ever afraid. He had never seen the Capuchin lose his cool, nor seem to doubt himself, which was reassuring. In the end, Father Gary knew he had to trust that God would protect him.

All through the bus ride home he sat deep in thought. He was beginning to see how what he'd witnessed that night would affect the rest of his life. He wondered how many people had such an evil force operating in their lives. Probably more than anyone realized. After just one week of participating in exorcisms, he was amazed that so many of his ideas about what constituted demonic possession had been reversed. Apparently it didn't have to be an all-or-nothing affair; there were obviously different levels. What constituted those levels or even why they existed would be questions to ask Father Carmine.

While the night's events had revealed several important things to him, perhaps what mattered most was his realization that if called upon he would be able to perform an exorcism himself. Maybe it had been the calm way that Father Carmine went about praying the *Ritual,* or the pastoral flourishes he brought into the process. It certainly didn't hurt that he had seen some pretty terrible things himself as an embalmer, which had prepared him in a way. Beyond the spectacle, what had touched him most was the victims' profound suffering. And while he knew what it was like to suffer, this suffering was like nothing he had seen before; it went beyond simple pain, much deeper. If he could do anything in his power to help these people, he felt it was his duty. 'These people suffer so much,' he thought. 'May God help us.'

CHAPTER ELEVEN

THE FALL

*The problems or crises which arise, due to no fault of our own,
are part of the human condition we call mystery and related to
our own vulnerability, our mortality.*

Father Gary Thomas, *Town Crier*, 1996

One of Father Gary's idols, the late Joseph Cardinal Bernardin –
who died of cancer in 1997 – wrote, 'Whenever we are with
people who suffer, it frequently becomes evident that there is
very little we can do to help them other than be present to them,
walk with them as the Lord walks with us.'[1] For Father Gary
such feelings of powerlessness had manifested in the form of
guilt. Whether administering last rites in a hospital, or comfort-
ing a spouse dealing with a nasty divorce, early in his life he felt
that here he was, helping people to overcome tragedy and yet
he'd got off relatively scot-free. While he certainly didn't wish
horrible things upon himself, he couldn't help but wonder, 'Why
hasn't anything happened to me?'

In the summer of 1997 that would all change. At the time, he
had been pastor of Saint Nicholas Parish for three years but
things had not been going as smoothly as he had hoped.

Unhappy that the sense of community he was trying to foster wasn't manifesting and feeling perhaps that he wasn't doing enough himself, he took some time off to visit a friend, Jim Michaletti, in the foothills of the Sierra Nevada Mountains.

The pair went for a hike with Jim's two golden retrievers (Buck and Spitz) to a place called Three Pools, which was near the Lion's Lake Reservoir. The day was incredibly hot, and Jim carried a backpack with a Bible and two water bottles. On the way out, they hiked up a dry riverbed, which snaked through the South Fork Stanislaus River canyon. On their way back, though, Jim decided they should take a different path. A little deer trail bordered the riverbed, and it seemed easier to negotiate. After a few minutes of paralleling the riverbed, however, the trail rose steeply until eventually the two were walking along the edge of a sixty-foot cliff. When they came to a section of the trail where some rocks were covered by moss, Jim's dog Buck slipped and tumbled over the edge, disappearing from view.

Imagining his dog twisted and dead among the rocks below, Jim left Father Gary and scrambled down the steep slope. When he got to his dog he was amazed to see that his only injury was a broken leg. Relieved, he began to climb back up to tell Father Gary the good news when he heard Father Gary shout 'Oh God!' followed by the sickening thud as his body hit the ground a few seconds later.

Jim was sure that Father Gary had died. Wracked with guilt at having 'killed a priest', Jim made his way over to Father Gary's bruised and bloodied body to discover that he was still alive, though barely. Father Gary's face was cut and one eye was basically a pool of blood. It also appeared that his kneecap was shattered. It was impossible to know whether he had any internal injuries. Since moving him was out of the question, Jim's only option was to run for help.

Racing to the South Fork Bridge a mile-and-a-half away, he flagged down a couple with a cell phone, then hurried back to stay with Father Gary. He waited an hour (along with a nurse who was hiking nearby and had heard Jim's calls for help) until rescue personnel finally began showing up – paramedics, members of the Tuolumne County Sheriff's Search and Rescue Team, and a few Stanislaus National Forest Rangers. Doing what they could to stabilize Father Gary, the paramedics called in a helicopter, which, when it arrived, hoisted Father Gary up in a metal basket, and flew him to a nearby abandoned golf course where he was dropped down on the ninth green. There, a life-flight helicopter was waiting to take him to Memorial Medical Center in Modesto. Nobody onboard thought he was going to make it.

At Modesto, the doctors immediately went to work on Father Gary in a series of operations, the first of which lasted about fourteen hours. His injures were extensive: the accident had fractured the c6 and c7 vertebrae in his neck, caved in a part of his skull, shattered his right wrist (this injury wouldn't actually be discovered until later), damaged the carpal tunnel, severed his orbital nerve, broken his kneecap, and turned his right elbow to dust. In addition his face was severely lacerated and bruised and would require over a hundred stitches. The big question was brain damage; his head injury was serious and the surgeons wouldn't know the extent until they opened his skull.

After surgery the doctors had good news. The brain membrane was intact and there wasn't going to be brain damage. He also wasn't going to be paralysed (apparently, he'd only broken two of the three bones in his neck instead of all three that can lead to paralysis), something they attributed to his probably falling directly on to the water bottles in the backpack that somehow cushioned the blow. The only real doubt was whether he'd be able to use his elbow again.

After staying at the hospital for ten days, he was transferred to Sequoia for twenty days and then ultimately to his parents' house to begin his rehab. Almost immediately, the post-traumatic stress began to take its toll. At times, the pain was unbearable. Unable to bathe or go to the bathroom by himself, he felt uncomfortable with his own body and stripped of all his dignity. His hair had been shaved for the surgery on his skull and, coupled with the bruises and numerous facial lacerations, he barely recognized himself in a mirror, an apt metaphor for how he felt about life in general.

Beyond this, he began to obsess about the cause of the accident, and about when, if ever, he was going to feel whole again. At the hospital Jim had half-jokingly called him 'Lazarus', because he appeared to have been raised from the dead. But now that he was in so much pain, Father Gary began to question his faith, wondering why God had allowed him to survive at all. He understood the plight of his parishioners in an entirely new way. 'Physical pain doesn't hold a candle to depression,' he thought.

At times his depression got so bad that he even contemplated committing suicide. Over and over he would ask the same question: Why did God save me on those rocks? Why didn't He let me die? In the end, the only thing that pulled him through was his reluctance to leave the world that way. Thinking about his parents quickly put an end to those thoughts – he would never burden them with that grief.

Going back to work – which he did in November 1997, at first easing in one day a week – helped him stop obsessing. He began taking medication and went to a trauma clinician. He also went to healing masses at Saint Joseph's in Capitola. Already a big believer in the Sacrament of the Sick (in which the priest prays for the person to be healed in 'body, soul, and in spirit'), he found the masses helpful not only for the blessings they bestowed, but also because they helped him reconnect with the healing ministry of Christ and with the power of prayer.

In August 1998, he went to a neurologist, Doctor Susan Hansen, who, in the process of doing an MRI, discovered that Father Gary's heart murmur had most likely caused his heart to throw a clot, in turn causing him to have a slight stroke before

the fall. The stroke would have caused him to be very disori-
ented, and as a result, he had probably just walked off the cliff.

The news was the final piece of the puzzle and healed him
body and soul. The realization that he hadn't done anything
wrong was a huge relief.

Because of this accident, Father Gary comprehended the depths
of suffering following a traumatic event and could respond in a
uniquely empathetic way with people who were convalescing or
depressed. He also saw the importance of prayer in the healing
process. As a result of the benefit he'd gained from the healing
masses he'd attended, he planned to conduct a weekly healing
mass at Saint Nicholas. But perhaps the most important thing he
took from his accident was that it helped him to understand the
concept that 'suffering was the cross', which ultimately brought
him closer to God. He could see now that 'suffering was a part of
life', and that 'nobody escapes this world unscathed'.

CHAPTER TWELVE

SUFFERING OF THE SOUL

This ministry is very hard, but I thank God because it has allowed me to grow very much. Being in touch with people who are suffering can be an advantage, because they can somehow teach you a lot about patience and a real Christian life. In this way I feel privileged, even if it is a very hard to be so in touch with the world of suffering.

Father Carmine De Filipis

'What you are saying is worthless!' the guttural voice growled at Father Carmine.

The Capuchin stood with his right hand on Sister Janica's forehead while in his left he held his crucifix against the back of her neck. She howled in pain.

Father Gary, sitting a few feet away, kept his eyes trained on the nun's face. He'd seen a number of exorcisms in the two weeks since her last visit – including several dramatic ones in which he heard the gruff, demonic voice speak – but he was still struck by the violence of Sister Janica's reaction to the prayer.

'I am stronger!' the deep voice bellowed. Sister Janica took several strained breaths that sounded more like screeches, 'Heeeeeeee! Heeeeeeee! Heeeeeeeee!' She bared her teeth.

'Adiúro te, maledícte draco, in nómine Dómini nostri Iesu Christi eradicáre et effugáre ab hoc plásmate Dei,' recited Father Carmine. I adjure you, accursed dragon, in the name of our Lord Jesus Christ, to eradicate yourself and depart from this creature of God.

Again the voice exploded: 'Really! Who do you think you are? You can't make me do anything. We are many!'

Father Carmine continued undeterred, 'Ipse Christus tibi ímperat, qui te de supérnis cælórum in inferióra terræ demérgi præcépit [Christ himself commands you who enjoined you to be cast down from the heights of heaven into the lower parts of the earth].' Again he repeated 'ímparat' a few times, accentuating it as he did, 'ímmmm-paaa-rat, ímmmm-paaa-rat'.

Sister Janica screamed. 'You think so?'

'Illum métue, qui in Isaac immolátus est, in Ioseph venúmdatus, in agno occísus, in hómine crucifíxus, deínde inférni triumphátor fuit. Da locum Christo, in quo nihil invenísti de opéribus tuis,' intoned Father Carmine. Fear that one, who was sacrificed in place of Isaac, who was sold in place of Joseph, who was killed in place of the lamb, who was crucified in place of man, and then was triumphant over hell. Give place to Christ, in whom you have found nothing of your works.

Sister Janica's demeanour suddenly shifted from snarling and prideful, to whimpering and whining. 'Basta,' she begged, in an almost inaudible whisper. 'Stop. Please stop.' She began to cry and curl up into a foetal position in the chair.

Father Carmine paid no attention to this change in tactics. 'Humiliáre sub poténti manu Dei [Be humbled under the powerful hand of God].' He repeated the word humiliáre, drawing it out in a slightly deeper tone, 'humiliaaaaare'.

'Basta!' the voice screamed, once again becoming enraged. 'Don't you know who you are talking to?'

Father Carmine put a few drops of holy water on his fingers

and pinched the bridge of her nose. She immediately thrashed wildly, shoving at Father Carmine and slamming herself backwards into the wall repeatedly. Her companion and Father Carmine tried to hold her, but she was too strong.

Unable to stand on the sidelines any longer, Father Gary tossed his *Ritual* book aside and jumped into the fray. He worried that she was going to hurt herself or possibly even Father Carmine. He threw himself between the chair and the wall. Sister Janica pushed back with such incredible force that it was all he could do to keep her from pounding a hole in the wall with her head.

For nearly twenty minutes he struggled to hold the woman back. When it was over, everyone was exhausted. When Father Gary glanced down at the metal chair, he was amazed to see that the back legs were bent completely out of shape.

After his third week, Father Gary had begun to recognize some of the Latin words of the *Ritual* and was generally only a few lines behind Father Carmine, keeping one eye on the page and another on the reactions of the victim. Usually, Father Carmine prayed fifteen to twenty minutes per person, but this varied – some got a simple blessing, while the more stubborn cases, such as Sister Janica, might go on for the better part of an hour.

Since there is no time limit specified in the *Ritual*, Father Gary wanted to know how Father Carmine knew when to stop. In the beginning he'd just assumed that an exorcist followed the prescribed prayers all the way to the end – including the litany, the gospel readings and the actual exorcism prayers. Instead, the reality proved very different.

'When the situation is bad, when you are dealing with a possession, in those cases you cannot pray for just fifteen or twenty minutes. It's not enough,' Father Carmine would later tell him. 'It also depends on how much time you have or the person has, as well as on their ability to resist the prayer.'

'But how can you tell when they have reached that point?'
Father Gary wondered.

'You know it, you see it,' Father Carmine assured him, 'and
you see that the person can't take it any more; they are in pain,
worn out.'

Most of the people Father Carmine saw had what Father Gary
would characterize as 'minor reactions', such as coughing or
yawning. However, he did see some more dramatic cases. One of
these involved a wholesome-looking brother and sister, both in
their mid-twenties, whom Father Carmine exorcized together.
During the *Ritual* the woman howled and groaned, her eyes
rolling back into her head, while the brother made noises similar to an elk. Each had dry heaves and spat up frothy foam. Their
mother, who had accompanied them, used her handkerchief to
carefully wipe off the spittle. The sight of her lovingly caring for
her children, who had been reduced to a sub-human level,
moved Father Gary tremendously.

When he had asked Father Carmine about this case, the
Capuchin responded that, while it was rare, people could be hit
with the same curse, and they could then be prayed over simultaneously. There was also the issue of time. On the night that
he had seen them, the waiting room was once again filled to
capacity.

Another case, involving a career woman in her forties, proved
to be extreme as well. Father Gary suspected something immediately when the woman – who appeared to have stepped out of
a boardroom – entered and eyed him suspiciously. Following her
into the room, Father Carmine had wasted no time, sprinkling
her with holy water almost before she sat down. The woman
reacted instantaneously. She grabbed the wooden chair and
swung it at Father Carmine, smashing it against the wall. Father
Gary, along with the woman's companion, had been forced to
jump in to keep her from trying it again.

In yet a third case, a mild-mannered housewife who had baked
a cake for Father Carmine was transformed into a grunting beast,

swearing at Father Carmine and saying in Latin 'We will never leave her!' only to smile politely at everyone when the exorcism was over fifteen minutes later.

The diverse reactions amazed Father Gary. He was learning that every demon has his own 'personality', even to the point that an exorcist can recognize them. Father Carmine told him that demons apparently vary their reactions from one exorcist to the other, so that if two exorcists pray over the same person at different times, they will see different responses. Or exorcists may experience the same exorcisms differently. Father Gary would have such a thing happen to him a few weeks later when he was witnessing an exorcism along with an American exorcist from Indianapolis. During the exorcism, Father Gary had the overwhelming sensation that the room was suffocatingly hot, while the priest from Indianapolis smelled a terrible overpowering stench.

Occasionally, Father Carmine would turn to him and fill him in on the history of the case: 'This person has been coming to me for three years and is afflicted by a curse' or 'this person has trouble studying, thanks to the demon'. Though few and far between, these little snapshots allowed Father Gary to piece together the tattered lives of some of the people who sought Father Carmine's help. Most, he learned, had either been involved in the occult or were victims of a curse.

Since learning about the causes of possession, Father Gary had wondered how to discern whether or not a person might be suffering from a curse, the symptoms of which seemed to border on superstition.

One woman complained to Father Carmine that her marriage had failed because of a curse. As Father Gary watched, however, it was clear to him that Father Carmine didn't believe her; and instead of praying the *Ritual*, he'd performed a simple blessing and admonished her not to believe in such notions.

Later Father Carmine explained that such cases are common

and warned, 'You must never believe when a person says to you "I have a curse on me". In the majority of the cases, it's not true. Especially if another person told them that they were cursed, never, never give credence to this other person's words. The people who have a real problem will never tell you that the cause is demonic. Usually it is the last thing they think about.' And even if Father Gary suspected a curse at work, Father Carmine cautioned him to proceed slowly and prudently. 'If you think the person might be cursed or have a problem, simply do a quick blessing over them. Tell them to calm down, that you are going to say a simple blessing, or pray the *Ritual* under your breath so they don't hear. If you told the person, "Yes it's true, you've got a curse on you and now I am going to exorcize you", you could do huge damage to their psyche.'

Hoping for some more clarity, he ran the question about how to discern the presence of a curse by Father Daniel, who described a scenario involving one: a young couple is engaged but the man's parents are against the match. The in-laws invite the woman over for dinner and give her something to eat, per-haps a piece of cake (sometimes bones are ground up into a powder and baked in the cake, as are bits of dried blood or other substances). Soon after she eats the cake, she begins to feel pain in her stomach or suffer from a severe headache. These 'symp-toms' always correlate with seeing her fiancé or going to church (because the agent of the curse is demonic). Armed with such a story, Father Daniel told Father Gary, if the exorcist prays a blessing over the person and she reacts negatively, it is highly likely that she is afflicted.

In the lore of exorcism, perhaps nothing is as infamous (because it is so spectacular) as the victim vomiting strange objects or copious amounts of fluid, sometimes even blood. Most of us remember Linda Blair's projectile vomit in the film *The Exorcist*, and Father Carmine had a case in which a woman vom-ited buckets of sperm. Such action typically signifies a curse; the person has eaten cursed food that he or she needs to eject.

Vomiting objects such as finely woven hair or beads, and even blood clots, are common indications of a curse as well. Or, in the case of a curse that was launched by sticking a sharp object such as a pin or nail into a Voodoo doll, the victim might vomit up a nail.

Note that exorcists believe these objects don't necessarily come from the person's stomach, but instead materialize in the mouth. In this way, such people are not harmed physically even though they appear to vomit sharp objects such as pieces of glass or needles. According to Father Nanni, spirits can modify the state of matter, even to the point of provoking 'materializations'. 'A person can vomit an object, but he doesn't have it inside from a material point of view. It is there spiritually, but for the person he feels it inside, a wasp stinging, or a scorpion stinging, the pain of a nail, and then he vomits and the object materializes outside the mouth.'

Other exorcists have seen things that defy explanation, such as pools of mysterious black liquid appearing on the floor, or live animals – including crabs or scorpions – vomited up. Father Carmine once saw a woman vomit a small black toad that was alive. When he went to catch it, it fizzled away into black saliva.

Psychotic patients swallow strange objects and expel them routinely. For this reason, the exorcist has to take these phenomena in context with other manifestations rather than simply depend on vomiting as a proof of a possession.

If the curse was carried out indirectly, say exorcists, it often turns out that objects from home, such as pillows, when blessed and torn open, reveal strange objects as well – perhaps pieces of metal or bones wrapped in twine, or braided hair. When they find these objects, exorcists usually say another blessing and burn them. Some objects, however, do not burn right away but need to be blessed repeatedly before they will ignite.

Just as surprising to Father Gary, however, were the times Father Carmine was unable to discern the cause of possession. In one such case involving a devout woman in her early thirties, she was neither a victim of the occult nor a curse. In the end he surmised that her possession must be for the 'expiation of sin'.

Beyond the different reactions of the victims, something about the relationship between the demon and the *Ritual* itself was peculiar. It seemed as if the demon were somehow stimulated by the prayers. When Father Carmine began the prayers, he and the victim entered into their own little world, as if surrounded by a bubble. Then, at the end of each exorcism, Father Carmine would either tap the person's forehead with his finger, or give a little pat, at which point the bubble would burst. Father Daniel would later explain to Father Gary that, when Father Carmine tapped people, he was essentially bringing them out of a trance.

Rather than being a continuous thing, demonic possession alternates between periods of calm and 'moments of crisis', when the demon manifests its presence – that is, takes over the person's body and speaks and acts through it. Between crisis moments, however, during periods of calm, it is possible for a victim to carry on as if nothing is out of the ordinary.

Typically, in hearing the word 'possession', one imagines an evil spirit as dwelling 'inside' a person. The Bible says: 'When the unclean spirit has gone out of a person, it wanders through waterless regions looking for a resting place, but finds none. Then it says, "I will return to my house from which I came." When it comes, it finds it empty, swept, and put in order. Then it goes and brings along seven other spirits more evil than itself, and they enter and live there' (Matt. 12: 43–5). While the primary purpose of this verse is to show that, once liberated, demons may return, it none the less illustrates the popular concept that demons reside inside a person, almost as if the body were a physical home. However, as Thomas Aquinas points out, pure spirits do not occupy space. Therefore when a demon 'possesses' a person, he is merely acting on that person.[1] According to Father Nanni, 'During a possession the demon is not present; it is connected like a pipe, and so he sends inputs into that person that the person can perceive.' Typically these 'inputs' can be a variety of things that the person can experience, such as voices or noises, or even thoughts. 'In this way, [the demon] tries to solicit the permission of our free will to evil, with the purpose of causing and reinforcing in us a growing dependence on him.'[2] The goal is always the same: to drive the person to desperation and isolation, to make him a willing 'slave' to the demon and sin.

'In the moment of the crisis, however, the demon is not only connected but he comes, he is there; and the prayer of exorcism forces him to be present because it provokes him and forces him to reveal himself,' says Father Nanni. 'The majority of people can resolve their crisis state with a prayer of thirty to forty minutes. I say "resolve" but I mean temporarily. When the state of crisis begins, you keep performing the exorcism until the demon gets tired and detaches himself, and so the person comes back.'

During an exorcism the demon suffers and causes suffering. 'Every exorcism is like hitting the demon with a bat. He suffers greatly; at the same time he also causes pain and weakness to the person he possesses. He even admits that he is better off in hell than during an exorcism,' relates Father Amorth.[3]

Just how a spiritual being might feel pain by being touched with material sacred objects is something of a mystery. 'There is some kind of relationship between the matter and the spirit. When they enter into a human body they are not in one place but all over the body. It is as if they somehow penetrate into the matter and so they also suffer the consequences of it. Saint Augustine talks about spirits as having some kind of matter to them; Saint Paul talks about spirits of the air, and the air is ethereal but it is still matter. However, we can't say for sure,' Father Nanni admits.

For the Church, these sacred objects (holy water, blessed oil, a crucifix) possess a kind of 'power' because they carry the blessing of the Church. 'Of course the object itself has no power; rather the power lies in that of Christ Himself which has been

placed upon the particular object,' writes Spanish exorcist Father
José Antonio Fortea.[4]

Most exorcists are affected by the intense suffering that they
see during their ministries. As Father Amorth wrote, 'The
strongest and most lasting impression, for a beginner-exorcist, is
coming in contact with a world where suffering of the soul –
more than of the body – is the norm.'[5]

Father Gary was particularly moved by just how personal this
pain could be. Not only did it touch the individuals, but it
affected the lives of their family, loved ones, and friends as well.

From the time she was a little girl, Anna,[6] now thirty-five, felt
that something was not completely right. 'I had problems but I
didn't know they were connected,' she said.

> When I was a little girl I heard noises that people around me
> couldn't hear, like the ticking of a watch. It bothered me a lot
> and I used to cry and ask my mom what it was but she would
> only tell me that she couldn't hear anything. So I started to
> think I was going crazy. I could also sense a presence in my
> room, and so I used to hide myself under the covers. My mom
> thought I was just 'acting out', but I was very scared.
>
> Around the age of seven or eight, I started to feel a choking
> sensation when I was lying down in bed and I had to stand up
> just so that I could breathe. Several times I almost choked to
> death and my mom had to pull my tongue out. I went to many
> doctors who told me I was perfectly fine, that all these things
> were just kid's fantasies.
>
> When I turned twelve, I became very interested in sex. My
> interest was very extreme, exaggerated. It was wrong of course
> but back then I didn't know. When I was fourteen I started to
> have intercourse, also in a very dirty way. For me it was
> normal but at the same time I had an immense amount of
> suffering going on inside. I had very low self-esteem and as a
> result I began to suffer from anorexia and even thought about

committing suicide many times. I felt terrible and became addicted to some drops that were supposed to help me sleep.

Meanwhile on the outside I always looked fine. I always had perfect makeup on, and I was well dressed. When I started working, all my salary went to buying clothes, drinks, going out to the clubs.

When I became addicted to the drops I was sixteen and my mum started to pray for me, but I found that out only later on. As a result, whenever I saw her I felt this intense hatred for her; I mean I really hated her. Now I know why, but back then I didn't know anything. Another thing was that whenever I saw Pope John Paul II on TV I used to run away or turn the channel immediately. And I never so much as put a foot inside a church, which was strange because even as a little girl I loved to attend mass.

This went on for some time until finally, when I was twenty-eight, a friend told me, 'Let's go to Saint John Lateran to get a blessing.' I was bad at the time. I couldn't sleep without the drops. I was anorexic. I was bulimic. I also had this weird sensation of a hand pressing on the small of my back, as if somebody kept his hand on me the whole time. A few days before going for the blessing, I started to say, 'No, I'm not going. Why should I go? I'm totally fine; all I need is to meet a guy and then I'll be fine.' Instead my friend made me go.

When I got to the church my head was pounding. I couldn't understand what people were telling me. I didn't have any reactions until I got in front of the priest, and then I burst into tears, sobbing and crying so much that I wasn't able to stop. The priest just let me go on. Afterwards, when I went home, I was no longer addicted to the drops – from one day to the next – and the weird sensation of the hand on my back disappeared. Even after this reaction, I didn't change my lifestyle at all until the day that I went to confess my sins. When the priest blessed me, I fell on the floor and started to scream, after which I didn't remember anything. The priest told my girlfriend to take me to Father Tommaso at the Scala Santa. I went and he blessed me and nothing weird happened. Later I met Father Alberto from Saint Anastasia, and he helped me to return to a spiritual path, to praying and belonging to a community of prayer.

When I started praying again, I began to feel a little better on the inside, but outside I got worse and worse. During the night sometimes all of a sudden I could not move, as if something was blocking me. I cried a lot during this time and I said to myself that I must be crazy. I told Father Alberto and he said, 'When this happens, start to pray.' It was very hard for me to pray because in those moments I couldn't remember the words of the prayers. At the beginning I remember saying simply, 'Help, help, help, Mary, Mary, Mary!' Then I started with the Hail Mary, and gradually those episodes went away.

One day Father Alberto prayed Psalm 90 over me and I began to vomit and feel really bad. As I was doing it I kept thinking, 'Why am I vomiting?' I felt like I was choking but I didn't know why. I also saw a strange vision of some kind of ritual in which people were chanting. Father Alberto told me that maybe I needed an exorcism. I said to myself, 'Who, me? I'm fine.' I told myself that I was just doing all this so that I could get attention.

About this time I met my husband and things got really bad, especially when we blessed the engagement rings. In that moment I lost consciousness and the demon manifested for the first time and told my husband that if he were to marry me, I would kill him.

From that point on, I started to feel really sick. I had problems with my ovaries, problems with my stomach, headaches. The worst thing that ever happened to me physically was that one morning I woke up with one side of my body totally numb. I went to the hospital and they diagnosed me with multiple sclerosis.

I had two major problems: first my arm and then my leg.

They were totally numb; I didn't feel them any more. The doctors were not very optimistic. I would have lost the use of my limbs sooner or later, but instead I followed the treatment of cortisone together with the blessings and in my case the illness froze completely. Slowly it is going away. The doctors want me to continue with the cortisone, but I would prefer not to do it – especially now that I put myself in the hands of the Lord. But I have to say that Father Alberto always tells me to do it because he says that the Lord put science in the hands of man.

Around this time I began seeing Father Francesco [Bamonte], and my husband came with me to the exorcisms. All this time I continued to doubt myself, to doubt that I needed an exorcism. I still thought I was making everything up to get attention. Father Francesco did a little test.

In order to prove that she wasn't imagining everything, Father Bamonte brought in a plastic shopping bag with an object sealed inside. He then ordered the demon in the name of Jesus Christ to reveal what the object was. At first the demon resisted, but eventually, as Father Bamonte insisted, the demon correctly identified the object: a pair of gloves that belonged to Padre Pio.

That scared me a little, but I knew then that I wasn't crazy, so I understood and I felt calm. I said to myself, 'OK, now we are going to get rid of him.'

After we got married we went on a pilgrimage for our honeymoon to various churches and holy sites around Italy, travelling to Saint Gemma in Lucca, a person I felt particularly close to since I read about her life. At the time I had been told that I couldn't become pregnant and so I asked for her intercession. As soon as I left Saint Gemma's tomb, I started to feel really bad. I was folded in two with pain in my ovaries and uterus. I was hospitalized and diagnosed with a cyst of five centimetres. When I got to Rome, it had grown to ten centimetres. I was supposed to have surgery but slowly it started to become smaller and smaller on its own, something I also attribute to the prayers of the community. (I was a member of a prayer group then and we always helped each other.) I also think that the prayers of my mother helped a lot as well. Anyway, I followed the therapy prescribed by the hospital and two months later I got pregnant, and now I have a wonderful eight-month-old baby.

When I got married I thought I would have been liberated, but it didn't happen. During the exorcisms the demon began to lash out at my husband. I said terrible things to him there, and it happened even at home.

I remember one night I sat down with my husband to have dinner. My husband blessed the food and after that I don't remember what happened. I woke up on the bed with my arms locked in front of me and my husband standing near by, out of breath, looking slightly shocked. When I asked him what had happened, at first he didn't want to tell me. While he had been blessing the food, the demon had manifested and told him, 'Pay attention because now you are going to choke. I know you are scared of me. You pretend you're not, but I know you are.' At one point the demon told my husband, 'You make me so mad because I can't touch you! I'm not allowed to touch you.'

Another time, my husband and I were watching a movie on TV one night about Pope John Paul II and at one point I broke down in tears. My husband tried to console me, saying, 'Don't cry, John Paul II is in the sky and he prays for you.' But then I turned on him and started to say bad words because it wasn't me. It was the demon.

Thank God my husband knew how to handle it. He didn't answer; he started to pray.

Throughout this time I kept having obsessive thoughts. Every time I had to come to see Father Francesco I had this thought in my mind like 'Where are you going? Now you are going to tell the priest a bunch of lies, you are going to look in his eyes and you are going to lie to him' and in my mind I told him the most terrible things.

I felt this constant heaviness on me. Like a weight. It was a chore to do anything. I couldn't clean, I couldn't wash my baby because it took too much of an effort. I was exhausted. Father Francesco prayed over me and I began to get better. Slowly I felt the weight lifting.

After the exorcisms I feel tired, but I can see things clearer and the pain goes away. Father Francesco has made me understand that I wasn't crazy. I wouldn't have believed that I was possessed but the exorcisms have helped me to understand it. I would never have imagined that things like this could happen but now I know. All I can say is that if the Lord created exorcists there must be a reason for it. Satan exists and works on people without them knowing it. If I hadn't had people praying for me, probably I wouldn't be here now.

Anna was eventually liberated in November 2006 (her liberation was recounted in the prologue) and remains free of the symptoms of possession. Father Bamonte believes that her possession was probably caused by a Satanic ritual performed on a relative of hers four generations ago, in which members of her family performed a ritual to gain power by sacrificing an infant to a demon (this was the ritual that Anna herself said she saw when Father Alberto prayed over her). And though he was never able to verify the claim, according to Father Bamonte, during the exorcisms, the demon would often hum the sing-song chant used by the participants of this ritual. The chant sounded like a jingle used in a TV commercial for a popular aperitif. When the commercial came on TV, Anna would feel compelled to quickly change the channel, without realizing why.

One day, after performing exorcisms, Father Gary decided to stay in San Lorenzo and have dinner with Father Carmine. While he considered Father Carmine to be a 'holy man', there was no denying that there was a distance between them. Much of it was cultural, and because of the language barrier as well. But there was something else, too – a sort of professional wariness that comes from two people meeting to perform an arduous task under unpleasant circumstances.

They ate inside a horseshoe-shaped dining hall that offered little in the way of decorations beyond the scuffs and dents that come from long and continuous use. The meal was staggered in two shifts, with Father Gary and Father Carmine sharing the space with about eight other friars. Since he was the superior, Father Carmine sat at the head of the table, while Father Gary took a place near the end, next to a lay man in his seventies who lived at the convent and taught English as a second language. As Father Gary talked and enjoyed dinner with the lay man, he noticed that Father Carmine's demeanour here was very different from what he displayed at his office. He appeared much more relaxed and conversed with the other priests as he presided over the meal. Because the juxtaposition was so striking, Father Gary realized that it must be hard for Father Carmine and his fellow exorcists to maintain any sense of equilibrium.

What Father Gary didn't realize was that, even though Father Carmine knew it needed to be done, he didn't like training new exorcists. 'Yes, apprenticeships are necessary,' Father Carmine would say later. 'In order to become an exorcist, you need to apprentice, to see and have experience; but you can't say it is an enjoyable thing. I prefer to teach beautiful things, good and holy things, things of God. Personally I thank God for this "job" because it puts me in touch with a supernatural world and so my faith grows as a result. However, that does not make it a beautiful job.'

CHAPTER THIRTEEN

A PASTORAL APPROACH

We can do only our best, and then we must leave the final deci-
sion up to God.

Father Candido Amantini, as quoted in *An Exorcist Tells*
His Story by Father Gabriele Amorth

By February Father Gary settled into a comfortable routine.
After morning mass he would usually do some reading, either up
in his room or in the NAC library. Then in the evenings on
Monday through Thursday he would see exorcisms at San
Lorenzo until dinner. On Thursday morning he would head out
to the Regina Apostolorum and then in the afternoon over to
his class on the history of spirituality at the Angelicum.

About this time, an American exorcist, Father Vince
Lampert, from the diocese of Indianapolis, got in touch. In
Rome to participate in the continuing education programme at
the NAC, Father Vince had recently been nominated exorcist
and figured that it would be a good idea to participate in a few
exorcisms while he was in town. Like Father Gary, when his
archbishop had appointed him exorcist he'd told him that 'he
had no idea what he was asking [him] to do'.

A slender, thoughtful man whose unedited bluntness comes off as a bit gruff, Father Vince is none the less very personable and quick to laugh at a good joke. Meeting one night for dinner in a trattoria near Saint Peter's, the two priests immediately hit it off. As they got to know each other, Father Vince filled Father Gary in about the circumstances that led to his nomination and his concern (like most American exorcists) that he had no training and wasn't sure where he should begin.

Father Gary, for his part, was candid about his own background. He had checked with Father Carmine about bringing Father Vince along, but he wanted to prepare him – remembering his own feelings of disappointment alternating with shock.

As he listened, Father Vince's favourable impression of Father Gary grew. This was not a priest who was out to bag demons and make a name for himself, but somebody who levelled with him and told him that some of the victim's reactions were downright 'odd'.

The two decided they would meet the following Monday at the Casa first and then together come to San Lorenzo on the bus.

Like any novice, Father Gary included, Father Vince had been growing increasingly anxious about what he might see during his first exorcism. He'd spent the previous day readying himself in the only way he knew, going to confession and spending extra time in prayer. He had purposefully tried to steer clear of films like *The Exorcism of Emily Rose* (some priests at the NAC had watched it one night) because he didn't want to be prejudiced. Before he left the NAC that afternoon, he told a few fellow priests where he was going; they replied that they would pray for him.

On the bus, his apprehension grew. Father Gary filled him in on the protocol and what he might expect to see, displaying a demeanour that helped calm his nerves. When they arrived at San Lorenzo, the usual crowd had already gathered in the courtyard. And as they waited, Father Gary gave Father Vince what little history he could on the various people.

After the first night, the two stopped to have a coffee and decompress. That night had been a particularly violent one. A woman in her early forties with sharp, attractive features and shoulder-length black hair had shaken so violently that to Father Vince she seemed to have levitated five inches off the chair, at which point Father Carmine had simply pushed her back down with the palm of his hand. Father Gary, who was momentarily engrossed in the *Ritual* book at the time, had missed it.

Father Vince had several questions. As he was wont to do, Father Carmine had pinched the bridge of the woman's nose, which Father Vince found strange. Father Gary chuckled, telling him that he'd had that same feeling himself. (Father Carmine would later explain that he pinched the nose because the demon enters through the person's senses.)[1]

Both of them, thinking ahead to the day when the fate of a person's spiritual well-being would rest in their hands, were keen to learn practical tips. Since the *Ritual* is imprecise on how an exorcism should be performed, their chief concerns were avoiding mistakes. Father Gary, for one, had read that if the exorcist went about it wrong, he could actually open himself up spiritually to an attack. One author had even gone so far as to suggest that if the exorcist touched the person during an exorcism, the demon could enter into him.

Father Carmine scoffed at this. 'Absolutely not. It's not a disease,' he would later say. However, there were dangers. Father Carmine was adamant about not engaging the demon.

'Whenever the demon talks, you should never listen to him. You should never ask questions to the demon in order to know something hidden; this is a very serious mistake. A priest is not to ask the demon anything that you don't already know the answer to [for instance, 'Why did you try to put yourself above God when you know He is all-powerful?']. Never ask questions so that the demon could be considered a source of information, never! First of all because he is a liar and so what he says can very well be a lie, and second because you can't give him the honour of being your source of information.'

The *Ritual* does permit the exorcist to ask the demon his name, which in the ancient Hebrew tradition is believed to give one a kind of power over another, also evidenced by the ancient practice that prohibited writing or pronouncing the name of God.[2]

The foundation for asking for the demon's name comes from the Bible, where Jesus asked the name of the Gerasene demoniac (Mark 5: 9). Early exorcists considered it worthy and codified it in the old 1614 *Roman Ritual*, which allows the exorcist to ask 'the number and name of the spirits inhabiting the person, the time when they entered into him and the cause'.[3]

'One of the first things that he struggles to avoid is to confess his name because to do so is some sort of half-defeat for him,' says Father Amorth.

A demon's name delineates the type of spirit it may be. Sometimes the names are purely functional, such as 'anger' or 'lust'; at other times they are recognizable names from the Bible, like Beelzebub or Asmodeus.

Even exorcists admit that there is a great deal of mystery to it. For instance, if the demon Asmodeus is present in several people that an exorcist prays over, why doesn't the demon recognize the exorcist? Shouldn't he be able to say to the exorcist, 'Hi, remember me? We met this morning.' In actuality, sometimes it does happen that an exorcist will pray over a person, even in another part of the world, and have the demon say, 'We fought each other five years ago in Jerusalem' – referring to an exorcism that the victim knows nothing about. However, this is rare, and the average exorcist (especially in Italy) may see Asmodeus three times in the same week without any acknowledgement from the demon at all. But according to one Italian exorcist, the actual name isn't that important. It may signify 'the army' of that particular evil spirit. In other words, a demon saying 'Asmodeus' is like a WWII soldier saying 'I'm a Royal Marine' or 'I'm under

Montgomery'. 'All that matters is that they give you a name, any name, so long as they respond to it,' says the exorcist.

For this reason, many exorcists actually prefer not to talk to the demon at all. Father Dermine, for example, doesn't even ask for the name. 'I don't ask anything because I don't believe them. I know this may sound disappointing, but demons are such big liars that I just continue with the prayer almost as if they weren't there.'

It can also happen that a demon will sometimes give a person's name, such as 'Adam'. A great debate exists among exorcists about whether or not the soul of a deceased person can cause a possession. The more theologically inclined exorcists say no (when a person dies, the soul goes straight to heaven, hell, or purgatory), while those who have spent some time in places like Africa (where the belief is widespread) say yes, it is possible. Father Nanni once prayed over a person who claimed to be the soul of a dead Mafia boss. After months of refusing to give any other name, Father Nanni did a little checking and discovered that the person in question never existed. On this occasion, the demon finally relented and confessed that he'd been trying to fool the exorcist all along.

In addition to the moments when Father Carmine was able to answer a few of their questions, Father Gary and Father Vince made it a habit to have a coffee or try to grab a bite afterwards. Through Father Gary's knowledge of the personal histories and Father Vince's understanding of Italian (since he was fluent in Spanish, he could make out more Italian than Father Gary could), the two would compare notes. During one of their late-night repasts, Father Gary explained to Father Vince something that had taken him weeks to understand – Father Carmine's practice of touching people on certain parts of their body with the crucifix. He was searching for the points that had been 'hit' by a curse. 'People will often be dedicated in certain rituals and cursed objects will be placed on the back of their neck.'

They also discussed actions they felt wouldn't be appropriate back home, like Father Carmine slapping people at the end of the exorcism. They talked at length about the fact that the majority of bishops in America knew little about the reality of exorcism. Both agreed that this lack of understanding needed to change.

As he continued to participate in exorcisms, Father Gary came to realize that while they could be gruelling affairs, perhaps the most arduous aspect was the endless repetition. Father Carmine ran San Lorenzo as though it was an outpatient clinic. He would pray over people for fifteen to twenty minutes, and then, after scheduling a follow-up appointment, they would go about their day. From talking to Father Daniel, he knew that many of the other exorcists in Rome had similar approaches.

Later, Father Gary would discover that each exorcist has his own system, in part because almost all had other duties to perform besides being an exorcist. Father Carmine, for example, was the superior at San Lorenzo and was busy with running the day-to-day operations of the basilica and parish, which meant he could schedule people only three to four days a week, usually in the evenings. So Father Carmine tended to lump the more severe cases on certain days and see fewer of them, perhaps five rather than ten. However, people also showed up unannounced looking for a quick blessing. One day a sanitation worker parked her miniature garbage truck outside in the courtyard, stomped in wearing her bright green reflective striped uniform, and asked the assembled throng whether Father Carmine was taking walk-in visits. As it turned out, he was not.

Then Father Gary considered the more entrenched cases, such as Sister Janica. The second time he had seen her, she seemed worse than before. On top of that, he reminded himself that she'd been coming to Father Carmine for nine years. Didn't the prayers of exorcism work?

People, Father Gary realized, are under a huge misapprehension that exorcism is a simple and quick procedure; that once an exorcist begins the *Ritual*, it is a fight to the finish that can last for days on end – until only one is left standing. An American exorcist in Scranton, Pennsylvania, coined the phrase 'drive-through exorcisms' to describe this won-and-done approach that the media and Hollywood films have made popular. Not surprisingly, this misconception is held by many who visit exorcists, most of whom go looking for a 'quick fix'.

'People don't understand what we do,' says Father Gramolazzo. 'People come to see us expecting to be healed right away. They think, "I have a headache because of the demon", "my job isn't going well because of the demon". People are not properly informed.'

Instead, as Father Gramolazzo explains, exorcism is more akin to a journey, with the exorcist acting as a kind of 'spiritual director' helping the victim to 'rediscover the grace of God' through prayer and the sacraments. This is one of the reasons why exorcists believe God allows people to become possessed in the first place. 'This message is extremely important,' insists Father Gramolazzo. 'This is why it takes so long for people to become liberated. It is a journey of faith for the person, the family and for the parish.'

Getting people to see it this way is not always easy for the exorcist. 'Half the battle is to change their whole purpose so they don't see it in the light of getting rid of a problem, but see it in the light of being more fully converted or being converted at all,' says English exorcist Father Jeremy Davies. 'That's the whole aim. It's what I'm always telling people week by week. And that's the most important thing – the exorcism is secondary to that.'

Simply put, the prayers of the exorcism weaken the power that the demon has over the individual. The healing, however, cannot happen without the full participation of the person. Victims of possession are exhorted to go to weekly confession, to recite the rosary daily, and above all to receive the Eucharist. 'I always say that the exorcism is 10 per cent of the cure; the remaining 90 per cent is the responsibility of the individual. What does this mean? It means that there is a need for much prayer, frequent reception of the sacraments, living a life according to the Gospel, using sacramentals [exorcized water, oil and salt],' writes Father Amorth.[4]

'I have people that I've been exorcizing for twenty years,' says Father Amorth.

Saint Alfonso de' Liguori says a very exact phrase, 'You don't always get to the liberation; you always get to some kind of relief.' This means that those people who in the past used to throw themselves on the floor just for a blessing, screaming and yelling, after years of exorcisms are calm; they can live their professional life and their careers. But every once in a while, they feel a little disturbance and so they come, people that in the past used to come every day or once a week, after a few years of exorcism they may come once every two months or every six months. What I mean is that they have a progressive improvement.

On 9 February, Father Gary climbed up the beige marble stairs and into the classroom at the Regina Apostolorum for the last time. While the second half of the course hadn't matched the quality of the first half, he was definitely looking forward to this last lecture, a roundtable discussion lead by three exorcists – Father Bamonte, Father Nanni, Father Amorth – and a fourth priest, Father Alberto, who ran a spiritual listening centre called the *centro ascolto*.

Bringing in the exorcists to talk about their ministries was a compromise for the course organizers. Originally, they had contacted the International Association of Exorcists (IAE) and asked for an exorcist to actually perform an exorcism in the classroom. Father Gramolazzo had told them, however, that, while the IAE thought the course was a good idea, exorcism wasn't a spectator sport. Putting a victim on the spot like that would only add to the suffering and cheapen the whole affair.

Father Gary was very impressed by the three exorcists as they filed into the classroom. Like Father Bamonte, Father Amorth wore a long black cassock that lent him an air of piety. Bald and wearing glasses, at eighty years old he walked with a slight stoop and took his time climbing the three steps that led up to the podium. He was hardly the larger-than-life figure that the media portrayed him to be, and instead exuded a more jovial and avuncular quality. Thankfully, despite the presence of such luminaries, the media wasn't obtrusive.

After opening prayers, Father Amorth spoke for forty-five minutes in a gravelly yet steady voice, his eyes fixed on a far corner of the room. The theme was familiar to those who followed his public appearances and read his numerous books: exorcism goes to the heart of what it means to be a Christian and is something that every priest should take more seriously. This was especially true, of course, for the bishops whose job it was to appoint exorcists. In interviews, Father Amorth had even gone so far as to say that any bishop who doesn't appoint an exorcist is committing a mortal sin.

After the break, Father Nanni spoke for half an hour about the crucial role of co-operation between the exorcist and his bishop, ensuring that only officially appointed exorcists performed the *Ritual*. In other words, just because someone had taken the course didn't mean that he could begin praying over people on his own. Since Father Gary was an official exorcist, this was a moot point, though it did remind him that he would need to work closely with his bishop once he had returned home.

Father Bamonte then discussed the importance of an exorcist having a team approach, stressing the need to have a close working relationship with a therapist or a psychologist. As he listened, Father Gary was struck again by the fact that Father Carmine didn't have such colleagues. Most victims brought a companion; but still, on certain occasions, Father Carmine would have been all alone but for Father Gary – something he planned never to do, even just for 'legal' considerations.

Father Alberto, who ran the *centro ascolto*, proved to be the most engaging speaker in Father Gary's opinion. The listening centre was basically a spiritual centre, staffed by two priests, two nuns, a therapist and an attached prayer group. It was a place for people with spiritual or psychological problems that they attributed to spiritual issues. The concept was similar to that in a book Father Gary had bought: *Stumbling Blocks or Stepping Stones: Spiritual Answers to Psychological Questions* by Benedict J. Groeschel. Father Gary was inspired by Father Alberto's emphasis on the continual need for people to practise the sacraments – especially confession – and bring prayer back into their lives, which he said people were filling with many other activities. And while not necessarily terrible, these distractions, as Father Alberto put it, were still exposing people to the wrong kinds of influences. First and foremost he wanted to create venues for people to pray. He'd set up a permanent chapel inside the Basilica of Saint Anastasia for Eucharistic adoration (a Catholic tradition of meditating in front of the exposed Eucharist). Of course Eucharistic adoration wasn't novel, but Father Gary liked the idea of people needing more 'quiet time' with God. He also appreciated Father Alberto's intention of getting back to the traditions of the Church. These approaches would also benefit him as an exorcist. While it might be hard to talk to people about demons, he could certainly tell them about the benefits of praying, and he would be practising 'preventative medicine', as Father Kevin Joyce recommended.

After Father Alberto finished, Father Gary was delighted that there was an entire hour just for questions and answers, which was so absorbing he could have sat there listening for much longer.

Father Amorth's response to one question made Father Gary chuckle: 'Everybody who is considering doing this needs to be apprenticed.' After all that trouble he went through to be able to apprentice! Knowing there were 185 dioceses in the United States alone – which meant that many exorcists would have to

be trained and apprenticed – it was impossible for him to con-
ceive that six overworked exorcists could all of a sudden tutor
185 priests. But if they didn't, who would?

Father Gary left that final day of the course feeling reinvigo-
rated about his calling as an exorcist. Not only had the course
given him the grounding he needed, but it had reinforced his
desire to help people. He could see now that rather than just
being on the fringe, there was also a strong pastoral element to
exorcism.

CHAPTER FOURTEEN

WINDOWS TO THE SOUL

The commander triumphs in victory; yet he could not have conquered if he had not fought; and the greater the peril of the battle, the more the joy of the triumph.

Saint Augustine, *Confessions*

As the evening dragged on, Father Gary noticed a shift in Father Carmine's demeanour. By 6.45, after the Capuchin had exorcized about nine people, his once-upright posture stooped heavily, braced against the wall by his left hand. Despite the freezing rain outside, his brown robe clung to him, heavily matted with sweat. Father Gary had no idea how his mentor maintained his stamina day in and day out.

By the end of February, Father Gary had seen over forty exorcisms, including some in which the reaction was so explosive that both he and Father Vince had helped subdue the person. One case involved a small bent-looking nun in her full habit, probably in her fifties but seeming much older, who had changed so completely during the *Ritual* that he no longer recognized her. He also saw Sister Janica a third and fourth time, each exorcism seemingly more violent than the previous one.

It came as no surprise when he learned that the repetitive nature of exorcism can be challenging for an exorcist. 'For me,' says Father Carmine, 'the hardest thing is that the liberation never happens right away. Sometimes you need years and years, and this methodical perseverance is not only very tiring, but the demon takes advantage of it in order to try to insinuate the poison of doubt, as if to say, "You are wasting your life and you are deceiving people."'

Exorcists also have to deal with the real threat of suicide. Father Daniel had told Father Gary of a time during an exorcism when he had to tackle a woman who tried to jump out of the third-storey window.[1]

In Italy, where every exorcist has a cell phone, it is common for an exorcist to receive several messages a day saying things like 'Today I am finally going to end it all!' or 'I can't go on without your help!' As Father Amorth relates in his book, *An Exorcist Tells His Story*, a woman seeing Father Candido threw herself out of the window between exorcism sessions. Faced with a daily environment that is this rife with suffering and desperation, many exorcists feel overburdened.

Father Gary began to notice that the exorcisms were starting to affect him as well. Even though he hated to admit it, he began to feel that he was in a rut. He realized Father Carmine saw many of the same people over and over again and neither their condition, nor the way he prayed over them, changed much. With the exception of the more dramatic cases, there was nothing new for Father Gary to see. Besides, he was just a passive observer; perhaps his attitude would change once he started his own ministry and felt the import of being in charge.

The big surprise was that while he found himself distracted sometimes during a ritual, he noticed that the exorcisms were affecting him outside San Lorenzo as well – and not in a good way.

Father Gary was aware that exorcists were prime targets for attacks by the Devil. Both the exorcism course and the numerous books he'd read had all pointed this out, some in lurid detail. 'He need only enter into the stream of our own inclinations, when we treat lightly things that lead us astray; he has only to press against that which already totters, to hold back that which seeks to rise. His influence spreads like a poisonous gas, which we inhale without knowing it,' wrote the Dominican theologian Antonin-Gilbert Sertillanges OP.[2]

Christian tradition has long held that the more a person's life reaches upward towards God, the more fiercely the Devil attacks. Numerous saints have suffered as a result of their devotions, including Saint Paul, Teresa of Avila, Padre Pio and Gemma Galgani.

In his book *The Dark Night of the Soul*, John of the Cross describes how God maintains a certain 'equality' among all things, so that we may attain grace comparable to our station. Just as a heavyweight prizefighter wouldn't have any trouble beating an amateur, so too would a saint's devotion ring hollow unless it was properly tested. The graces that we receive through prayer and the gifts given us by the good angels do not escape the notice of Satan, says John of the Cross, 'partly so that he may do that which he can against them according to the measure of justice and that thus he may not be able to allege with truth that no opportunity is given him for conquering the soul, as he said concerning Job'.[3]

It is for this reason that Saint Paul warns early Christians, 'Discipline yourselves, keep alert. Like a roaring lion your adversary the devil prowls around, looking for someone to devour. Resist him, steadfast in your faith, for you know that your brothers and sisters in all the world are undergoing the same kinds of suffering' (1 Paul 5: 8–9).

Father Gary had decided to quit drinking over a decade before because of the effect it had on him. He wasn't a big drinker at the time, but he noticed that if he even drank a glass or two of wine with dinner, he would feel the edges of his self-control starting to slip. Upon arriving in Italy, however, a place synonymous with wine and three-hour meals, he'd decided to relax that stricture a little. The Casa often served wine with lunch (as was the custom), and now and again he allowed himself to enjoy a glass. And while things had been fine for the first half of his stay in Rome, once he'd started participating in exorcisms it was as if somebody, or something, had hooked his libido up to a satellite dish and images streamed in.

Sexual temptation is one of the main dangers an exorcist faces. 'We have to be very careful sometimes [towards] the people we exorcize because they can really arouse some desires in the exorcist,' says Father Dermine. Some of the women who sought help from Father Carmine were quite attractive, and during the exorcisms a few would actually try to tear their clothes off, or rub themselves. The surprising thing was that Father Gary's temptations came not during the exorcisms but afterwards. Unable to overcome them on his own, he went down to the chapel in the Casa, or over to the little Church of Santa Rita, which was right around the corner, and prayed silently for God to give him strength. When the thoughts didn't go away, even after intense prayer, he began to get upset with himself. Had he opened a door that had allowed a demon to attack him?

While exorcists admit that their ministry can sometimes be a heavy burden, it would be a mistake, they say, to overstate the power of the Devil. As Father Amorth writes, 'A priest who is afraid of the Devil is like a shepherd who is afraid of a wolf. It is a groundless fear.' 'The Devil,' says Amorth, is already 'doing us as much harm as he possibly can'.[4]

And so rather than fear him, exorcists say, it is better to emulate saints such as Teresa of Avila, who proclaimed, 'If this Lord is powerful, as I see that He is and I know that He is, and if the devils are His slaves (and there is no doubt about this because it's a matter of faith), what evil can they do to me since I am a servant of this Lord and King? Why shouldn't I have the fortitude to engage in combat with all of hell?'[5]

While exorcists don't have a patron saint, many feel a strong devotion to Mary. In the traditions of the Catholic Church, Mary holds a particular place of honour: 'Throughout her life and until her son died on the cross, Mary's faith never wavered. She never ceased to believe in the fulfillment of God's word. And so the Church venerates in Mary the purest realization of faith.'[6] And because of this acceptance of God, Mary represents a parallel arc that is the exact opposite of the Devil's. 'God made [Satan] magnificent in his nature and he corrupted himself; God made Mary humble in her nature (a human being and, as such, inferior to the angels) and she sanctified herself.'[7] The Bible cites this hostility between Satan and Mary. In talking to the serpent who tempted Adam and Eve in the Garden of Eden, God says, 'I will put enmity between you and the woman, and between your offspring and hers, he will strike your head, and you will strike his heel' (Gen. 3: 15). Thus many statues of Mary depict her crushing a serpent beneath her feet.

Many exorcists invoke Mary during the ritual. 'The demon is so terrified of her that he will never pronounce her name. He'll say "that woman" or "she destroys me",' says Father Amorth.

'The Marian prayer, especially the rosary, is a very powerful weapon in the fight against Satan,' explains Father Bamonte. 'That is why [Mary] insists so much that we pray the rosary; the rosary is a prayer that really whips the demon into a frenzy.' On numerous occasions Father Bamonte has beseeched Mary for help only to have the person he is praying over say 'She is here!' or 'You can't imagine what I would do to you if she weren't stopping me!'[8]

After weeks of dealing with the temptations, Father Gary concluded they had to be demonic in nature; there was just no other way to explain their intensity. The realization helped. The course had warned him about such a possibility so rather than let it intimidate him, he took it in the greater context of the spiritual path that all Christians undertake. As Saint Paul said, 'God is faithful, and he will not let you be tested beyond your strength, but with the testing he will also provide the way out so that you may be able to endure it' (1 Cor. 10: 13). As such, even though he was a target, he knew God would eventually provide him with the means to overcome it.

It also helped to have the support of family and colleagues. He talked a lot of his problems out, calling his parents at least once a week. He also opened up to a circle of priests at the Casa whom he had either known before coming to Rome or who had an interest in exorcism. He especially liked talking to the seminarians at the NAC because he felt they might one day find themselves in a similar situation.

A few of the priests at the Casa were curious enough to want to participate in exorcisms. Some had even had past experiences of their own – praying spontaneous prayers of deliverance over people – and were eager to confirm that what they had seen was real.

Father Gary even made a believer out of Sister Rebecca when he stopped to chat with her at the library, telling her about his experiences out at San Lorenzo.

Other distractions helped take his mind off the events at San Lorenzo and his increasing internal struggles. He had always been a huge fan of classical music, finding it 'uplifting' and 'inspiring'. In fact, his parents had played some of his favourite composers, such as Vivaldi and Bach, while he was incoherent in the hospital after his accident. So on weekends he went to nearby churches such as San Ignazio, San Marcello, and the Dodici Apostoli as often as he could to listen to the free concerts. Once he saw a performance of Rachmaninov at the performing-arts centre, and on another occasion he dragged another priest from the Casa out to Saint Paul's Basilica in the pouring rain to listen to a Vatican-sponsored concert.

A few parties at the Casa also helped, including the Feast of Our Lady of Guadalupe, which he thought brought many of the priests out of their shells. He took it upon himself to organize the

Saint Patrick's Day celebration, asking one of the Irish priests to make Irish coffee and decking out the refectory in green. He even enlisted the help of a real Irish fiddler to come and play for a couple of hours, all of which made the party a huge hit.

For Father Gary, being a priest was all about human interaction. He found it ironic when a parishioner who was going through marital problems told him he was lucky that he didn't have to worry about such stuff. (The irony is that, as a pastor, he had around a thousand families to look after.) 'People assume that as a priest I don't have any problems, but I do. We all do,' says Father Gary. 'Yes it's true that I don't have some of the problems other people have, such as dealing with the stress of raising a family; but it's also true that I come home to an empty house every night.' He loved to get out and be among people and continually looked for ways to include them. For him, community was paramount, belonging to a family that comes together to celebrate Christ's love.

Since that first day in January when Father Carmine had accepted him as an apprentice, Father Gary had felt a huge disconnection with the victims when the ritual began, despite the cramped space and the bizarre intimacies. All that changed during an exorcism one Saturday in late February.

As usual, Father Carmine had given him no idea what to expect. When he'd stepped into the office at ten that morning, he was surprised to see Father Daniel, of all people, waiting. 'So how'd you get involved in all of this?' Father Gary asked and got a brief sketch of the case before them: the woman was from southern Italy and, because her diocese had no exorcist, she travelled to Rome for exorcisms. Father Daniel happened to be a friend of the priest who often accompanied her.

Father Gary would have liked to hear more, but in walked three people – a Franciscan in his mid-forties with close-cropped hair and neatly trimmed beard, followed by a plain-looking couple in their early sixties. Wearing a rumpled suit, the man kept his eyes lowered as he entered while the woman, Giovanna, her hair short and slightly dishevelled, had a hard, calcified look about her, as if the weight of some unseen burden was slowly grinding her to dust.[9] She immediately caught Father Gary's attention because she looked very disturbed and eyed him warily.

Without wasting time, Father Carmine took Giovanna into the small room and everyone followed – Father Carmine and the two Franciscans in their brown robes, Father Gary in his black clerics. All four priests had on their stoles. The second Father Carmine closed the door, the mood in the room became very subdued. Giovanna sat down in the chair and, even though the ritual hadn't begun, she began to twitch nervously. Everyone's eyes were fixed on her, and Father Gary could tell immediately that something was unique about this case – he felt a strong sense of foreboding in her presence.

Father Carmine tossed some holy water from his squeeze bottle in her direction saying, 'In nómine Patris et Fílii et Spíritus Sancti [In the name of the Father, Son, and Holy Spirit].'

Giovanna immediately let fly a blood-curdling scream that chilled Father Gary to the bone. She quickly stood and scooped up the metal chair with one hand, wielding it over her head like a club while Father Daniel, the family priest, and her husband quickly jumped in to stop her from hurting anyone. Wrestling her back down into the chair, Father Carmine didn't hesitate in placing his hand on top of her head and invoking the Holy Spirit, even as she kicked and fought against the hands that held her back.

After a prayer to Saint Michael the Archangel, Father Carmine skipped straight through to the exorcism prayers: 'Deus, humáni géneris cónditor atque defénsor, réspice super hunc fámulam tuam, quam ad tuam imáginem formásti et ad tuæ voca glóriæ consórtium . . . [God, Creator and defender of the human race, look down on this your servant whom you formed in your own image and now call to be a partaker in your glory . . .]' he said.

The demon wasted no time in manifesting. 'You have no power over me!' he growled at Father Carmine in the typical guttural voice.

'Exáudi, Deus, Humánæ salútis amátor, oratiónem Apostolórum tuórum Petri et Pauli et ómnium Sanctórum, qui tua grátia victóres exstitérunt Malígni: líbera hunc fámulum tuam ab omni aliéna potestáte et incólumen custódi, ut traquíllæ devotióni restitúta, te corde díligat et opéribus desérviat, te gloríficet láudibus et magníficet vita [Hear, God, lover of human salvation, the prayer of your apostles Peter and Paul and of all the saints, who by your grace emerged as victors over the Evil one: free this, your servant, from every foreign power and keep her safe, so that restored to peaceful devotion, she may love you with her heart and may serve you zealously with her works, may glorify you with praises and may magnify you with her life],' Father Carmine prayed.

'You don't really believe those children's stories do you?' the demon scoffed. Once again the voice reminded Father Gary of a sound a dog might make were it able to speak. It was a deep, dark evil sound that seemed to come from the depths of the woman's stomach.

'Ooooooooooohhhhhhhh,' she moaned over and over as she fought back with even more violence, forcing Father Gary to jump in to help restrain her. The family priest grabbed her legs while Father Gary and Father Daniel held her arms; Giovanna's husband wrapped his own arm around her torso even as she growled and spat at Father Carmine.

Father Gary had never seen this strong a reaction. Giovanna's face had transformed, displaying a sneering look of pure hatred, with her eyes remaining open. Usually in the rare instances when the eyes stayed open, people had mild reactions to the prayers. In stronger cases victims typically closed their eyes to avoid looking at the sacred objects in the room. This time, however, not only were Giovanna's eyes open, but she boldly glared at the various people in the room.

'Exorcízo te, vetus hóminis inimíce: recéde ab hoc plásmate

Dei. Hoc te iubet Dóminus noster Iesus Christus, cuius humíli-tas tuam vicit supérbiam, lárgitas tuam prostrávit invídiam, mansuetúdo calcávit sævítiam [I cast you out, old enemy of man: depart from this servant of God. Our Lord Jesus Christ com-mands this of you, the humility of whom conquered your pride, the generosity of whom laid low your envy, the gentleness of whom trampled upon your cruelty].'

Again the voice exploded: 'Don't you know that he died on the cross? And you are still following him! We are stronger! We are stronger! We win! We win!'

Father Carmine poured some holy water into her eyes, and she struggled violently to shake free, shouting 'Basta!' and screaming. He continued, undeterred. 'Obmutésce, pater mendácii, neque impédias hanc fámulam Dei Dóminum benedícere et laudáre. Hoc tibi ímperat Iesus Christus, sapiéntia Patris et splendor ver-itátis, cuius verba spíritus et vita sunt [Be silent, father of lies, and do not hinder this servant of God from blessing and praising the Lord. Jesus Christ commands this of you, the wisdom of the Father and the splendour of truth, the words of whom are spirit and life],' he intoned. Again he repeated the word 'ímparat' (com-mands) a few times, accentuating it as he did, 'Ímmmm-pa-rat', in an effort to force the demon to acknowledge his inferiority.

Giovanna bared her teeth. Thick globs of mucus and saliva oozed from her mouth and ran down her chin. 'Shut up! Do you know who I am?' the deep voice growled, 'Don't treat me like a pig! Look what I can do to this old woman, look what I can do!' Again her body shook violently, prompting all four men to jump in again to stop her from hurting herself.

'Non mi toccare [Don't touch me]!' the demon shouted. After a few minutes, Giovanna calmed down enough that Father Gary and the others could relax their grip. She continued to drool, making no effort to stop the saliva from dribbling on to her shirt. Already there was small puddle beneath her feet. The family priest grabbed some paper towels and handed them to the Giovanna's husband, who dutifully wiped her mouth.

Father Carmine was just starting another prayer of the *Ritual* when, without warning, Giovanna turned towards Father Gary, fixing him with unblinking eyes full of hate. He noticed something incredibly unnatural about her eyes, which appeared somehow thicker than normal, almost like 'coke bottles', the irises unusually large and black. Even more striking, however, was that a presence seemed to be missing. Her eyes seemed almost dead, the gaze reminding him of the lifeless eyes of cadavers he had seen on the embalming table.

Trapped in the headlights of that 'dead' stare, Father Gary felt suddenly exposed, insignificant as the eyes bored into him. In this profound moment, he knew he was looking straight into the presence of pure evil. Refusing to be cowed, he quickly recomposed himself and refused to waver. 'I'll be damned if I am going to let this demon intimidate me,' he thought. And moments later the demon looked away from Father Gary and fixed his eyes on someone else.

The exorcism continued for over two hours, throughout which Giovanna continued to drool and fight violently while staring at everyone in the room in turn. Father Carmine interspersed psalms with both the revised and the old *Ritual*. More than a few times, she passed out. Knowing this as a trick the demon will sometimes use to prevent his host from hearing the prayers, Father Carmine simply said a blessing or threw holy water on to her and she sprang right back up. Father Gary jumped in to hold her down on numerous occasions.

As they neared the three-hour mark, Father Gary wondered how much longer they could continue. While all the men in the room were spent, especially Father Carmine, Giovanna showed no signs of slowing down, even though, Father Gary imagined, she had to be exhausted. Finally, when it looked like Father Carmine might pray the *Ritual* for the tenth time, he abruptly stopped and slapped Giovanna a few times on the forehead to bring her out of her trance.

It took her a full five minutes to recover and even then she seemed rather confused. Because she was unable to stand on her own, Father Daniel and Giovanna's husband carried her out of the room and laid her on Father Carmine's couch. Before long, she began grunting and cursing again.

'Did this do any good at all?' Father Gary asked Father Daniel.

Looking grim, Father Daniel responded that the possession was very entrenched. Giovanna had been undergoing exorcisms for more than forty years, and her case was considered one of the most severe that many of the exorcists in Rome (including Father Amorth and Father Gramolazzo) had seen.

'How did it happen?' Father Gary asked.

Father Daniel explained that she had been cursed by her mother when she was still in the womb. The mother, a poor woman from a small rural village, had originally tried to terminate the pregnancy on her own; when that failed, she had cursed her own baby.

As they were talking, Giovanna began to shout once again, letting fly a string of blasphemies, at which point her husband and the family priest took her away. When she'd gone, Father Gary turned to Father Carmine, curious to know why this case had been so violent.

'This is a very powerful demon,' Father Carmine said, explaining a little bit about what he meant. It was then that Father Gary learned that, just like the angels, demons have an entire hierarchy to their existence.

The Bible indicates that there is a hierarchy of demons. The 'ruler of the demons' is mentioned in the Gospel of Matthew (Matt. 9: 34), while Jesus refers to this hierarchy when he said 'the Devil and his angels' (Matt. 25: 41). Moreover, since the demons were once angels, it seems logical to assume that they were once connected to the angelic hierarchy.

The Bible mentions nine different orders of angels: seraphim (Isa. 6: 2); cherubim (Gen. 3: 24); thrones (Col. 1: 16); dominations (Col. 1: 16, Eph. 1: 21); virtues (Eph. 1: 21); powers

(Col. 1: 16, Eph. 6: 12); principalities (Eph. 6: 12); archangels, and angels (Rom. 8: 38). Three archangels appear in the Bible: Michael (Dan. 10: 13, 21; 12: 1; Jude 9; Apoc. 12: 7), Gabriel (Dan. 8: 16, 9: 21), and Raphael (Tobit 3: 17). Commonly these nine orders are called 'choirs,' since their principal job is to sing the glory of God.

Though many writers have attempted to address this hierarchy, perhaps the most well known is a man who lived about 500 CE called Pseudo-Dionysius, so named because he was mistaken by later writers as the convert of Saint Paul, Dionysius the Areopagite (Acts 17: 34).[10] A neo-Platonist, Pseudo-Dionysius grouped the nine choirs of angels into three hierarchies: the 'Supreme Hierarchy', consisting of the seraphim, cherubim and thrones; the 'Middle Hierarchy,' with dominations, virtues and powers; and the 'Lower Hierarchy,' made up of the principalities, archangels and angels. For Pseudo-Dionysius, this hierarchy constituted a sacred order of beings who were arranged in their likeness to God in descending order and who in their duties presided over the government of the world. Each hierarchy acted as a kind of 'mirror' that 'receives the rays of the supreme Deity which is the source of light . . . and pours it forth again abundantly, in accordance with God's law, upon those below itself'.[11]

More than a few theologians have pointed out the rigid and arbitrary nature of this structure. In the Bible, Michael appears as the leader of God's angelic army; and yet here, archangels are near the bottom of the scale.

When talking about the hierarchy, it's impossible not to see the limits of human reasoning at work. If angels are incorporeal spirits living in a world that we as humans can't even begin to comprehend, then how could we pretend to know their various ranks? Irenaeus had doubts about a structured hierarchy of angels as did Saint Augustine, who wrote: 'That there are in heaven Thrones, Dominations, Principalities and Powers, I firmly believe; that they differ among themselves I have no doubt; but as to saying what they are, and in what way they differ . . . I must admit I do not know.'[12]

Today, a majority of Catholic theologians lean towards the hierarchy as proposed by Thomas Aquinas, who adopted the Pseudo-Dionysius model, but used a slightly different distinction between the choirs – that of varying degrees of intelligence.

According to Aquinas, each angel is a distinct individual constituting a species unto itself. As a result each angel and demon varies slightly from the next, though rather than differing in materialistic ways, spirits vary in the degree of their perfection as spiritual beings – in other words, in their ability to manifest their powers.

Yet, as with any intellectual theory, other factors must be taken into consideration. In a practical sense, this is also true when it comes to demons, exorcists say.

The demons of the highest hierarchy always have biblical names like Satan, Beelzebub, Asmodeus, Zebulun, Zebuin and Meridiano. As Father Carmine explains, 'They are usually followed by many others who are secondary and are the ones who go to possess a person because they have been ordered to by their leader.' Satan, of course, as the most powerful demon, is always present to some extent in every possession, but almost never is he 'physically' present.

The key to being able to differentiate between the types of demons is by their level of intelligence. 'You don't measure the power of the demon by the strength of the person, but by the intelligence of the demon who talks,' says Father Gramolazzo. 'They will always manifest a profound knowledge of theology.' In addition, a stronger demon will always be able to resist the prayers of exorcism longer than a weaker one, and he may be able to pronounce sacred names such as Jesus or Mary, names that a weaker demon will never say. Instead of using names, they will simply say 'He is destroying me' or 'she is burning me'.

While the hierarchy of the angels is based on love, there is no such concept in 'hell', say exorcists. The demons keep their former angelic ranks, but the only thing that unifies them is their hatred for God and man. The demons of the lower ranks obey the stronger ones, not out of obedience but out of fear. 'They are like slaves,' says Father Nanni.

Exorcists have seen this firsthand when a more powerful demon blocked a weaker demon from leaving a person's body during an exorcism even though the prayer caused him great pain. This is also evident when there is more than one demon present. The weakest demon will always manifest first. 'The strongest tend to hide; in the mean time they send out the smaller ones,' says Father Nanni.

Some demons seem to be actively antagonistic towards one another. Father Daniel (who became an exorcist briefly in Rome in 2006) had to schedule two possessed people he was seeing on different days. The instant they saw each other, their demons would manifest and become so violently enraged that they would often come to blows. And yet, even while some apparently despise each other, other groups seem to be able to work together. A stronger demon – or perhaps the leader of the possessing demon – will often come to the aid of a weaker demon. Most often, this will happen during the ritual, in which the exorcist will discern that he is dealing with a stronger demon, or in between exorcisms, when the character of the demon (and its name) will change from one session to the next.

As for Giovanna, there was no way for Father Gary to know the hierarchy of her demon. He had been too engrossed in reining her in to hear whether Father Carmine had addressed the demon by name. Later, Father Daniel would speculate that the case was one of the rarest of rare instances – an actual Satanic possession.[13]

On the way home from San Lorenzo, the bus was jammed with tourists and Saturday-afternoon commuters wearing bulky winter coats. The windows were fogged from breath and body heat and the overhead fans blasting hot air. Father Gary had only been able to get a few feet inside the front door and stood crushed between the driver's compartment and the mass of bodies swaying along with the lurching bus. It was a weird juxtaposition to be surrounded by so much humanity after the events he'd just experienced at San Lorenzo. Replaying the exorcism in his mind he couldn't get over the way the demon had looked at him. The gaze seemed to penetrate his very soul, as if the demon had been able to read him.

Numerous exorcists have attested that they are constantly watched by the demon. Many, if not all, have had strange moments when their lives are touched by an evil presence. Father Bamonte remembers an exorcism when a demon somehow knew that he was suffering from rheumatism. 'How are your bones feeling this morning?' the demon asked him sarcastically. Father Carmine once had a demon mock a recent trip he had taken, saying, 'How stupid you are to think that visiting Lourdes would actually help you,' even though he hadn't mentioned to the person he was praying over that he was going.

'The spiritual dimension is adjoining to the material one – [angels and demons] live between us and they see us but we do not see them,' explains Father Nanni. 'From a biblical perspective, their function is one of catching every mistake we make in order to throw them in our face.' It's for this reason that on numerous occasions Satan is referred to as 'the accuser'. 'Then I heard a loud voice in heaven proclaiming, "Now have come the salvation and the power and the kingdom of our God and the authority of his Messiah, for the accuser of our comrades has been thrown down, who accuses them day and night before our God"' (Rev. 12: 10).

'This means that the demon is always actively watching people and he gets pleasure when he sees that they are not faithful to God and, as a result, take his side,' says Father Nanni. 'He wants humankind to rebel against God as well, and this is the one "accusation" that he can level against an individual at the Last Judgement that has the most weight.'

For the next few days the experience of having the demon lock eyes with him would continue to dog Father Gary. He wondered what kind of effect such a direct connection would have on him. After his hiking accident, he'd often wondered if God had saved him for a reason. Over the years when something would happen in his life he would think, well, maybe this is the reason why. After some time, he stopped worrying about it. However, when he looked back on the series of events that had led him to Rome, there did seem to be a logical sequence at work. His time in the mortuary, his accident, his depression, his belief in healing prayer – had God somehow been grooming him to be an exorcist all along? Ultimately he couldn't say; but he knew that as a result of those experiences he would certainly be more motivated to try. And if this was really what God wanted him to do, then even if the Devil were somehow watching him, so was God; and that's all that mattered.

CHAPTER FIFTEEN

LIBERATION

The Devil's main trick is to make people think that they are unworthy of God's forgiveness. This is the biggest lie that the demon gives us, not making us believe in God's mercy.

A Charismatic individual who assists Father Bamonte
during exorcisms

Father Daniel and Silvia, a hollow-eyed woman of thirty-seven with thinning hair, sat together on a bench across from the shrine.[1] Silvia, wearing a scarf and heavy jacket to ward off the night air, kept her eyes focused on the statue of Mary while Father Daniel, his dark brown robes partially hidden under a black parka, prayed the rosary softly under his breath. It was nearly midnight and the shrine was deserted. Eyeing his watch, Father Daniel wondered if the demon's promise would turn out to be true. Two months before, the demon had proclaimed his departure for this very night. Father Daniel, who normally didn't put much stock in what demons said, remained sceptical. This time, however, over the course of several exorcisms in Rome, the demon had been very precise, giving not only the date, but also the time and place – at the stroke of midnight in Lourdes, France.

Silvia continued to finger her rosary beads as she prayed, rocking slightly. Father Daniel was trying not to get his hopes up. Her possession had been a terribly trying case, lasting more than twelve years (though he had been praying over her for only eight months) and bringing her to the brink of suicide.

As the minute hand ticked closer to midnight, Father Daniel wondered what would signify her liberation. Would the demon depart violently or would she vomit up a talisman? He braced himself. His mind returned to the rosary, and he lost track of the time. They continued to pray for several minutes when suddenly Silvia let out a deep, guttural sigh, as if some invisible hand were pushing on her abdomen: 'Huhhhhhhhhh.'

He looked up, studying her. She had a slightly puzzled expression on her face.

He scrutinized her carefully to see if the sigh were a prelude to something more. Silvia sat completely still. Finally she turned, looking a little unsure.

'How do you feel?' he asked.

'Fine,' she said, thinking about it.

'Anything else?' he persisted.

She shook her head no.

He waited for her to add something, but she didn't. Remembering, he looked down at his watch and saw that it was only a few minutes after midnight. She was not wearing a watch herself so was unaware of the precise time.

'Let's say a prayer of thanksgiving together,' he suggested, secretly hoping that this wasn't a nefarious ruse on the part of the demon.

They prayed for several minutes, while Silvia's mood continued to lighten. She wiped away tears as the realization of what had happened dawned on her. The demon was finally gone.

A week later, back in Rome, still hesitant to declare victory, Father Daniel sent her to Father Amorth, who prayed over her. After two sessions in which she showed no reaction, he said another prayer of thanksgiving, sang a hymn, and declared her 'healed'. Silvia's long ordeal was indeed over.

Since it can take a long time for a person to become liberated, Father Gary had yet to see it happen, though Father Carmine had told him about improvements in some of their 'regulars'. At one point, Sister Janica hadn't been able to even get out of bed. Another young woman who had been unable to study was now going to the university full-time. But for Father Gary, who had only recently met these people, it was hard to gauge any true advancement. On one occasion, he thought Sister Janica seemed a little better. After one exorcism towards the end of his stint with Father Carmine, she actually smiled at him and kissed his hand.

Exorcism is not a magic formula. There are three factors, say exorcists, to consider when it comes to liberation: the behaviour of the victim, the action of the exorcist, and the permission of God. All three are important, yet obviously to varying degrees. Essentially, liberation comes when the Spirit of God commands the demon to depart. In an exorcism, of course, it is the exorcist who, as a representative of the Catholic Church and by invoking the name of Jesus Christ, does this. And while this action is important, God is still the one doing the work. As Sicilian exorcist Father Matteo La Grua states, 'Liberation is a gift from God, and God can liberate when He wants and how He wants, even without the intervention of man.'[2] The effectiveness of God's presence, however, depends in large part on the co-operation of the victim and to a lesser extent on the faith of the exorcist. A good analogy is a person who burns an ant by focusing sunbeams through a magnifying lens – the sunlight represents the Spirit of God and the lens the person who accepts God's love, focusing it on the ant, which of course is the demon.

In order for any exorcism to work, victims must co-operate with the exorcist. They must renounce the demon and any sins or actions that may have led them to become possessed; they also should pray and return to practising the sacraments. (Not everybody has to be a Catholic, or convert, to become liberated, though some do. Father Amorth says he has exorcized Muslims and Hindus on rare occasions, but mentions that he will pray the *Ritual* using the name of Jesus Christ. 'I also ask them to fulfil their spiritual duties. For example, Muslims have the obligation to pray and so I tell them to do so. Otherwise I tell them to be a good person, an honest person who fulfils their professional and moral duties.')[3]

The sacrament of reconciliation, say exorcists, is incredibly important. 'Exorcism can drive a demon out of a person's body; confession can drive evil out of a person's soul. Confession not only forgives, but heals our soul and fills it with light,' writes Father José Antonio Fortea.[4]

This process can be particularly drawn out when the person has strayed far from God, or in some cases has joined a satanic cult, say exorcists. Another difficult hurdle to overcome is the victim's inability to forgive. 'Sincere forgiveness, which includes prayer on that person's behalf and having masses said for the person's conversion, often breaks open a deadlocked situation and helps speed up the healing,' writes Father Amorth.[5]

This is a difficult process for the possessed person to undergo, and the demon will attempt to stop it, say exorcists, attacking internally (by convincing the person that he or she is only crazy, not possessed, and so doesn't need an exorcism) or by intervening directly (for instance causing such fatigue that the victim can't get out of bed). According to Anna, when she was close to liberation, the demon almost convinced her that she was imagining everything, even putting the thought in her mind that Father Bamonte was trying to take advantage of her by recording her exorcism to write about it in a book, for his own benefit. Father Bamonte freed her from this obsession by tricking the demon into guessing the contents of a sealed envelope. When the demon knew what was in the envelope, Anna says her conviction was affirmed. After this incident, Anna's sense of desperation faded and she began to pray with renewed vigour.

Obviously an exorcist needs to have a strong spiritual core. 'An exorcist must live an intense life of prayer and not be afraid,' says Father Bamonte. 'If you don't have a strong spiritual life, if you don't have the protection of your faith, how can you be able to fight? Praying, loving God, not committing sins – those are the weapons an exorcist uses.'

Some demons may be more difficult to cast out than others. The duration of the possession is the first and most important element. A person who has been hit in infancy and then doesn't see an exorcist until adulthood is going to have a much harder time getting rid of the demon that has now become almost a part of his or her identity, say exorcists.

The strength of the demon can also be another factor, though apparently the most difficult cases always involve a curse. As Father Carmine explains, 'There remains a connection between the victim and the one who caused the curse. In those cases it's difficult because it's about the hatred of other people toward the affected person.'

Unlike a natural illness for which treatment usually brings relief, exorcists claim that the process is reversed in demonic possession. Once the demon is discovered, he fights hard to resist the prayers of the exorcism. But even though the person suffers, these attacks are, in a larger sense, an indication that the victim is headed in the right direction, say exorcists.

'It can happen that when a person who has been possessed for a very long time, gets close to God, he can be hit by a series of bad events. I know this may sound strange, but this is a good sign because it means that the demon is losing; that's why it is reacting like that. You don't have to be discouraged; it is a good sign. I always say, "Don't be scared of the demon, be scared of the sin,"' advises Father Bamonte.

As the exorcist continues to pray the *Ritual*, and to pray for the victim to return to God, the power of the exorcism begins to weaken the demon. There are several signs that indicate the demon is close to leaving. 'He is weaker in the voice, in the ability to manifest in the crisis; he leaves sooner every time. .When those exorcisms become weaker and weaker, when the possession time gets shorter and the temporary liberations come sooner than before, it means that he is getting weaker. Also outside of the exorcism the person's life is more normal,' Father Nanni says.

At the moment of liberation the demon may offer a 'sign' that he is leaving. If the person has been hit by a 'spell', then the demon may indicate that liberation will come when a certain object is vomited. It may even be expelled through the anus or secreted through the skin. Exorcists have seen it all. Father Carmine once saw a woman sweat a green mucus-like substance through her skin. Another sign may be the demon saying a prayer or reciting a hymn.

In certain cases, the exorcist may ask for a sign that is directly connected to the suffering the demon may be causing. Father Daniel claims that he once asked that a woman become pregnant as a sign of liberation because the demon had been preventing it. Sure enough, he says, a month after the woman's liberation, she became pregnant – something that she had been trying unsuccessfully to do for five years.

An outward sign is generally not necessary, say exorcists. 'If the person lives in peace, is no longer disturbed by the demon, can pray, and lives in the grace of God, you know she is liberated,' explains Father Nanni. 'If you go back to pray and during another exorcism the crisis starts again, then it means only that the liberation was just temporary.' As a precaution, many exorcists will continue to pray over people a few times even after they have been liberated.

Once the person has been liberated, it is said that the demon will often try to return. Exorcists generally offer a prayer of thanksgiving (Father Davies uses the Gloria, which Catholics recognise from the Sunday liturgy) and ask that the Holy Spirit fill the void left by the departing spirit. In addition, the newly liberated person must continue to live a Christian life and not fall back into the habits or sins that caused the possession in the first place, or else, exorcists claim, there is a high risk of becoming possessed again, this time worse than before (Matt. 12: 43–5).

In 2003, Beatrice, a 46-year-old married woman[6] who worked as biologist in a medical lab, began experiencing odd phenomena – freak accidents, objects moving around the house on their own, a mysterious force that pushed her mother to the ground, breaking her arm. A year later, burn marks began appearing on all her clothing, always in the same place – on the thigh – and always the same size. Thinking she was losing her mind, she eventually found her way to Father Bamonte, who discerned the presence of three demons. After a gruelling two-year battle involving weekly exorcisms, Beatrice was finally freed.

> The first of December 2006, a day which seemed like any other, was the day in which God permitted my liberation. To tell you the truth, my mood had been pretty down for a few days because, after a period of relative calm on the part of 'that one' [the demon], I went back to the old times, when I used to scream, to be agitated and to attack everybody either verbally or physically. While in the past I was usually conscious, feeling as if I was split between the sensations of my own life and those from the demon (to the point of even fearing that I was hallucinating, or that those were just the manifestation of my psychosis), in the last couple months I entered in a deep state of trance. I could only feel rage and the other atrocious sensations of that monster which manifested and at the end I could remember only a few things, almost nothing.
>
> This new situation unfortunately made me think that things, for some mysterious reason, were getting worse. As a matter of fact, e en if I continued to trust in God's divine

mercy and in the protection of the Blessed Mother, these strong reactions made me think that the demon had somehow regained some strength and that, as a result, the day of my liberation was still very far off. In spite of that, every day I kept giving my life to the Lord and to the Immaculate Virgin.

In the previous session I had a huge amount of saliva coming out of my mouth, as if I was 'expelling' all the evil that I still had inside, but in the end 'that one' seemed to still be there. The day in which he left though, it was a special day: it was the Friday after the feast of Christ the King, two days after it would have been the first Sunday of Advent and in one week the Feast of the Immaculate Conception would have started (actually my husband and I had already started reciting the novena for two days). It was basically a marvellous coincidence of sacred events. The exorcism started as usual with the prayers following the formula of the rite; the only difference that manifested after a while was a strong reaction by the demon to the words 'For Christ, with Christ and in Christ'. It seemed as if he had never heard them before. He started to become very agitated, he lost all his usual arrogance and became desperate. He tried to bite the hands of the people that were trying to hold him or to throw away the crucifix that the exorcist had put on my chest and also (with my great sorrow) to spit on it. All of a sudden (I don't remember the sequence of the events; maybe it was when the exorcist invoked Mary) I felt hit by a huge wave of a very bright white light, it was all-encompassing, a light that I could perceive and feel as well and it gave me a sensation of very sweet peace while for the demon it provoked atrocious pain.

Once again I felt like I was splitting, dividing between my own sensations and 'his'. If I closed my eyes I could see in my mind's eye that we were in a deep shadow and so I knew that the light that was embracing me was a spiritual one. Closing my eyes again I could also perceive that this same light was stabbing the eyes of the monster like a thousand swords.

Meanwhile the monster was screaming, moving like crazy, saying that the veil of Mary (whom he referred to as 'that one') was suffocating him and causing him a huge amount of pain, to the point of causing him to go into terrible, indescribable spasms. Towards the end he launched a scream as he never did before and I felt rent in two, as if somebody turned me inside out.

Then all of a sudden there was calm and silence and I opened my eyes coming out of the trance by myself. Then Father Francesco [Bamonte] blessed me, ending the rite. I had no idea that something out of the ordinary had happened. In fact, as I said, the three days leading up to the exorcism were terrible for me and all through that time I had felt a growing rage and a huge sense of mental confusion mixed with a lack of hope. I was familiar with all those kinds of emotions but I never felt them in such an intensive way. It seemed as if my life was about to end. After the exorcism, I started to feel a little better again and from that moment I started to improve more and more.

During the exorcism two Fridays later I remained conscious; and even though I closed my eyes, when Father Francesco checked them in order to see how my pupils looked, they stayed in the normal position. From the very beginning of the rite my mind started to form thoughts in which I denied with all my will any kind of 'co-operation' with the demon; I told 'him' that with the help and the strength of God, I would never allow him any kind of power over me, something I had never been able to do before.

When the rite was nearing completion, Father Francesco suggested to his helpers that they open the Bible and read a passage. One of them opened the Bible at random and they read a passage from the Gospel of Luke in which Jesus reads in the synagogue of Nazareth. 'When he came to Nazareth, where he had been brought up, he went into the synagogue on the Sabbath day, as was his custom. He stood up to read, and the scroll of the prophet Isaiah was given to him. He unrolled the scroll and found the place where it was written: The Spirit of the Lord is upon me, because he has anointed me to bring good news to the poor. He has sent me to proclaim release to the captives and recovery of sight to the blind, to let the oppressed go free' (Luke 4: 16–18). That passage of the Gospel was the marvellous confirmation of what had just happened: the Lord liberated me! While I was crying tears of joy, I started to thank the Lord and the Immaculate Virgin, which I will continue to do for as long as I live.[7]

For many years, the scientific and medical community scorned the idea that a person could be 'healed' through prayers or ritualistic ceremonies like exorcism. Today, however, the ability of certain healing rituals to offer genuine relief is no longer disputed – numerous anthropologists have documented[8] that people have recovered from problems varying from depression, addictive behaviour, or anxiety to even more severe ailments, including life-threatening diseases, through such ceremonies.[9] So how does science account for 'anomalous healing'?

At the core of these experiences lies the difference between 'healing' and 'curing'. According to Stanley Krippner and Jeanne Achterberg in the book *Varieties of Anomalous Experience: Examining the Scientific Evidence*, for many indigenous people 'healing' means restoring a person's physical, mental, emotional, or spiritual capacities, while 'curing' usually refers to overcoming a disease that is primarily biological in nature.[10]

Scientists and doctors have tried a variety of methods in an attempt to explain how anomalous healing experiences may actually work. In looking at spirit possession in Haiti, for example, scholar Steve Mizrach came to the conclusion that Voodoo possession can be considered a kind of psychotherapy or 'folk therapy'.[11] In addition, I. M. Lewis, author of *Ecstatic Religion: A Study of Shamanism and Spirit Possession*, surmised that the 'psychologically highly charged atmosphere' of a séance could be

effective in treating certain neurotic or psychosomatic disturbances; adding that even in the case of organic illnesses, he
thought it might also provide a benefit simply by strengthening
the patient's will to recover.[12]

More than a few cognitive scientists have pointed out the
potential benefits of an exorcism in treating people with dissociative identity disorder (DID). Dr Mazzoni, for example,
believes the exorcist gives some people a way out by saying that
their problems are caused by an outside entity and therefore they
are not the cause, which, she says, 'allows the patient to make a
clean break . . . People get cured of demonic possession because
basically the priest becomes the therapist and the priest is the
one who is able to take control of the bad part of the person.'

In comparing exorcism with the 'traditional' approach to
treating DID, Dr Steven Jay Lynn notes that the former may
actually be more beneficial:

> In a way the exorcist's ritual is a lot clearer because if the ther-
> apist believes that the person cannot be cured until they know
> all about the underlying personality system, and recover all
> the memories and have succeeded in integrating all the per-
> sonalities – the person or patient can go through a tremendous
> amount of emotional pain in trying to recover memories,
> especially if they're not real memories. Now an exorcism is a
> pretty clear-cut procedure that doesn't really depend on this
> extensive background of work with the person so I would
> think that it may in fact be much more effective in helping
> people 'get better', quote, unquote.

Dr Richard Gallagher, however, says that that's not really the
purpose of the *Ritual*. 'I wouldn't do it for mental-health purposes,' he says. 'If you are dealing with a suggestive individual or
an individual who is deluded into thinking they are being
attacked by the demonic I personally think that an exorcism is
a bad idea. I am sure that there are some people who argue that

an exorcism can be psychologically therapeutic but again that is not the primary reason that it is being done. It's being done because [the exorcist] thinks there is a genuine demonic entity involved and they need spiritual help.'

Interestingly, neuroscience is also beginning to weigh in on this subject as well. Dr Jeffrey Schwartz, a neuropsychiatrist at the University of California Los Angeles, has discovered a way to treat obsessive compulsive disorder (OCD) that sounds very similar to how exorcism is practised in certain circles. In looking at the disorder, Dr Schwartz saw how the plasticity of the brain actually made people's compulsions stronger if they gave in to them, since the neural pathways increased in number when used. Because Dr Schwartz believes that the brain has the capacity to rewire itself if given the correct set of instructions, he created a four-step programme that he said could address the problem naturally. Similar to having a religious person give a demonic name to the compulsion, the first step in Dr Schwartz's programme teaches the patient to say that the problem is the result of the OCD and not the patient themselves. According to Dr Schwartz, reattributing is a particularly effective technique in helping the patient to redirect their attention away from the demoralizing effects of engaging in compulsive behaviours.[13]

These healing rituals may also work because of the placebo effect. Psychologist Dr Michael E. Hyland, from the University of Plymouth in the United Kingdom, has done extensive research into placebos, which he prefers to call 'therapeutic rituals'. 'I don't like the word placebo because, one, it implies that we know what the cause of it is, and the other is that we know the mechanism and we don't.' He first became interested in placebos as a way to 'personalize' therapy. 'It doesn't really matter what the therapy is, therapies work, that is the one thing you can be sure of,' he says. 'Now the question is why do they work? That is a much more controversial issue.'

According to Dr Hyland, the conventional wisdom on

placebo says that it works because of expectancy, but he thinks there might be other mechanisms involved. 'It isn't just the expectation that you are going to get better or be healed; there is actually a far more complex process.'

Dr Hyland has come up with something he calls motivational concordance. 'Our research suggests that two mechanisms are involved. One is the well-established mechanism of response expectancy. The other is a motivational mechanism where people gain therapeutic benefit by engaging in therapeutic rituals that are concordant with self-defining or self-actualizing goals. That is, when people self-actualize as part of therapy, then this produces therapeutic benefit through a motivational, non-expectancy-dedicated pathway.' Put differently, when a person feels as if their needs are being met through therapy, then this can help them to get better by motivating them to get really engaged with the therapy.

Most importantly, Dr Hyland's research showed that it doesn't necessarily matter if the person undergoing the ritual believes in it, what really matters is how it 'feels' to them. 'The ritual is basically concordant with your motivations. So, for example, if we look at prayer as a therapeutic ritual and people know about it, we see those psychological mediated effects, some of which might be expectancy.' In other words, spiritual rituals tend to work for spiritual people.

However, Dr Hyland is quick to point out that it is not entirely clear how and why the placebo effect works. 'Even so I can only explain ten per cent of the variance, I can't explain much variance.'

One of the theories he looked at in the hope of going deeper was quantum entanglement, the principle stating that when two particles become entangled, then an observation made on one particle has an instantaneous effect on the behaviour of the other particle, no matter where that particle is. If true, quantum entanglement could help to explain how things like healing from a distance, or the power of prayer, actually work.

At present, however, Dr Hyland is not entirely convinced that there is enough evidence to support this theory. 'People say since funny things happen in the quantum world they must also happen in the macro world, and that may or may not be true.'

For sheer ingenuity, perhaps no one has gone further in trying to debunk the world of the transcendent than Canadian neuroscientist Michael Persinger, who conducted a series of experiments in which he tried to prove that the major components of certain 'mystical' experiences, especially near-death experiences (NDEs), could be re-created by stimulating the temporal-lobe region of the brain with electric current. In order to do this, Persinger created a magnetic device – which he termed the 'God helmet' – that was supposed to be able to simulate the sensations that accompany mystical experiences and NDEs, namely floating outside the body, having a sense of profound meaning, seeing a tunnel of white light, and so on.

As some critics have noted, however, the results of his experiments are far from conclusive, mostly leaving people with a feeling of slight wooziness, and not the coherent and lucid experiences described by those claiming to have had NDEs.[14] Even British author and evolutionary biologist Richard Dawkins, who used the helmet in 2003 and felt nothing more than a shortness of breath and slight twitching in his leg, said he was 'very disappointed' by the results.[15]

In addition, some have pointed out the faulty assumptions behind the concept. As Bruce Greyson states in *Varieties of Anomalous Experience: Examining the Scientific Evidence*, 'Correlating a brain state with an experience does not necessarily imply that brain states cause the experience; the brain state may alternatively allow access to or simply reflect the experience.'[16] As one critic put it, knowing how a television set works doesn't necessarily shed light on the origin of the signal.[17]

Inherent, of course, in the failures of some of these theories, say religious believers, is the problem of trying to weigh and measure that which may not fit into a laboratory, namely spirits. Believers decry the attitude of critics that they say discounts the value of faith and tries to skew the argument towards the scientific (and especially materialist) canon, an argument that might be paraphrased something like this: since we can prove a possible natural cause for the occurrence of something, then the onus is on you to show us the proof of your 'supernatural' cause. This implies that any 'proof' of a supernatural cause would have to be scientific in order for it to be considered legitimate. But are scientific standards really the only criteria that matter? In his refutation, theologian John Haught describes a concept that he calls 'layered explanation', which can be illustrated by answers to the question: Why does a pot of water boil on a stove? One answer is to say that the water is boiling because the H_2O molecules are moving around and making a transition from a liquid state to a gaseous one. Another answer would be that the water is boiling because someone turned the stove on. A third answer could be that it's boiling because a person wants a cup of tea. All are valid answers but offer very different levels of understanding.[18] For a person of faith, the scientific explanation seems only valid to a certain degree.

Perhaps not surprisingly, some doctors and scientists are trying to bridge this supposed gap between science and religion.

In their book, *The Spiritual Brain*, neuroscientist Mario Beauregard and journalist Denyse O'Leary argue against the belief that humans are nothing more than 'biological automatons', and that spiritual experiences are simply the result of synapses firing in the brain. Instead, using a variety of scientific analyses, the authors propose a non-materialist view of neuroscience in which the mind is separate from the body. For instance, in looking at Dr Schwartz's study on OCD and the way patients were able to reorder the neural pathways of their brain, Beauregard and O'Leary stipulated that, for this to work, there must be some outside agent running the show.

Similarly, in looking at 'mystical experiences' (defined by the authors as 'the experience of certain, mystical contact with a higher truth or a greater power underlying the universe'[19]), Beauregard used brain-scan imagery on a group of Carmelite nuns who were in a deep contemplative state in order to find out which areas of the brain are most active during such states. The scans showed that when these nuns reported having mystical experiences, rather than being isolated to a single area of the brain (the left temporal lobe, for example) the experiences neurally engaged different regions of the brain responsible for a variety of functions, including self-consciousness, emotion, visual and motor imagery and spiritual perception.[20] To Beauregard and O'Leary, this suggests that these mystical experiences are not only as complex and multidimensional as people who have them claim they are, but are the products of a healthy and functioning brain and not some simple 'trick' or defect of the brain.

Dr Craig Isaacs, a psychiatrist from San Francisco, California, who also happens to be an Anglican priest, is another person trying to bridge the divide. In the course of his work in both areas, Dr Isaacs has treated numerous patients for mental illness. However, he is convinced that some of the people he has seen are suffering from a demonic possession, and in that case he has prayed prayers of deliverance over them.

According to Dr Isaacs, the key to distinguishing between the two is in differentiating the source: 'Is the ego perceiving something from within the psyche or is it coming from outside the soul?'[21] In other words, is the person imagining that he is speaking to a being (such as a child who has an imaginary friend) or is he really contacting a separate entity, something that Dr Isaacs referrers to as the 'wholly other'. In his research, Dr Isaacs has discovered five qualities that the ego experiences when encountering the wholly other: first, the patient experiences a vision or voice as coming from outside themselves, from a wholly other; second, the experience is otherworldly or spiritual in nature; third, the experience is accompanied by numinous fear or awe; fourth, there is unusual clarity associated with the experience; and fifth, when a vision is involved there is almost always some form of luminosity, either a shadow or a beautiful light.

The criteria are not common to psychosis, claims Dr Isaacs. And depending on the therapist's school of thought, he says, one may address this problem inadequately or not at all.[22]

Dr Isaacs believes in the concept that a human being consists of a 'tripartite nature', comprised of body-soul-spirit, an idea that comes from 1 Thessalonians 5: 23. This understanding can then be carried over into illness, he claims, for if a person is tripartite, then so too would be the various sicknesses that could affect him or her in one or more of these functions.[23]

In this model, sickness of the body is caused by disease, normally cured through medicine, while the second category, sickness of the soul (that is, neurotic and psychotic behaviours) is caused by 'a breakdown in one of [the soul's] functions', the cure for which can be psychotherapy or prayers of inner healing. The third category, 'sickness of the spirit', is caused either by personal sin or the demonic and can lead to what Dr Isaacs calls 'existential neuroses' – in which the patient may feel 'a loss of freedom or the loss of meaning in life'. If the cause is sin, then the patient will be helped through repentance and forgiveness; if demonic, then through an exorcism or a prayer of deliverance.

Since all the functions of a human being are interrelated, any illness in one function can affect the others. 'Thus, spiritual illness may also be seen to affect the volition of the soul, or an illness of the soul may affect the actions of the body,' says Dr Isaacs.[24]

While it is clear that advances in science and medicine *have* been able to explain why many people claiming to be possessed by an evil spirit may actually feel a genuine sense of healing after undergoing an exorcism, several questions still remain. Paranormal events – mind-reading, levitation, speaking in

previously unknown foreign languages – continue to elude
scientific explanation. Perhaps one day science will be able to
explain why these things happen. Until then, however, it
would seem a betrayal of the tenets of scientific curiosity to
discount a whole range of experiences affecting the lives of so
many people simply because they defy such explanation.

CHAPTER SIXTEEN

ORGANIZING THE MINISTRY

The profession of exorcism has meaning if we as exorcists, through possession and exorcism, prove that God is not only present but stronger. This is a path of faith and I always tell that to the families I meet with in a parish where there is a possessed person. It is through the grace of God that these people can redis-cover the evangelical message of our faith.

Father Giancarlo Gramolazzo

In late March, Father Gary's bishop, along with other priests from the diocese of San Francisco and San Jose, came to Rome for the ceremony creating Archbishop Laveda as cardinal. And though only in town for a week, the bishop found time to talk with Father Gary about his new assignment. Back in November, when Father Gary was just four months into his sabbatical, his bishop had asked if he would be willing to take over as pastor of Sacred Heart Parish in Saratoga, California. The two sat in the reading room of the Casa, one day, discussing the post and Father Gary's desire to bring renewal to the Parish.

With that business out of the way, his bishop asked him how the exorcism training was going, no doubt half-expecting to hear a few dry remarks about a classroom, lectures and textbooks. Instead he was shocked when Father Gary told him that he'd seen around fifteen exorcisms that week alone.

'You mean you've actually *seen* an exorcism?' his bishop asked.

'I've seen about sixty,' Father Gary said, correcting him.

His bishop listened intently as Father Gary briefly described some of the scenes out at San Lorenzo. He mentioned Father Carmine's – and other Italian exorcists' – complaints that some bishops didn't take them seriously. As he talked, Father Gary was careful to reiterate how grateful he was to have had the opportunity to come to Rome and study. 'Without the training, I wouldn't have known the first thing about how to proceed,' he told his bishop. It was a natural segue into the practical concerns of getting other American exorcists trained. 'If every diocese is supposed to have an exorcist then we have a hell of a lot of work to do.' It just wasn't practical to ask priests to come all the way over to Rome for four months to take the course. One positive development came in the form of a conference in the Midwest that he was planning to attend in August. Apparently the co-ordinators were attempting to organize something modelled on the conferences of the International Association of Exorcists. This seemed like a good place to start.

He and his bishop also needed to establish a protocol for when someone approached him about exorcism. Since he'd need to get his bishop's permission before proceeding, a system had to be worked out. His bishop promised that they would set it in place when Father Gary got back.

In the meantime, Father Gary shared his ideas about the kind of 'exorcism team' he wanted to assemble. Because he was still concerned about discernment, he planned to err on the side of caution and vet potential 'patients' through either a psychiatrist or a psychologist. The challenge would be to find competent doctors who believed in the possibility of demonic possession but who weren't overzealous about it, something Father Gary realized could be just as harmful as being too sceptical. In addition, he anticipated having a medical doctor and perhaps a historical theologian (something recommended by an exorcist at the Angelicum). Beyond the medical team, he'd enlist Father Kevin (also for his ability to speak Spanish) and a couple of other priests as possible helpers. He didn't think he was going to use a prayer group just yet (something Father Bamonte had recommended). Because Father Carmine had told him how ashamed people could feel, he thought it prudent to avoid distractions or potential embarrassment that might result from bringing strangers into the room. At the minimum he would do what Father Carmine did, which was to offer up the person's name at mass.

As their meeting came to a close, his bishop told him he was impressed with Father Gary's intentions and reiterated his support.

Even before meeting with his bishop, Father Gary had been thinking about the day when he would have to perform an exorcism. He already knew – based on his own experience with depression – that he wanted to establish a measured, calm approach that could help put people at ease and create the right kind of environment for healing. He had been turned off by some of the more 'fundamentalist' books he had read attributing just about every problem under the sun – doubt, fear, alcoholism, greed – to a demon. He found that 'theologically troubling'. As C. S. Lewis so famously said in *The Screwtape Letters*, 'There are two equal and opposite errors into which our race can fall about the devils. One is to disbelieve in their existence. The other is to believe, and to feel an excessive and unhealthy interest in them.'

For this reason, he planned on starting out small. The first thing he'd probably do would be to ask a series of questions: Do you go to mass? Do you worship or pray? Have you been to confession lately? If the answers were no, he would most likely get the sufferer to start going back to church and the sacraments before he would perform an exorcism. Of course, he would still offer a simple blessing.

But would it be that easy to convince people to follow this cautious approach?

He knew from his experiences at Saint Nicholas, where some of his techno-conscious former parishioners had to have the latest piece of gadgetry, that it wasn't going to be easy to ask people to slow down and invest their time in something that might not show immediate results. 'We are a culture of instant gratification,' he would later say, voicing a criticism that virtually every exorcist shares.

Months later, Father Vince would have a similar experience when trying to get a woman who came to see him to return to mass. 'It is almost like people want to believe in the extreme,' says Father Vince. 'I am happy to pray with people; but if I tell them that they need to start going back to the church and taking advantage of the sacraments, they look at me like I am crazy for actually suggesting that they practise their faith. And I know if I told them to go out and do the extreme, "Go stand on your lawn and swing a dead chicken around your head and you will be fine," they would do that. But just going to mass or confession – they think that is kind of mundane.'

There would be other challenges as well, some of them uniquely American. Whereas Italy is basically a monocultural (predominantly Catholic) society, America is anything but. In Father Gary's estimate, in the diocese of San Jose alone, more than 100 different languages are spoken. There is a sizeable Vietnamese community in town, as well as a large Hispanic population. He would have to know a little about the cultural mores of the various immigrant groups (as well as their traditions) if he were to become an effective exorcist.

Father Gary didn't pretend to have all the answers. He hoped to be able to share information and get advice from some of the other exorcists in the US who might have more experience. He had talked to Father Vince as well as to an exorcist he knew in Nebraska about the need to begin networking. The problem was the paucity of exorcists. Father Gary had heard the number was somewhere around fourteen officially appointed exorcists in the entire United States.[1] In addition, as he'd shared with his bishop, some of these exorcists had received no formal training beyond being handed the *Ritual*. Just trying to work out a common approach would present a challenge, let alone battling a demon.

At the beginning of Lent, Father Gary began participating in mass every morning at one of the old titular houses, original house churches used by early Christians when nascent Christianity was still outlawed.[2] Each morning he would get up around 5.30 and set out from the Casa along with about sixty other priests to walk to one designated for that day of Lent. Typically, the priests would take turns saying mass at the different places. When it was Father Gary's turn, he said mass in San Martino ai Monti, a tiny church where it was rumoured that the Nicene Creed had been read aloud for the first time. The experience offered him a very real reminder of the traditions of the Church and once again helped him to reconnect to the roots of his faith.

During this time he also continued witnessing exorcisms three days a week out at San Lorenzo, along with Father Vince. Almost all the people were repeat cases, and by now Father Gary was an old hand and knew what to expect, though there were still a few surprises. During one exorcism, a woman seemed to come out of the trance on her own and say in a normal voice, 'OK, I'm fine. You can stop praying now.' Father Carmine studied her carefully and then threw some holy water on to her, causing the demon to explode with rage.

After the sessions, Father Gary and Father Vince continued to compare notes over a coffee. Father Gary was still frustrated that there wasn't much time to ask questions. The language barrier persisted as well, even for Father Carmine. After one evening of exorcisms, Father Gary suggested that the three of them schedule an hour to sit down and talk and have the English-speaking lay man he'd met at dinner translate for them.

A few weeks after meeting with his bishop, Father Gary was asked to give a talk to a group of priests in the continuing-education programme that Father Vince had regaled with stories from San Lorenzo. Worried that they might one day have to perform an exorcism themselves, they asked Father Gary if he'd be willing to share his knowledge as well.

The talk took place in the common room of the NAC, used by the seminarians as a sort of TV and games room that included a large collection of travel guides. About sixteen priests, most in their mid-fifties, showed up for the talk. Perhaps not surprisingly, all had at least one story to tell, either about a candle that mysteriously blew out while giving a blessing in a windowless room, or having run-ins with parishioners who claimed to be cursed. One priest from Amityville, New York, even described an order of nuns in the diocese that he said had begun practising Wicca.

Father Gary was his usual candid self, tucking his Roman collar into his front shirt pocket and telling the priests some of the lessons he'd learned in his training: take the person seriously, ask questions, don't rule out the possibility of demonic possession but don't rush to judgement, and always be conscious that the person is suffering deeply. 'Evil takes many forms, and I think becoming more aware of it through our own spiritual lives will make us better priests. If we want to be able to guide someone else, we have to be aware of evil while not being paranoid about it. But I think if we are oblivious to it, or our own prayer life doesn't cause us to enter into the deeper mystery of it, then I don't think we are serving our people well.'

When the talk was over, everyone clapped.

Afterwards, Father Gary and a friend ate at a noisy, packed

pizzeria located just off Corso Vittorio Emanuele II. He was happy with how the talk went, but in truth had something else on his mind. In a little over two weeks, it would be time for him to return to California.

Sitting in the packed pizzeria, a huge spillover crowd mingling in the street outside, reminded him how much he enjoyed the energy of Rome. And now that his sabbatical was coming to an end, he realized how much he would miss it.

A few days later, Father Kevin Joyce flew out from San Francisco, and Father Gary went out to the airport to meet him. The two had a great deal to discuss. Father Kevin had been sent a few cases by the bishop during Father Gary's absence and was eager to get Father Gary's opinion. One woman in her early thirties claimed to have balls of energy fly out of her. At times her fiancé didn't even recognize her. A Hispanic man claimed to hear demonic voices and even see demons from time to time. More than a few times Father Kevin had been called out to bless parishioners' houses.

As Father Kevin listened to what Father Gary had to say about these cases, both became so engrossed that they got on the wrong train and found themselves heading into the countryside rather than towards the centre of town.

Father Kevin could see right away how 'passionate' and 'excited' Father Gary was about all that he had learned. Impressed with the new confidence and sense of spiritual growth that he observed in his old friend, he described Father Gary as a 'changed man', and observed, 'I think with this training you will be a real asset to the diocese.'

'I hope,' Father Gary responded.

Because Father Carmine was out of town for a few days and thus not available to talk with them, Father Gary instead contacted Father Daniel (who was so busy that he could be reached only between nine and ten in the evening) and asked whether he'd come over to the Casa to answer a few questions. The three

sat in the break room for two hours talking about exorcism.
Father Gary had already discussed many of the topics with the
Franciscan, such as the best way to go about blessing houses; but
other topics were new, such as how to recognize the presence of
a curse, and about the efficacy of using blessed oil, water and salt,
specifically having the possessed person cook with them. In certain cases, Father Daniel even asked people to put a few drops of
holy water into the washing machine to purify their clothes,
which he said helped.

Father Daniel also discussed practical issues specific to the US.
For example, he suggested that before Father Gary perform an
exorcism on anybody, he might want to draft a consent form for
everyone to sign. Father Daniel offered another piece of advice
that resonated: 'Never bless a home without making sure the
whole family is present. It's a great opportunity to perform a little
catechesis, and that way you can also see if the problem isn't
related to the house but instead the family.'

When they were finished, the two agreed to stay in touch.
Father Gary thanked the Franciscan and promised to let him
know what happened with his ministry when he got back to the
States.[3]

On the Thursday before Holy Week, Father Gary and Father
Vince went out to San Lorenzo for the last time. Father
Carmine had a light load that day and they saw only a couple
of people until five that afternoon, when the three sat down in
Father Carmine's office and talked for about an hour and a half.
Father Carmine had finally arranged for the English-speaking
lay man at San Lorenzo to act as a translator so Father Gary had
no trouble getting answers to all his questions, such as why
Father Carmine put holy water in the person's ears, or where
the demon went when it wasn't tormenting the person. There
were also unexpected moments of levity. Since the *Ritual* mentions that the exorcist should fast, Father Gary wanted to know
whether Father Carmine did this. Once the question had been

translated, Father Carmine responded by laughing and patting his protruding belly. 'I don't fast from food,' he said, smiling. But then he went on to tell Father Gary that he did fast from other things, such as TV and alcohol, and stated, 'I have to deal with many humiliations. This is not an easy ministry.' Apparently he felt these humiliations were a form of 'fasting' as well.

Near the end of the discussion, Father Carmine turned to Father Gary and said, 'It's too bad you have to go home now.'

Father Gary thanked Father Carmine for being such a kind and generous teacher, saying it would not have been possible to have even contemplated performing the ministry without his invaluable training.

As he and Father Vince were getting ready to go, Father Carmine imparted one final piece of advice: 'During the prayers of exorcism, remember that you are never addressing the person in front of you; you are always invoking the power of God. If you start focusing on this presence of evil in front of you as if your own self is dealing with it, you will get yourself into trouble because that is not what you are doing; it is what God is doing through you.'

As a token of his appreciation, Father Gary gave the Capuchin a silver-plated image of Padre Pio and thanked him again.

With that, as Father Gary and Father Carmine shook hands, the Capuchin patted him on the back in a brotherly way. 'Fai il bravo,' he said just before Father Gary left. Be good.

In the days following his visit with Father Carmine, as he organized his things for his return trip to the States, Father Gary reflected on his time in Rome. Not only had his training opened up his eyes; it also changed the way he approached his priestly ministry. In many ways he felt like Father Daniel, who said that now that he knew the reality of the spirit world, he felt more responsibility to do something to help people. To go back now to the way he was before would be like 'turning my back on God'.

At the start of April, the city slowly shifted gears as the bundled-up days of winter were replaced by the leafy *passeggiate* of spring. Father Gary had really been looking forward to celebrating Easter in Rome. He appreciated the holiday more so than the overly commercialized Christmas. For him, Easter was always about baptism and perhaps an apt time to start a new chapter in his priestly ministry. Father Kevin, who had been in Assisi on a retreat for a few days, returned in time for the two to participate together in the Triduum – the three-day period of Holy Thursday (the day of the Last Supper), Good Friday (the day Christ was crucified) and Holy Saturday (the night of the Great Paschal Vigil). On Thursday night Father Gary went to the mass of the Lord's Supper and afterwards out to dinner with Father Kevin. On Good Friday, he went to the Vatican for a three-hour service and, by coincidence, ran into Father Carmine, which allowed him another opportunity to say *grazie*. On Holy Saturday night he went up to the NAC for the Easter Vigil, which he found 'glorious' and deeply spiritual. It also presented him with a chance to say goodbye to many of the seminarians and priests, some of whom he had grown close to and with whom he intended to maintain friendships.

When he stopped and thought about it, he had never imagined that his sabbatical would have turned out this way. It had been an incredibly 'enriching' experience. When he'd told some of the seminarians that he was heading home, a few had said how much they wished they could go home, too. 'Oh no you don't,' he shook his head. 'I have had ten months without stress, and now I have to go home to a set of unknowns.'

Beyond a new parish, perhaps the biggest of these unknowns was about his own abilities as an exorcist. That demons existed he didn't doubt, but would they respond to him the way that they had responded to Father Carmine? Would the prayers of exorcism work for him? In addition, he worried about the prospect of having to confront a demon on his own. During the exorcisms that he'd witnessed, most of the demons had directed their attention at Father Carmine, and as an observer he had remained relatively isolated from that exchange. But as an exorcist, he would now have to bear the brunt of it himself. Would he be able to do that? There would be no way of knowing until he actually performed an exorcism himself.

CHAPTER SEVENTEEN

THE EXORCIST

Once when I was a young man, trees were trees, mountains were mountains and rivers were rivers. When I grew up, trees were no longer trees, mountains were no longer mountains and rivers were no longer rivers. But when I became old, trees once again became trees, mountains became mountains and rivers became rivers.

Zen poem

Father Gary began the morning as he always did, by reading the obituaries. It was a habit he'd picked up from his days in the funeral business. Back then, of course, he'd checked the listings for professional reasons – noting which funeral homes were handling the services. Now he did so to see if he recognized any names. He'd lived his whole life inside the confines of the South Bay and Silicon Valley, and during that time he'd come to know the community as only a parish priest can, from the minutiae to the milestones – baptisms, weddings and, yes, funerals. Spared the grief of recognizing anyone on that particular day, he moved on to the sports pages, devouring both the *San Jose Mercury News* and the *San Francisco Chronicle*.

After finishing his morning routine, Father Gary walked to

the parish offices. As always, there was much to do and never enough time. The key, he realized, was to keep his expectations low. As he passed the church – which had nearly triple the capacity of his former parish, Saint Nicholas – and the school (kindergarten to 13–14 years old), his mind wandered back to Rome. There was a square patch of asphalt with some trees that served as the drop-off area for the kids; perhaps for no other reason than its shape, he'd dubbed it the *piazza*.

His first order of business had been to meet with the staff and let them know just how involved he planned to be in the running of the parish. Initially kind and encouraging, he had no problem putting his foot down if somebody didn't pull their weight.

One thing Father Gary had yet to discuss with his staff was exorcism. At some point he planned to sit down with Father Kevin and go over the specifics of his exorcism team, but for the moment he figured there would be plenty of time before he had to hash it out. Later that morning, however, while he was chatting with the parish administrator in the conference room, his secretary tentatively knocked. Unsure, she paused for a second as if weighing each word carefully. 'There is a couple here for an exorcism.'

Father Gary froze. I don't believe this, already! he thought, then advised her calmly, 'Tell them to wait in the front room, I'll be down when I finish up here.' After his secretary left, he turned to the parish co-ordinator, who was eyeing him expectantly. 'There are some things I'm going to have to clear up with you. I can't go into it now, but we'll talk later.' Wrapping up the meeting, Father Gary pulled himself away and headed downstairs.

The couple was waiting in a small room just off the entrance to the parish office. As he entered the room, they stood up from the couch and he shook their hands. Their ages were hard to guess but he thought perhaps early thirties. The woman, Stephanie, had a very plain appearance and kept her eyes down, while the man, Chris, did most of the talking.[1] As they began to tell their story, Father Gary recognized their case as one that Father Kevin had mentioned in Rome. In fact, the couple had seen Father Kevin but weren't happy with how things were progressing. 'I need an exorcism,' Stephanie announced.

Chris described how, at odd times of the day and for no apparent reason, Stephanie would suddenly be overcome by what he called 'attacks' on her mind (which sounded to Father Gary like mood swings). According to Chris, she would become enraged beyond any rational thought. One such 'attack' had left her walking on the side of the road while Chris sat dumbfounded in the car. It wasn't until Chris brought it to her attention that she became aware of what she was doing.

Thinking that the problem might be spiritual in nature, Chris tried a spontaneous deliverance prayer over her and something amazing happened. During the prayer Stephanie felt 'hot spots' on various parts of her body – either her forehead or stomach or the back of her neck – and simultaneously felt that entities were leaving her. Chris also confirmed that while praying he'd felt warm balls of energy releasing from her.

Perplexed, Father Gary dug deeper, asking a little about Stephanie's past, specifically if she had any involvement in the occult, and if there was any particular event that had prompted this.

The problem had begun the previous March, when an older woman she knew approached her at their church and gave her a hug. This innocuous act, however, suddenly turned into something very bizarre as she heard the woman's voice change into a gruff demonic growl. The episode triggered an unpleasant memory of being abused by her father as a child, during which he also spoke in the same gruff demonic voice. In addition, there was some strange relationship with a minister from her church, whom she described as being obsessed with her (she'd stopped attending her church because of it).

At that point she'd gone to see Father Kevin, who sent her to an internist, who gave her a clean bill of health. She then went to see a clinical psychologist, an agnostic. He told her that she seemed fine and that maybe her problem was 'spiritual' in nature.

After this she returned to Father Kevin, who recommended she see a Catholic therapist. That didn't work out because Stephanie had refused to be interviewed without Chris being present, something the psychiatrist wasn't comfortable doing.

In the meantime they'd searched for other priests who might be willing to help them but had been turned away each time. One priest even said, 'I hope it's not something I can catch.' Sensing that they were desperate and unsure where to go, someone in the vicar's office at the diocesan chancery ultimately directed them to Father Gary.

Father Gary could see that Stephanie was clearly distressed. It upset him to think of the flippant remarks made by priests who turned her away in such a callous manner.

He told her that he'd recently been trained as an exorcist in Rome but that he'd yet to actually perform an exorcism himself. But, he said, 'I am willing to meet with you.' He cautioned them, however, not to expect quick results. 'We're going to have to start addressing this from the bottom up, and it may take some time.'

Stephanie was noticeably relieved. Here at last was an exorcist, and an officially appointed one at that, who was willing to help. 'Thank you,' she said.

Contacting his bishop, Father Gary relayed the details of the story. The bishop told him not to proceed with anything until Stephanie got a full psychiatric evaluation.

Without his team in place, Father Gary scrambled to locate a person who might assist him. Thinking back to his days at Saint Nicholas, he contacted a female clinical psychologist whom he knew to be very devout, but she felt the case was out of her league. He got in touch with another female clinician who seemed more willing to help. Father Gary then met with her for two hours and, after asking about her perspective on concepts such as demons and Satan, he was satisfied that she was equipped to give a competent analysis.

At first the couple balked at having to see another doctor. But when Father Gary told them, 'If you are even going to contemplate this as a possibility, you have to do it,' they relented.

In the interim, Father Gary prayed a simple blessing over Stephanie and anointed her with the sacrament of the sick. She showed no reaction during the blessing but claimed to feel better afterwards.

After evaluating her the following week, the psychologist could find nothing clinically wrong.

In the meantime, Father Gary consulted with an American exorcist on the East Coast who was associated with the upcoming exorcism conference in August, to ask his advice. The exorcist told Father Gary that he had seen symptoms such as Stephanie's many times.

Armed with this information, Father Gary went back to his bishop, who gave him the go-ahead for the exorcism, reminding him to have the couple sign a release form beforehand (an American prerequisite). Father Gary called Stephanie and told her the news. The exorcism was scheduled for the following Saturday.

During the week, Father Gary was too busy with the details of the parish to spend much time on the exorcism. He did take the parish co-ordinator and his secretary aside and fill them in about his appointment. Now that the cat was technically out of the bag, it was likely that more and more people would be calling (or showing up unannounced) so it would be better if his staff knew. In addition, at Father Kevin's suggestion, he downloaded from the Internet the 1952 version of the *Roman Ritual* for exorcism. Since he was a little out of practice with his Latin, it would be much easier to pray this version because he was allowed to do it in English.[2]

The morning of the exorcism he was anxious. While he had

witnessed nearly eighty exorcisms, this would be the first one he'd be performing. Chris would be present and assisting him if he needed a hand.

He decided to conduct the exorcism in one of the unused offices.[3] The room was tasteful and small, without a lot of furniture that might get in the way. Rather than skip straight through to the exorcism prayers as Father Carmine had, he resolved to pray the entire *Ritual* from start to finish. He didn't want to leave anything to chance.

He began the *Ritual*, reciting the litany of the saints in Latin, and then moved on to the gospel reading in English, followed by a brief homily. After the homily, he had both Stephanie and Chris renew their baptismal vows, 'Do you renounce Satan? And all his works? . . .' Once that was finished, he began the exorcism prayers, using a wooden crucifix that had been hanging on the wall in his office and touching it to the back of her neck as he did so. 'I cast you out, unclean spirit, along with every Satanic power of the enemy, every spectre from hell and all your fell companions . . .' As he prayed, he tried to keep one eye on the page and the other on Stephanie, who sat placidly on the couch, showing no sign of reaction. After the first prayer, he shifted the crucifix, placing it on the top of her head, and began the second prayer. When he was ready to move on to the third prayer, he placed it on her forehead. After he'd finished, he offered them both communion.

The whole exorcism had lasted about an hour, and as far as Father Gary was concerned, the woman had shown no outward reactions to the prayers.

'So what did you feel?' he asked her.

'I felt this heat on my head, but then it went away,' she said. 'At one point I felt this thing kind of pull out of my stomach and leave.'

Afterwards he sat in his office and went over the details. The exorcism had turned out to be pretty uneventful. Was there something he'd overlooked? Or was Stephanie faking? Was she perhaps trying to get Chris's attention? Father Gary's experiences in Rome had taught him to be circumspect; but since this was his first exorcism, he couldn't be sure. As he analysed it, he remembered that it was possible for demons to hide – maybe that's what had happened. He knew that exorcism wasn't an exact science and that he would become more competent with experience. Beyond that, he wondered anew how Father Carmine had the stamina to see so many people. Just this one exorcism had tired him out, and there were days when Father Carmine had seen twelve people. No wonder he had skipped to the heart of the *Ritual*.

He saw Stephanie and Chris a few more times over the following months, and each time her reaction was the same – she sat perfectly still and afterwards described having a burning sensation where he'd touched her with the cross and then the feeling of entities leaving her. He began to wonder why, if a demon was present, he hadn't manifested yet.

In August he flew out to the exorcism conference being held in the Midwest, hoping to get some practical tips about Stephanie's case, as well as to network with other exorcists. At Father Gary's instigation, Father Vince also attended the conference and the two swapped stories about how things were going in their ministries. Father Vince had seen a few people already, though he hadn't prayed the *Ritual* over anybody yet. He met one woman he believed might be possessed but she'd failed to return after he instructed her to attend mass and confession in conjunction with any formal help he'd provide. She basically walked out, telling him that if he wouldn't help her right then and there, she'd go somewhere else. He discovered later that she'd gone to a local prayer group that told her that she could be freed only when she had devoted herself to prayer and her rosary beads turned the colour gold.[4]

The conference was run by a group of charismatic lay people who sometimes assisted American exorcists in their ministry.[5]

The day started with prayer before breakfast at 7.30, followed by morning lectures until 11.15, then daily mass and lunch. The afternoon consisted of classes from three to five, followed by an early dinner; then, at seven, there was an hour of questions, after which everyone gathered to pray prayers of deliverance over one another. Both Fathers Gary and Vince felt a little awkward about this.

Father Vince spoke with one of the course organizers, telling her that since demonic possession was uncommon, it made no sense to ask priests 'to pray over each other to get rid of all the demons that are in us'. It also turned him off that some priests seemed too eager to become exorcists. One priest boasted that he exorcized his rectory at least once a month, including his telephone, because he was concerned that people on the other end of the line might be possessed.

According to Father Vince, one conference organizer claimed that Satan was trying to derail the conference by knocking out the sound system. She exhorted everyone to pray to get things back on line. Father Vince reminded her that there had been an electrical storm the previous night, and that a blown transformer was most likely the culprit. A few minutes later, relates Father Vince, a technician came in and fixed the equipment. Sure enough, everything worked. Father Vince found this a clear example of the American tendency to gravitate toward the extreme.

The conference did have its moments, though. Father Gary found the talk on the sacrament of reconciliation and the spirituality of mercy and the Eucharist as a weapon against evil influences to be very helpful. It also gibed with what he'd learned back in Rome – a fundamental job of an exorcist is to bring people back to the sacraments.

On the whole, Father Gary was pleased with the direction of the conference in its effort to train exorcists as had the course in Rome. He thought the organizers might have gotten more interest if they had held it at a Catholic site (as they would do the following year) so that more bishops would attend. More than anything, he envisioned a course sanctioned by the National Conference of Catholic Bishops, which would help legitimize the rite of exorcism, something that was desperately needed.

After he returned from the conference, Father Gary prayed over Stephanie again, while Chris was present. Wondering if they were getting anywhere, he asked if she really wanted these spirits to leave. When she answered 'yes', he reminded her that she was going to have to become more proactive and start praying every day. 'You can't just rely on me to do all this for you.'

As the sessions progressed, however, Chris and Stephanie became more exasperated. Why weren't these prayers 'curing' Stephanie the way Chris's numerous books described? While she did report some improvement, Father Gary's exorcisms didn't seem any more effective than what she had experienced when Chris prayed over her.

Feeling that her advancement wasn't fast enough, the couple decided to try another exorcist. Father Gary gave them the name of an exorcist in a nearby diocese and wished them well. He still wondered if he had missed something, or hadn't done it right. He still questioned whether or not the prayers of the *Ritual* would work for him. Despite the fact that Stephanie said she *felt* better, it was hard to gauge. Even in the milder cases that Father Carmine saw, Father Gary detected at least some external reaction to the prayer.

When the couple returned a month later saying that they weren't happy with the other exorcist either, Father Gary knew there was more to the story. It wasn't just him. In fact, he was beginning to feel ambivalent about their case. Knowing from his experiences with Father Carmine that people can get addicted to exorcism as if it were a kind of 'identity', he told them he'd be willing to see them again but they would have to shift gears and slow down. Disappointed, the couple had no choice but to agree.

*

Over the course of the following year, Father Gary saw more people, some from as far away as Oregon. A woman in her fifties said that demons were around her all the time; a Filipino man thought that his brother-in-law had put a curse on him; and another man claimed to be haunted by the ghost of a dead relative. A few times he needed Father Kevin to translate for Spanish-speaking victims, and on one occasion another priest helped out when he saw an older woman who spoke only Vietnamese.

In a few of these cases he performed the *Ritual*, but in the vast majority he simply prayed prayers of deliverance or offered a blessing if he suspected the cause was not demonic. Sometimes, when people wouldn't take no for an answer, he prayed a simple blessing over them while cautioning them to seek help through therapy.

Father Gary would also bless houses. One family in San Jose claimed to have witnessed various odd phenomena, including a ghostly apparition that would sometimes appear at the foot of the children's bed and a room that always seemed to be filled with an icy chill. Despite blessing every room in the house, Father Gary failed to uncover any curses or infestations that would explain the activities.

The fact that so many people were seeking him out came as a big surprise. Even after witnessing so many exorcisms in Rome, he still thought his services would rarely be called upon in America. And because he had been so busy, there'd been little opportunity to carry out some of the ideas he'd formulated in Rome. For instance he had yet to meet with the youth ministers in the parish and talk to them about the dangers of the occult. However, he had been able to open up a little chapel off the parish offices for daily Eucharistic adoration.

In January 2007, Father Gary e-mailed Father Carmine to let him know how things had been progressing since his return from Rome, mentioning some of the cases he'd witnessed and his hope that the ministry of exorcism would soon be seen in a more credible light. Having forgotten most of his Italian, he wrote the message in English.

A few weeks later, Father Carmine responded in Italian to his e-mail, delighted to have heard from his former protégé. He was even happier that Father Gary had written in English, saying that it would give him a much-needed opportunity to practise his language skills, a favour he hoped to reciprocate by responding in Italian.

In closing his e-mail, Father Gary had asked the Capuchin how things were in Rome. Was he still seeing lots of people? Father Carmine had responded by saying that the situation was as bad as ever. In some cases, he was getting people sent to him from other countries in Europe. One woman had sought him out from Germany, where there were no exorcists, he said:

> You know how tragic the situation is as far as that goes. I believe that we have to pray a lot for the theologians and bishops that they teach a doctrine that is truly and completely Catholic instead of one which is easier and more accommodating. All of humanity suffers because of a doctrine that is incomplete and unbalanced. But we put our faith in the hands of the *Madonna*. I praise God that there is a priest like you who can help a lot of poor and suffering people. Be simple and strong! And pray for me, because I need it . . . We will remain united in our prayers.

Several months after receiving Father Carmine's e-mail, Father Kevin got in touch with Father Gary about a case he thought he should investigate. The parents of a young Central American woman, Maria, who lived in a nearby diocese, had reached out to him, hoping that their daughter could receive an exorcism. A week later, Father Gary found time during a busy afternoon to sit down with the three.

The sullen and downtrodden appearance of Maria, a 27-year-old originally from Honduras, immediately alerted him that something might be amiss.[6] The defeated look the parents gave him reminded him of what he'd seen in people accompanying victims whom Father Carmine had prayed over in Rome.

As in the past, he started by asking Maria to tell him her story.

Ever since the age of seventeen, she said, she had been hearing voices and seeing demons, which would always tell her 'You belong to us'. Worried, her parents had taken her to see a witch doctor while they were living in Honduras. When he'd performed a ritualistic exorcism, Maria had entered into a trance and flopped around on the ground. After that, the problem seemed to abate for a time. However, recently it had come back again.

Father Gary continued to probe, noting that Maria had no history of drug abuse; and as far as he could surmise, she appeared sane. According to her parents, the witch doctor had told them that the troubles were most likely related to a curse.

Intrigued, Father Gary told the three that, while he was willing to help, the best course of action would be for Maria to get a psychiatric evaluation. In the meantime, however, he told them he would be happy to pray a simple blessing over her. (Remembering his training, he also suspected such a blessing might help unmask a demon if there was one.)

Without much fanfare, Father Gary picked up a three-ringed binder that contained some prayers that he had photocopied from various books and downloaded from the Internet. The prayers he liked most were printed in the back of Father Amorth's book, *An Exorcist Tells His Story*. Selecting one of these (originally from the Greek *Ritual*), he extended his hand toward Maria, intoning: '*Kyrie eleison*, God, our Lord, King of ages, All-powerful and All-mighty, you who made everything and who transform everything simply by your will. You who in Babylon changed into dew the flames of the "seven-times hotter" furnace and protected and saved the three holy children. You are the doctor and the physician of our soul. You are the salvation of those who turn to you.'

Almost immediately Maria's body began to twitch, her legs rocking back and forth. As he noticed this, Father Gary tried not to betray what he was thinking: here was his confirmation. He prayed:

> We beseech you to make powerless, banish, and drive out every diabolic power, presence, and machination; every evil influence, malefice, or evil eye, and all evil actions aimed against your servant Maria. Where there is envy and malice, give us an abundance of goodness, endurance, victory, and charity. O Lord, you who love mankind, we beg you to reach out your powerful hands and your most high and mighty arms and come to our aid. Help us, who are made in your image; send the angel of peace over us, to protect us body and soul.

Maria suddenly screamed. She began thrashing violently on the couch. Then, much to Father Gary's amazement, her facial muscles tensed in such a way that her appearance completely changed, and she took on the visage of an adder. Even her mannerisms seemed to become snakelike. Her eyes, which had become dead black discs, bored into him while her tongue shot in and out like a snake's.

As he beheld this transformation, his heart pounded in his chest. 'This is really happening,' he thought. He wasn't hallucinating. He threw some holy water on to Maria and she lunged at him, but was grabbed at the last minute by her parents, who were sitting on either side of her. Deep hatred poured out at him through her black eyes. There was no doubt in his mind that, if he had been alone with her, she would have long since attacked him. No longer a spectator, it was up to him to see this through to the end.

'May God keep at bay and vanquish every evil power, every poison or malice invoked against us by corrupt and envious people. Then, under the protection of your authority may we sing, in gratitude, "The Lord is my salvation; whom should I fear?"'

She kicked and strained, trying to break free.

The struggle continued for a few more minutes, until he decided that it was probably better if he didn't push things too much at this early stage. She needed a solemn exorcism, not a simple blessing. It would also allow him a chance to prepare more. For now it was enough to know that the prayers had generated a strong reaction.

Once the blessing was finished, Maria immediately calmed down and her face returned to normal. As she slumped down in her chair to catch her breath, Father Gary left to get a consecrated host, thinking that perhaps communion would do her good. When he re-entered the room with the Eucharist, however, she nearly jumped out of the window, and probably would have if it weren't for her parents once again wrestling her back down on to the couch. When she had recovered sufficiently, Father Gary finally gave her the wafer, but though she received it, she was unable to swallow it. Worrying that the demon might be coming back, Father Gary quickly unscrewed the cap from his holy water and handed it to her, saying, 'Here, wash it down with this.' Finally, the host went down.

When it was over, the mother approached Father Gary to thank him. She told him that while her daughter's reaction to the prayers had been similar to the exorcism in Honduras, this time it was much more intense.

After the family had left, Father Gary sat for a moment in his office to collect his thoughts. He had been through a tremendous change since being nominated exorcist in 2005. And while many of these experiences had touched him deeply – exposing him to a deep level of human suffering that he never knew existed – something particular about this case definitely stood out. Beyond the sensational, a profound element to it gave him hope. He was finally able to put aside his doubts once and for all about whether the *Ritual* would work for him. 'These prayers do have power,' he thought. It was a visceral reminder that the age-old conflict between good and evil, sin and salvation, was far from over. Not only did this validate his calling as a priest, and his choice to become an exorcist, but it was also a powerful confirmation of one of the deepest mysteries of his faith. Even though evil existed in the world, there was a way to defeat it.

AUTHOR'S NOTE

In the autumn of 2005, when I heard that a Vatican-affiliated university was offering a course entitled 'Exorcism and the Prayer of Liberation', I thought it might be a PR stunt. Did the Church still believe in exorcism? It was intriguing that the course would be open to non-priests, with some of the lessons taught by psychologists and criminologists. Living in Italy as a freelance writer and journalist who'd spent time in the Rome bureau of the Associated Press, I knew how hard it could be to crack the wall of secrecy surrounding the Vatican. Add to that the mystery surrounding exorcism, and I saw the class as a rare opportunity. Not knowing what to expect, I thought there was at least an article in it.

At the time, I knew almost nothing about exorcism. Like most people, I immediately thought of Hollywood movies. Yet, while films such as *The Exorcist* were reportedly 'based' on true stories, the cinematic packaging and special effects made it hard to separate fact from fiction.

The first day of the course, however, changed any such preconceptions I had about exorcism. Not only was the ultra-modern classroom an odd setting to see priests, Franciscan friars, and nuns of various orders listening to lectures on the powers of Satan, but, to my surprise, I found the students themselves to be anything but the 'superstitious' or puritanical priests portrayed in popular culture.

When I first met Father Gary I was immediately impressed by his honesty and transparency. The two of us struck up a friendship based on a strong desire to immerse ourselves in what we were learning.

As I became acquainted with the details of Father Gary's life, the writer in me began to realize that his journey presented a unique window into the world of exorcism. Here was the chance, I thought, to see what it is like to be an exorcist, told from the perspective of someone just getting started.

In truth, though, the thought of writing about demons and exorcism wasn't at the top of my list – my wife, for one, didn't find the subject all that appealing. I must say that there were days when I wondered whether it might be better for me to leave things well alone, lest my own life be invaded by an unseen 'spirit'.

Despite being raised a Catholic, I was ambivalent about demonic possession. In fact, in the interest of full disclosure, when I began this book I was more of a 'cultural Catholic' than a practising one. Sure, I went to mass now and then, at Christmas and Easter; but, beyond that, I probably wasn't the best person if you were looking for someone with whom to discuss the deeper mysteries of the faith. On the contrary, my approach was more journalistic than anything else. I wanted to know what the Church actually taught about exorcism. And in the case of Father Gary, I wanted to know what it took for a person to be willing to stand in a room and do battle with a demon, if in fact there were demons at all.

As a lay person, the first thing that surprised me about exorcism was that not many priests knew anything about it, especially not American priests.

Most, if not all, American books about exorcism were a little outdated, written in the 1970s and 1980s. In Italy, however, it was a different story, and almost immediately I found myself turning to these books, a vast majority of which (such as *Possessioni diaboliche ed esorcismo* by Father Franceso Bamonte and *Il Dito di Dio e il Potere di Satana: L'esorcismo* by Father Gabriele Nanni) were written since 2004. These books provided not only detailed theological analysis, but also first-hand accounts of what performing an exorcism is actually like. And the more I read, the more curious I became. Once Father Gary began participating in exorcisms, I was able to add his interpretations. However, I also knew that if I wanted to tell this story, I would have to enter into the world of the exorcist, and the only way to do that would be to witness an exorcism.

My first behind-the-scenes look at exorcism occurred when I began to interview the various exorcists on their 'home turf'. Here and there I would catch a glimpse of what existed on the other side – a group of people hounding Father Tommaso outside the sacristy of the Scala Santa; Father Bamonte wiping away a puddle of holy water off a chair so that I could sit down for our interview; sitting in Father Carmine's waiting room while a woman screamed and banged around in his office. Perhaps the most surprising thing was that far from being located in some hilltop monastery, many of the exorcisms were performed in churches located in the heart of Rome. In fact it was quite common to be talking to an exorcist while groups of tourists paraded around taking photos of religious iconography. One bizarre aspect of researching this book was this juxtaposition of these two worlds – talking to a victim of demonic possession or hearing an exorcism and then emerging into the bright sunshine and chaotic streets of Rome.

Each exorcist I interviewed was compelling in his own right: I warmed to Father Bamonte's boyhood exuberance, Father Nanni's movie-star good looks and intellectual demeanour, Father Amorth's avuncular joviality and penchant for dramatic rejoinders, and Father Carmine's salt-of-the-earth unpretentiousness. All were patient and gracious with me no matter how many questions I stumbled through in my less-than-perfect Italian.

I also found their candour to be refreshing. Many of the books

I'd read had ordered everything into neat little boxes, yet here were exorcists with years of experience telling me that there were still things that couldn't be known.

Then there were the victims. Like Father Gary, not only did I find their apparent normality to be surprising, but I also found them to be very credible, even likeable people. These were not people who struck me as trying to fool the exorcist, but sincere individuals who were struggling with something even they seemed at a loss to understand. Later, when I participated in exorcisms along with Father Carmine, this impression was only reinforced.

Many people assume that an exorcist is out to prove that people are possessed; however, with each of the Italian exorcists I talked to, I found the opposite to be true. It is also wrong, I think, to assume that the Church is on one side promoting belief in spirits while the secular world is on the other, trying to debunk such notions. Stroll down to the local New Age bookshop to see the tremendous popularity of angels, 'channelling', and 'astral travel', not to mention the numbers of ghost whisperers and therapists who practise 'spirit releasement'.[1] Take away officially appointed exorcists, and people will still seek out exorcisms, or pay 'psychics' to rid their homes of evil spirits. Seen in this light, the concept of an exorcism course offering lectures by psychologists and other experts in the field to help 'train' priests is a good idea, even if only to give people some sort of standards.[2]

The writing of this book became a journey of sorts for me as well. It helped me to reconnect with my faith in a way that I never expected when I began researching exorcism. Over the course of the three years I spent writing and conducting my research, I met many individuals like Father Gary, whose service and dedication to those who suffer showed me how much good we can do when we set aside our egos and reach out to help people.

While I was writing, people often asked me whether anything

strange had happened to me. Besides the odd shutter bang on a windless day or the ill-timed power outage costing me some of my work, both of which I attribute to coincidence, there was one experience I cannot explain.

I was driving home one afternoon, after an interview with a woman who suddenly entered into the trance state and started screaming at a picture of Mary on the wall. All at once my car was completely filled with the scent of flowers. In an offhand way, I thought, 'Oh, that's nice. Where is this coming from?' Then I found myself unconsciously smiling. I remembered that before the exorcism took place, Father Bamonte had told me that the Virgin Mary often came to the aid of the woman, and so during her outburst I'd said a little prayer asking Mary to help. I certainly didn't imagine that this tiny gesture had any real impact on her case. Father Bamonte went on to perform the exorcism, and the woman continued to scream for nearly an hour.

At the time, I had only a vague recollection that certain people reported smelling flowers in connection with Mary and other mystical experiences. Was my car being flooded by the scent of flowers somehow connected to what had happened earlier that morning? I wasn't so sure. The smell wasn't coming from outside the car (when it happened I'd been driving by a sheep farm notorious for its foul odour). It could have been coming from my air conditioner (though I had never smelled it before). It could have been an olfactory hallucination, for all I knew. But in hindsight I've come to realize that an explanation is beside the point. Even though this experience lasted only a few minutes, it touched me deeply. Was this some angelic being or Mary trying to tell me that she'd heard the pathetic cry of a person struggling to come to grips with his own faith in order to help a fellow human being? Was some part of my subconscious feeding impulses to another to convince myself of my own transcendence? I guess I'll never know. One thing is certain, whatever it was filled me with an immense sense of joy.

ACKNOWLEDGEMENTS

I am grateful beyond measure to the courageous and candid contributions of Father Gary Thomas, and to his indefatigable generosity and kindness. Quite simply this book would not have been possible without him and I can't thank him enough.

I am very grateful to all the people who appeared in this book but especially to Father Francesco Bamonte, Father Gabriele Nanni, and Father Carmine De Filippis, who not only took time out of their ridiculously busy schedules to answer my questions, but were also vital in opening up the world of exorcism to me. Special thanks also to Father Gabriele Amorth, Father Aldo Buonaiuto, Father Jeremy Davies, Father Francois Dermine, Father Giancarlo Gramolazzo, Father Kevin Joyce, Father Vince Lampert, and Father Tiziano Ripetto.

Numerous other priests shared with me their time and personal stories. Some made it into the book but many did not. Thanks to Father Avelina, Father Pedro Barrajon, Father Steve Bigler, Father Bernie Bush, Monsignor John Esseff, Father Paul Hrezzo, Father Brenden Lally, Father James LeBar, Father Gerardo Menchaca, Father John Michet, Father Bill O'Callaghan, Father Serge Propst O.P., Father Mike Simone, Father Johanus Sweetzer, Father Mike Tomaseck, and Father Antonius Wall.

Father Basil Cole O.P. not only helped me to navigate the teachings of Thomas Aquinas on the angels, but also read sections of the manuscript offering valuable feedback.

The same can be said for Father Jeffrey Grob, who provided invaluable insight into the *Ritual* of exorcism, and Father John A. Farren O.P., who donated his time and expertise to give the manuscript a critical read.

Thanks also to Monsignor James Checchio at the North American College for allowing me access to the treasure trove that is the NAC library, and to Sister Rebecca for making the difficult task of wading through all that material less daunting.

Doctor Richard Gallagher gets my sincerest thanks for sharing with me his knowledge and expertise and for his willingness to appear in the book. I was very sorry to hear that Dr. Barry L. Beyerstein had passed away in the spring of 2007. He was doing amazing work in the field of bio-psychology and I know he will be missed.

A special thank you to all the victims who were willing to share their stories with me. The experience of baring your soul to a complete stranger is never an easy thing to do and I was truly humbled by the courage of these people.

I can not say enough about my amazing agent Christy Fletcher, who got on board early and whose determination and dedication never faltered. She patiently guided me through my first foray into the world of publishing with an almost Zen-like calm. Thanks also to Peter Robinson and Sam Copeland in the UK who believed in the project and who were able to find a perfect home for the manuscript at Simon & Schuster UK.

Special thanks are in order for my wonderful US editor JillEllyn Riley. Thanks also to James Marriott and Hugo De Klee for their painstaking work reading and correcting the manuscript on the UK side. A huge thank you to Kerri Sharp at Simon and Schuster UK for her encouragement, dedication, and unwavering support of the book.

Thanks also to Paolo Alei, Lori Armstrong, Pierpaolo Balani, Richard Brener, Dr. Tonino Cantelmi, Melissa Chinchillo, Carlo Climati, Sam Copeland, Marta Falconi, Merideth Finn, Beau Flynn, Natalie S. Higgins, Dr. Michael E. Hyland, Dr. Craig

Isaacs, Dr. Steven Jay Lynn, Swanna MacNair, Dr. Giuliana A.L. Mazzoni, Jim Michaletti, Michael Petroni, Howard Sanders, Kate Scherler, Claudio Vignozzi, Tripp Vinson, Lorien Warner, Christopher Winner and Sara Wolski. Thanks also to the Thomas family for their time and memories.

Every writer needs a good support group and I have been particularly blessed in that respect. Thanks to Scooter Leonard for helping to instill in me a love of writing. To my good friend and mentor Randolph Wright who through skill and tact was able to steer me through the minefields of some of the earliest drafts.

I owe a huge debt of gratitude to Eric Blehm, who opened door after door for me and helped to keep me afloat throughout the whole process with his encouragement, sage advice, and commiseration. A simple thank-you would not be enough.

To my parents, Tom and Nancy Baglio who have always believed in me and supported me over the years. And to my entire American and Italian families for their unconditional support and enthusiasm, I could not have done it without you guys. My son Noah, who constantly reminded me what really mattered. And lastly to my brilliant and multi-talented wife Sara who not only translated and transcribed most of my interviews but who also put up with my long absences and never-ending doubts. I know it wasn't easy but your support never wavered. For that, and so much more, I offer you my eternal love and gratitude.

NOTES

Notes on citations: for the sake of maintaining the narrative flow, I have kept citations in the text to a minimum. Unless specifically noted in these endnotes, direct quotations appearing in the text are taken from my interviews.

Prologue
1 The material for this exorcism came primarily from two sources: the transcript of an audio recording of the exorcism taken by Father Bamonte; and an interview with the victim, in which she recounted her visions and feelings during the exorcism.
2 Saint Gemma is one of the few Catholic saints reported to have been attacked by the Devil during her lifetime. As a result, possessed people often pray to her for strength. Born near the Italian town of Lucca on 12 March 1878, Gemma had many mystical experiences. At a very early age, she dedicated herself to a life of intense prayer and claimed that Jesus, Mary and her guardian angel appeared to her. Constantly ill, she developed meningitis when she was twenty and attributed her cure to the intervention of deceased Passionist priest Gabriel Possenti, later canonized. At twenty-one she received the stigmata, which appeared on Thursday evenings and healed by Saturday mornings, leaving a whitish mark where the deep wounds had been. Throughout her life she felt constantly tormented by the Devil. In one diary entry, she describes the Devil raining blows down upon her back for several hours. She died at the age of twenty-five.
    In this case, the woman had always felt a strong connection to Gemma, even visiting her tomb in Lucca on her honeymoon.

Introduction
1 The first version of the *Catechism of the Catholic Church* was published in French in 1992, translated into English in 1994. The creation of the

Catechism was undertaken in 1985 when Pope John Paul II, guided by the 'spirit of the Second Vatican Council' convoked an extraordinary assembly of the Synod of Bishops to 'study its teachings in greater depth in order that all the Christian faithful might better adhere to it and to promote knowledge and application of it', CCC, p. 2. In 1986, Pope John Paul II entrusted the drafting of it to a group of twelve cardinals and bishops led by then Cardinal Joseph Ratzinger, who became Pope Benedict XVI in 2005. The book is considered the source of all authentic Catholic doctrine.

2   Chas S. Clifton, *Her Hidden Children: The Rise of Wicca and Paganism in America*, p. 11.

3   Numerous self-help spirituality books have become bestsellers in recent years, such as Eckhart Tolle's *The Power of Now: A Guide to Spiritual Enlightenment*, New World Library, 2004, and *A New Earth: Awakening Your Life's Purpose*, Penguin, 2008, which both had sales into the millions.

4   Reported in 'God Told Us to Exorcize My Daughter's Demons. I Don't Regret Her Death' by Elizabeth Day, *Daily Telegraph*, 26 November 2005.

5   From 'Crucified nun dies in "exorcism"', BBC News Web site, 18 June 2005. Story was originally reported in the *Agence France-Presse*, 2005. In February 2007, the priest was sentenced to fourteen years in jail for the crime. See 'Priest jailed for exorcism death', BBC News Web site, 19 February 2007.

In another famous case in Germany in 1976, two priests were charged with negligent homicide when a young girl they were exorcizing, Anneliese Michel, starved to death. The episode provided the basis for the movie *The Exorcism of Emily Rose*. For more, see *The Exorcism of Anneliese Michel* by Felicitas D. Goodman, 1981.

Chapter One / Rome

1   John L. Allen, Jr., *All the Pope's Men*, p. 161.

2   Jesus Caritas is based on the teachings of Charles de Foucauld, who was born in Strasbourg, France, in 1858. Losing his faith as a youth, Foucauld served as an officer in the army in North Africa and went to explore Morocco in 1883. After returning to France, he undertook a pilgrimage to Jerusalem, where he became a Trappist monk for seven years. Ordained in 1901, he desired to live as Jesus had, among 'the most abandoned'. He spent his time in the deserts of northern Africa and established the groundwork for founding a religious family, centred on the gospels. He died before its creation, however, when he was killed by marauders in 1916.

Members of the group meet once a month to share scripture, pray before the Eucharist, and share a review of life. http://www.jesuscarita-susa.org/

3 The latest of these appearances occurred on 6 June 2008. Both of Father Amorth's books, *An Exorcist Tells His Story* (1999) and *An Exorcist: More Stories* (2002), were European best-sellers. He has been featured in many publications, including the *Daily Telegraph* ('Vatican to create more exorcists to tackle "evil"' by Nick Pisa, 30 December 2007) and the *New York Times*, 1 January 2002.

4 In 2002, Father Amorth originally told the Italian news agency ANSA that 'behind Harry Potter hides the signature of the king of the darkness, the devil'. He also decried the books' attempt to differentiate between 'white' and 'black' magic when 'the distinction does not exist because magic is always a turn to the devil'. The diatribe was then picked up and ran in numerous periodicals and Web sites, most notably in an article in the *New York Times*, 1 January 2002: 'A Priest Not Intimidated by Satan or by Harry Potter'. As recently as 15 January 2008, an Italian scholar spoke out on the Harry Potter books in the official Vatican newspaper, *L'Osservatore Romano*, saying that the books fall into 'the old Gnostic temptation of confusing salvation and truth with secret knowledge'. In addition to attacking Harry Potter, Father Amorth has also been quoted as saying that both Hitler and Stalin were possessed by the devil, *Daily Mail*, London, by Nick Pisa, 28 August 2006.

5 These quotes are all taken from 'The Smoke of Satan in the House of the Lord', by Stefano Maria Paci, first printed in *30 Days*, June 2001, pp. 30–1.

6 Founded in 1968 by Don Oreste Benzi, the Associazione Comunità Papa Giovanni XXIII was established as a way to reach out to young people who 'would never have managed to make it on their own'. Now present in eighteen countries, the association works for the betterment of the marginalized, including former drug addicts, prostitutes and victims of cults. http://www.apg23.org/cgi-bin/pagina.cgi

7 For more information on tarantism, see *Ecstatic Religion: A Study of Shamanism and Spirit Possession* by I. M. Lewis, pp. 36–8, 80–3.

8 Marlise Simons, 'Paris Journal; Land of Descartes under the Spell of Druids?' *New York Times*, 30 April 1996.

9 Given the secretive nature of sects, it is hard to know if these numbers reflect an accurate picture. In *Sette sataniche* (*Satanic Sects*), Italian psychiatrist Vincenzo Maria Mastronardi and psychologist Ruben De Luca point out the near impossibility of knowing the true numbers of satanic

sects in existence, p. 92. To further complicate matters, some scholars cast a wide net when it comes to categorizing certain beliefs as 'satanic', including Voodoo and Wicca. According to one expert, Satanism can be seen as a form of extreme cynicism. 'It is a way of seeing the world as a jungle, where only the strongest survive. A world in which all limits are absent, bad examples are on offer and in which the perfection of television's role models is countered with the search for extremes, for power at all costs', Carlo Climati, as quoted by journalist Nicholas Rigillo, 'Satanic murders just the tip of an iceberg, claims Roman church' from the Australian Web site 'The Age', 5 January 2005.

10 Father Gramolazzo told me that the International Association of Exorcists had been looking at the possibility of starting a training programme for many years as well, but had been unable to organize it.

11 Founded in 1941 in Mexico by Father Marcial Maciel, the Legionaries of Christ is currently one of the fastest-growing Catholic organizations in the world, with a presence in over twenty countries, and a large lay movement known as Regnum Christi. The Legion is mostly considered 'right wing' because it is dedicated to advancing the Church's social agenda as expressed by the Holy See. It has always been strongly supported by the Vatican, especially by Pope John Paul II. Liberals see the group as antithetical to the modernization that was ushered in by the Second Vatican Council. For more on the Legionaries go to: www.legionariesofchrist.org/

Chapter Three / Going Back to School

1 A concept developed by Saint Augustine, in his work *The City of God*, in which he contrasted the declining glory of the Roman Empire and its citizens' worldly pursuits to that which will be won by the inhabitants of the City of God, who shun all such earthly pleasures in favour of a spiritual path.

2: Four of Jesus's exorcisms are presented in great detail in the New Testament: (1) the man in the synagogue at Capernaum (Mark 1: 21–8; Luke 4: 33–6); (2) the Gerasene demoniac (Mark 5: 1–20; Matt. 8: 28–34; Luke 8: 26–39); (3) the Syrophoenician woman (Mark 7: 24–30; Matt. 15: 21–8); and (4) the epileptic boy (Mark 9: 14–29; Matt. 7: 14–21; Luke 9: 37–43).

3 Despite being labelled the Gerasene demoniac, Matthew locates the exorcism in the town of Gadara, closer to the Sea of Galilee than Gerasa is. Much has been made of the obvious exaggeration associated with this exorcism. For instance, in his book *Mary Magdalene*, Bruce Chilton

suggests 'Legion' is really a stand-in for Rome and all the 'evils' that the Roman Empire represented to the Jews at the time, pp. 38–40.

4 The Jews also believed in exorcism, as documented by the historian Flavius Josephus who lived in Palestine (*circa* 37–100). In one exorcism recounted by him, the Jewish exorcist Eleazar used a root attached to a sacred ring to draw out a demon though a person's nose, Josephus's *Antiquities* 8.46–8.

5 Jesus was charged by the Pharisees with invoking the name of Beelzebul, 'the chief of demons', also known as 'Beelzebub', which was tantamount to an accusation of witchcraft. Some scholars say the name 'Baal Zebub', meaning 'Lord of the flies' is actually a corruption of 'Baal Zebul', 'Lord in high places'. It is first used in 2 Kings 1: 2–16, to denote a foreign god. It has been reported by scholars that during the exorcisms of the time, certain exorcists did invoke Beelzebul's name (which according to the Christian tradition would have worked only in removing the appearance of an evil spirit, similar to a witch doctor performing a curse and then 'healing' the person by removing it). See Bruce Chilton's *Mary Magdalene*, p. 29; and *By the Power of Beelzebub: An Aramaic Incantation Formula from Qumran (4Q560)*, Douglas L. Penney and Michael O. Wise, pp. 627–50.

6 Irenaeus, writing in the second century CE (Christian Era) says, 'By invoking the name of Jesus Christ . . . Satan is driven out of men.' In his *Apology*, Tertullian writes: 'Let a person be brought before your tribunals, who is plainly under demonical possession. The wicked spirit, bidden to speak by a follower of Christ, will as readily make the truthful confession that he is a demon, as elsewhere he had falsely asserted that he is a god' (Chapter 23). And in his apologetical work, *Against Celsus*, Origen counters the pagan philosopher Celsus's view that Christian exorcisms are accomplished through magical rites, stating that 'the strength of the exorcism lies in the name of Jesus, which we pronounce while, at the same time, we announce the facts of his life.' Origen even claims that the name of Jesus is so powerful that a non-Christian can use it with success (as witnessed by the Jewish exorcists in the Gospel of Mark (9: 38–41).

7 In *The Prince of Darkness*, Jeffrey Burton Russell quotes Tertullian as saying, 'If the Son of God has appeared . . . to destroy the works of the Devil, he has destroyed them by delivering the soul through baptism.' Russell also notes that, until the year 200, baptism was preceded by a series of exorcisms that were separate from the rite itself, reflecting the belief of early Christians that the Devil had a hold over mankind thanks to original sin, p. 72. Among other things, Tertullian incorporated a

234

234234234234234234

234234234234

234

234

In addition, many critics of exorcism simply assume that all disease was attributed to the presence of 'evil spirits'. The Greek Hippocrates (460–377 BCE), for one, wrote in his treatise *The Sacred Disease* that mental illnesses have natural causes. About epilepsy, known as 'sacred disease' at the time, he wrote: 'It is not in my opinion, any more divine or more sacred than other diseases, but has a natural cause, and its supposed divine origin is due to men's inexperience, and to their wonder at its peculiar character', from *The Sacred Disease* I (W. H. S. Jones and E. T. Withington, *Hippocrates*, 4 vols, Loeb Classical Library, 1923).

14 Existentialism's emphasis on individual interpretation undercut the foundation for ontological truth, which Thomas Aquinas said formed the 'essence' of a thing. As John Nicola wrote in *Diabolical Possession and Exorcism*, 'Relativism in ethics urged the individual to judge the morality of a given act not on general principles of law but in its concrete moral milieu', p. 77. In this way, priests became less bound by tradition and more apt to follow their own interpretations.

15 'My dear brothers, never forget, when you hear *the progress of enlightenment* vaunted, that the devil's best trick is to persuade you that he doesn't exist!' *'Le Joueur généreux'*, pub. 7 February 1864; translation by Cat Nilan, 1999.

16 Father Daniel is a pseudonym.

17 For many years, it was used by Father Candido Amantini, a Passionist monk who was the chief exorcist in Rome during the 1960s–80s.

Chapter Four / Know Your Enemy

1 Evil is considered to be the lack of good that should otherwise normally be present in an object. Theology typically divides evil into two categories: physical and moral. Examples of a physical evil would be something harmful such as an accident, illness or disaster. But moral evil occurs when an individual knowingly makes a choice to commit an evil act. In the Church, moral evil is considered more base than a physical evil because it stems from the free-will choice of man. In other words, when we commit a moral evil, we intentionally commit that sin. For more, see *Catechism of the Catholic Church*, 309–14, pp. 91–3.

2 Thomas Aquinas writes in the *Summa Theologica*, 'Augustine says (De Civ. Dei xi, 50) that the angels were not passed over in that account of the first creation of things, but are designated by the name "heavens" or of "light". And they were either passed over, or else designated by the

names of corporeal things, because Moses was addressing an uncultured people, as yet incapable of understanding an incorporeal nature; and if it had been divulged that there were creatures existing beyond corporeal nature, it would have proved to them an occasion of idolatry, to which they were inclined, and from which Moses especially meant to safeguard them', *Summa Theologica* I, 61: 1.

3   Gabriele Nanni, *Il Dito di Dio e il Potere di Satatana: L'Esorcismo* (The Finger of God and the Power of Satan: Exorcism), p. 15.

4   Any number of books address this topic; see, for example, Jeffrey Burton Russell's books, *The Prince of Darkness*, p. 33, and *Satan, The Early Christian Tradition*, pp. 26–8; also, Edward Langton, *Essentials of Demonology: A Study of Jewish and Christian Doctrine, Its Origin and Development.*

5   The ancient world was rife with fear of demons. In addition to the Assyrians, the Babylonians also believed in a complex hierarchy of evil spirits. For instance there was *Pazuzu*, a god associated with the howling north winds who was responsible for leaching the soil and destroying crops. Another was *Lilitu* (an early forerunner of the witch of medieval tradition), a creature that was part human and part bird who 'roamed the night draining men of their bodily fluids'. See Jeffrey Burton Russell, *The Prince of Darkness*, pp. 15–16.

6   *Catechism of the Catholic Church*, 325, p. 95.

7   For more on Thomas Aquinas's extensive writings on the subject, see: *Summa Theologica* I, 50, 1; 14, 8; 19, 4.

8   Pie-Raymond Régamey, OP, *What is an Angel?* Translated from the French by Dom Mark Pontifex, pp. 20–1.

9   See the *Catechism of the Catholic Church* 391, p. 110.

10 Pope John Paul II, 'Creator of the angels who are free beings', Catechesis on the Angels, general audience, 23 July 1986, as published in *L'Osservatore Romano* weekly edition in English. One theologian says, 'Pure spirit is pure love . . . Love has created them and controls them; and their perfection consists in their likeness to God', Pie-Raymond Régamey, OP, *What Is an Angel?* Translated from the French by Dom Mark Pontifex, p. 42.

11 General audience by Pope John Paul II, on 23 July 1986, titled 'Creator of the Angels Who Are Free Beings', from the Global Catholic Network (EWTN) Web site.

12 Because of the exalted nature of the angels, once they sinned, they could never go back on their decision. Thomas Aquinas deals with this point extensively and equates the angelic fall with human death. 'Now it is

clear that all the mortal sins of men, grave or less grave, are pardonable before death; whereas after death they are without remission and endure for ever', *Summa Theologica* I, 64, 2.

13   From the online *Catholic Encyclopedia: The New Advent*: 'The *poena damni*, or pain of loss, consists in the loss of the beatific vision and in so complete a separation of all the powers of the soul from God that it cannot find in Him even the least peace and rest.'

14   There is no mention in the Bible of Satan being connected to Lucifer. In *Satan, The Early Christian Tradition*, Jeffrey Burton Russell notes that the association was most likely established by Origen when he linked the Prince of Tyre and the Dragon to Satan, pp. 131–3. According to Father Amorth, Lucifer is a very common name among demons, while Satan is rare. In Father Amorth's opinion, during an exorcism, if the eyes of the victim roll upwards, this signifies the presence of Lucifer or his army, while if they roll down it means that the person has been possessed by Satan or members of his army.

15   Pope John Paul II, in a general audience on 13 August 1986, taken from *L'Osservatore Romano* weekly edition in English.

16   The Council of Trent (1545–63) affirms this story as a dogmatic element of the Church. 'Let him be an anathema who does not admit that the first man, Adam, after having transgressed God's commandment, in the earthly paradise, immediately lost his holiness and the justice in which it had been established, and incurred, by committing such an offence, the wrath and indignation of God and subsequently death, with which God had previously threatened him, and with death, captivity under the dominion of him who, from that instant after that, had dominion over death, that is to say the Devil, and that Adam, by committing this offence, suffered a fall both in his body and his soul. From the Eternal World Television Web site 'The Council of Trent, Session V, June 17, 1546', http://www.ewtn.com/library/COUNCILS/TRENT5.HTM

17   For more, see Jeffrey Burton Russell's *Satan, The Early Christian Tradition*, p. 73; and *The Angels* by Pascal P. Parente, pp. 20–3.

18   *Catechism of the Catholic Church* 329, p. 96.

19   Thomas Aquinas addresses the intelligence of angels in the *Summa Theologica* I, 58, 1–7.

20   Thomas Aquinas says 'Only a being endowed with an intellect can act with a judgment which is free', *Summa Theologica* I, 59, 3.

21   In *Summa Theologica* I, 54, 3, Thomas Aquinas writes, 'An angel is called "intellect" and "mind", because all his knowledge is intellectual: whereas the knowledge of a soul is partly intellectual and partly sensitive.'

22 A. M. Lépicier, *The Unseen World*, p. 27, from *The Angels*, by Pascal P. Parente, p. 29.
23 Thomas Aquinas addresses this notion extensively in question I, 52, 1 of the *Summa Theologica*. 'A body is said to be in a place in such a way that it is applied to such place according to the contact of dimensive quantity; but there is no such quantity in the angels, for theirs is a virtual one. Consequently an angel is said to be in a corporeal place by application of the angelic power in any manner whatever to any place.'
24 Pascal P. Parente, *The Angels*, p. 38.
25 Preternatural is derived from the Latin *prætor* meaning 'beyond' the natural, as opposed to supernatural, which comes from the Latin *supra* meaning 'above' the natural. In this way, an angel's abilities are said to be beyond human understanding, though still falling within the confines of the natural world, while God's are above nature.
26 Thomas Aquinas writes: 'For even a man by doing what is beyond the power and knowledge of another, leads him to marvel at what he has done, so that in a way he seems to that man to have worked a miracle', *Summa Theologica* I, 114, 4.
27 Thomas Aquinas addresses this in the *Summa Theologica*, I, 57, 3. 'This manner of knowing future events exists in the angels, and by so much the more than it does in us, as they understand the causes of things both more universally and more perfectly.'
28 'It is a great mystery that providence should permit diabolical activity, but "we know that in everything God works for good with those who love him"' *Catechism of the Catholic Church* 395, p. 111. Thomas Aquinas called the Devil's work part of the natural order, 'In another way, indirectly, as when anyone assailed is exercised by fighting against opposition. It was fitting for this procuring of man's welfare to be brought about through the wicked spirits, lest they should cease to be of service in the natural order', *Summa Theologica* I, 64, 4.
29 Thomas Aquinas, *Summa Theologica* I, 114, 3.
30 It is important to note that according to the International Association of Exorcists (IAE), these categories do not constitute a sequence of events that leads automatically to possession, which some authors have suggested.
31 Born in Siena, Catherine was a mystic who was said to have received visions of Hell, Purgatory and Heaven. The Devil supposedly appeared to Catherine in various forms, including once as an angel of light, to tempt and assault her. She wrote extensively on the discernment of spirits.
   A powerful reformer of the Carmelite Order, Teresa was born in Avila,

Spain. Considered to be one of the foremost writers on mental prayer, Teresa later became one of only three women ever to be named as a doctor of the Church. A mystic, Teresa was troubled by demonic visions as well as physical attacks that she attributed to the Devil. Once, the Devil attacked her in the form of a small black 'creature' that she chased away with a jar of holy water.

The Curé d'Ars, John Vianney, was born near Lyons, France, in 1786. Patron saints of parish priests, Vianney was reputed to have a preternatural gift of knowing the past and future, and was also said to have a gift for healing. Vianney was also believed to be attacked by the Devil, who would harass him all night with shouts and loud noises and, in one famous incident, set his bed on fire. During the last ten years of his life, he spent between sixteen and eighteen hours a day in the confessional.

32 Francesco Bamonte, *Possessioni diaboliche ed esorcismo*, p. 76.
33 Anthropologists refer to demonic possession as being 'involuntary' so as not to confuse it with the various rituals in which a shaman or witch-doctor is said to invite a possession to take place (usually for the purpose of imparting knowledge or healing). The same also goes for the practice of glossolalia (speaking in tongues) in which individuals are said to be possessed by the Holy Spirit.
34 Father Amorth compares the cultural atmosphere of today to the decadence of the declining years of the Roman Empire.
35 This quote is taken from a personal interview with Italian exorcist Father Gabrielle Nanni. For more on Father Nanni, see Chapter Six.
36 Ibid., Father Gabriele Nanni. The person is not literally taken over by the demon, it is just that his actions comply with the demonic, i.e. he is full of pride, hate, rage, engages in illicit activity, crimes, etc. In this case, say exorcists, the demon does not need to make his presence known. It is only when the person wishes to turn his life around that the demon manifests to put a stop to that.

Chapter Five / Opening the Door
1 Jeffrey Burton Russell and Brooks Alexander, *A History of Witchcraft, Sorcerers, Heretics and Pagans*, p. 61. The authors write: 'Evidence that this [misinterpretation of Catharist doctrine] occurred comes from fourteenth century Italy, where heretics believed that the Devil created the material world. Since the Devil was the creator of the world, he was – more powerful than God, and should be worshipped in his place.'
2 For more on the Hellfire Club see Geoffrey Ashe's *The Hell-Fire Clubs*, 2001.

3   Pride, avarice, lust, wrath, envy, gluttony, and sloth.
4   Francesco Bamonte, *Possessioni diaboliche ed esorcismo*, p 46. A variant of the famous phrase 'Do what thou wilt' by Aleister Crowley, who called himself 'The Great Beast'.
5   According to author Michael Cuneo, a variety of factors contributed to this phenomenon, including, among other things, an explosion in charismatic-style deliverance ministries coinciding with the growth in psychotherapy that took place during the 1980s. A few scandalous testimonials – some later debunked as fabrications – such as *Michelle Remembers* by Michelle Smith, which detailed the horrors of ritual abuse, also fanned the flames. For more, see *American Exorcism* by Michael Cuneo, pp. 51–5, 195–209.
6   The McMartin preschool in Los Angeles was well covered in Paul and Shirley Eberle's The *Abuse of Innocence*, *The McMartin Preschool Trial* (1993); Debbie Nathan and Michael R. Snedeker's *Satan's Silence: Ritual Abuse and the Making of a Modern American Witch Hunt* (1995); and Jeffrey S. Victor's *Satanic Panic: The Creation of a Contemporary Legend* (1993).
7   The information in this section is complied from interviews with Fathers Francesco Bamonte, Gabriele Amorth, Gabriele Nanni, Giancarlo Gramolazzo, Françoise Dermine, Fra Benigno, Jeremy Davies and Carmine De Filippis.
8   *Patrologia graeca*, ed. P.J. Migne, LX, p. 293, from Corrado Balducci, *The Devil*, p. 119.
9   *Catechism of the Catholic Church* 2116, pp. 569–70.
10 In the Bible, Jesus rebukes his disciples James and John when they wish to 'bring down fire from heaven' in order to punish the Samaritans who refuse them hospitality. For more on this concept see: Francis MacNutt, *Deliverance from Evil Spirits*, pp. 97–119.
11 John Nicola, *Diabolical Possession and Exorcism*, p. 95.

Chapter Six / In My Name
1   Series 'Is It Real?' on exorcism, Episode 8, Season 1, 29 August 2005.
2   According to the *Catechism of the Catholic Church*, 'Sacramentals are sacred signs which bear a resemblance to the sacraments. They signify effects, particularly of a spiritual nature, which are obtained through the intercession of the Church',1667, p. 464. For more on sacramentals, see *Catechism of the Catholic Church* 1668–79, pp. 464–7.
3   *Catechism of the Catholic Church*, 1673, pp. 465–6.
4   Francis MacNutt, *Healing*, p. 167.

5   Praenotanda, No. 13, *De exorcismis et supplicationibus quibusdam*, trans-
    lated by Pierre Bellemare of Saint Paul University. Also number 1172 of
    the Code of Canon Law states that a potential exorcist should have piety,
    knowledge, prudence, and integrity of life.

6   Jeffrey Grob, unpublished dissertation 'A Major Revision of the
    Discipline on Exorcism: A Comparative Study of the Liturgical Laws in
    the 1614 and 1998 Rites of Exorcism', Saint Paul University, Ottawa,
    Canada, p. 53.

7   Jeffrey Grob, ibid., p. 54.

8   Charisms are said to be gifts bestowed by the Holy Spirit to devout indi-
    viduals, including such abilities as healing and discernment of spirits. For
    more on charisms, see Chapter Seven.

9   In his *Apologetics*, Tertullian added this practice, which some experts say
    is connected to the act of Jesus breathing on his disciples at Easter. For
    more, see *Apologetics 23.16; Tertullian: Apologetical Works and Minucius
    Felix: Octavius*, p. 74; 1, 415.

10 Jeffrey Grob, unpublished dissertation 'A Major Revision of the
    Discipline on Exorcism: A Comparative Study of the Liturgical Laws in
    the 1614 and 1998 Rites of Exorcism', Saint Paul University, Ottawa,
    Canada, p. 48.

11 Corrado Balducci, *The Devil*, translated by Jordan Aumann, OP, p. 167.

12 As early as the eleventh century, people began to augment the official
    formulas of the Church with their own gestures, incantations and even
    medicines. A general sense of superstition grew attached to the rite of
    exorcism, which fed into the already growing hysteria of the age, marked
    by an exaggerated fear of the Devil and witchcraft. Perhaps one of the
    most infamous cases illustrating the hysterical climate surrounding exor-
    cism during the sixteenth century was Marthe Brossier, a 25-year-old
    woman who alleged that her neighbour had bewitched her, causing her
    to become possessed. The neighbour was jailed and Brossier was paraded
    from village to village by her father – as a sort of travelling sideshow –
    and repeatedly exorcized in public. Jeffery Grob, ibid., p. 78. See also
    Sarah Ferber, *Demonic Possession and Exorcism in Early Modern France*, pp.
    40–59.

13 Though a number of people were involved in the process of compiling
    what would later come to be known as the *Ritual*, two stand out as having
    arguably contributed the most. The first was a Franciscan named
    Girolamo Menghi (1529–1609) born in Viadana, Italy, and considered to
    be one of the most important exorcists of the sixteenth century. Menghi's
    work, the *Flagellum daemonum* (Scourge of the Devil), contains seven

exorcism prayers as well as helpful advice for exorcists on discerning spirits. For more on Menghi, see *The Devil's Scourge*, Weiser Books, 2002. The second figure was Peter Thyraeus (1546–1601), a Jesuit from Germany who was instrumental in revising the criteria used for determining whether a person was possessed or not. Prior to Thyraeus, the signs used by exorcists to determine possession varied greatly from region to region. His most important work was *Daemoniaci, hoc est: de obsessis a spiritibus daemoniorum hominibus*, published in 1598. Thyraeus divided the signs of possession into two categories, those that are attributed to the intellect and those attributed to the body.

For this information, I am indebted to the research conducted by Father Jeffrey Grob, and his unpublished dissertation 'A Major Revision of the Discipline on Exorcism: A Comparative Study of the Liturgical Laws in the 1614 and 1998 Rites of Exorcism', Saint Paul University, Ottawa, Canada.

14 In 1952, Pope Pius XII released the new edition of the *Roman Ritual*, slightly updating some of the language in the criteria section pertaining to mental illness and psychology. In addition, the strictures on what constitutes demonic possession were loosened up. Where the original states, 'Signs of possession are the following . . .,' the revised language states, 'Signs of possession may be the following . . .' Considerable consternation followed the release of the 1998 *Ritual*, with Father Amorth perhaps the most vocal critic of the revision, characterizing it as watered down. Much less important, the order of the prayers was also reversed. In January 1999, a year after the *Revised Ritual* was released, the Congregation for Divine Worship and the Discipline of the Sacraments announced that, if requested by the diocesan bishop, it would grant a priest the permission to use the former rite of exorcism contained in the 1952 edition of the *Roman Ritual*. Many exorcists prefer to pray the older *Ritual* for a variety of reasons, some simply because they know the older *Ritual* by heart so don't have to read it. The 1998 *Ritual* has also gone through various revisions since it was released, the most recent in 2005 (Jeffrey Grob, ibid.).

15 In certain difficult cases where the presence of a demon may be hard to diagnose, some exorcists, including Father Amorth and Father Bamonte, prefer to use the deprecatory prayer as a tool for discernment. In addition, other exorcists might incorporate elements of the deprecatory prayer into spontaneous prayers of deliverance; not, however, the imperative formula.

16 In the Catholic tradition, for someone to be considered a candidate for canonization (sainthood), they first must pass through a series of steps,

the next to last of which is beatification. Essentially, when a candidate for sainthood (a person known for their holiness and sanctity of life) dies, the bishop of the candidate's diocese begins collecting documentation and testimonies associated with the individual (a period of five years must pass after the candidate's death before this process can officially begin). After this has happened, the Congregation for the Causes of Saints will then begin a formal investigation, looking into such things as the candidate's faith, the doctrinal purity of their writing, their humility, and especially if any miracles have been granted through their intercession. Candidates at this stage are awarded the title Servant of God. The postulator then collects this material and presents it to a council of nine theologians who must take a vote. For beatification, evidence must be presented of a miracle having been performed in the candidate's name after their death. For the candidate to become canonized, literally have their name written into the canon, there must be evidence of another miracle having been performed after their beatification took place. For more on this process, see 'New Laws for the Causes of Saints', Congregation for the Causes of Saints, 1983, www.vatican.va/roman_curia/congregations/csaints/index.htm

17   Praenotanda No. 19, *De exorcismis et supplicationibus quibusdam*, translated by Pierre Bellemare of Saint Paul University.

18   Gabriele Amorth, *An Exorcist Tells His Story*, pp. 79–80.

19   Father Nanni, *Il dito di Dio e il potere di Satana. L'esorcismo*, pp. 257–62.

20   Being threatened by demons is quite common, so much so that some exorcists have devised little 'tricks'. One exorcist prefers to recite Luke 10: 17–20 when intimidated: 'And the seventy returned again with joy, saying Lord, even the devils are subject unto us through thy name. And he said unto them, I beheld Satan like lightning falling from heaven. Behold, I give unto you power to tread on serpents and scorpions, and over all the powers of the enemy: and nothing shall by any means hurt you.'

21   For example, Somalis believe that evil spirits (jinns) often lie in wait to take possession of unsuspecting passersby. 'These malevolent sprites are thought to be consumed by envy and greed and to hunger especially after dainty foods, luxurious clothing, jewelry, perfume and other finery … . The prime targets for the unwelcome attentions of these malign spirits are women, and particularly married women', *Ecstatic Religion, A Study of Shamanism and Spirit Possession*, p. 67.

22   Gabriele Amorth, *An Exorcist Tells His Story*, pp. 194–5.

23   For its sheer level of hysteria, no book has perhaps surpassed Malachi

Martin's *Hostage to the Devil*, in which the author, a former Jesuit priest, describes in lurid prose the physical and spiritual dangers that await any priest who dares to perform this ministry. Numerous critics have cast doubt on the veracity of Malachi's claims, including even some of his disciples. In his book *People of the Lie*, psychiatrist M. Scott Peck, who credits Martin as one of his sources for his knowledge about exorcism, writes: 'From my experience I suspect Martin may have overemphasized the physical dangers [of exorcism].' M. Scott Peck, *People of the Lie*, p. 189.

Chapter Seven / Searching for an Exorcist

1   The church was once a part of the Lateran Palace. In the sixteenth century, Pope Sixtus V renovated the site and had the steps moved to their present location. Upon entering the building, the visitor is immediately faced with three flights of stairs, the one in the centre being the Holy Steps. The Sancta Sanctorum, which is protected by a large grille, and a small chapel are all located on the second floor.

2   Similar to Fatima in Portugal, six villagers at Medjugorje claim to have seen Mary on the mountainside daily since 1981. While the Catholic Church still has yet to make any kind of official statement as to the authenticity of the claims, the site has become a major pilgrimage destination on a par with other Marian sites. Many people have claimed to have their rosary beads turn to gold, or seen other strange lights. On a trip to Medjugorje in 1998, Father Gary, along with his parents, saw the sun spin (a common miracle associated with the site), though nothing similar happened this time.

3   Lumen Gentium, No. 12, from Gabriele Amorth, *An Exorcist Tells His Story*, p. 157.

4   Though the porch had to be rebuilt when the church, which was located next to a Nazi supply dump, was accidentally bombed during World War II by the Allies in 1943. More than 3,000 citizens were killed during the attack.

Chapter Eight / The First Night

1   Born in Pietrelcina, in the south of Italy, in 1887, Padre Pio became a Capuchin novice at sixteen and was later ordained in 1910. In 1920, Padre Pio was purported to have been kneeling in front of a crucifix when he received the stigmata. The blood from the wounds carried with it the particular scent of flowers and when he died, in 1968, they miraculously healed without leaving a mark. Padre Pio was also said to have

the ability to read the inner hearts of the people who confessed to him, and numerous miracles – such as bi-location (appearing in two places simultaneously) – were attributed to him. The gloves that Padre Pio wore to cover the stigmata were also said to effect miraculous cures. On more than one occasion during his life he was said to have fought with the Devil, who appeared to him in various forms – including a 'monstrous dog' with smoke billowing from its mouth – in order to torment him.

Chapter Nine / Discernment

1   Cognitive therapists use this rationale to illustrate how a person claiming to have multiple-personality disorder (MPD) might have that condition reinforced by a therapist who requires that an individual 'inhabit' these personalities through hypnosis and past-life regression. This in turn not only legitimizes those personalities in the person's mind, they say, but it can also create an 'alter' where none existed. As Nicholas Spanos points out, a majority of MPD cases (80 per cent in one study) do not enter therapy complaining about having more than one personality. It's because of this that Spanos says 'the procedures used to diagnose MPD often create rather than discover the multiplicity', *Multiple Identities & False Memories: A Sociocognitive Perspective*, p. 235. Another problem, according to academic psychiatrist Dr Richard Gallagher, is that a person suffering from a mental disease might not get the proper medical treatment if he is led to believe his problem is 'spiritual'.

2   No. 16 of the Praenotanda, *De exorcismis et supplicationibus quibusdam* (*DESQ*), translated into English by Pierre Bellemare of Saint Paul University.

3   No. 14 of the Praenotanda, *DESQ*, translated into English by Pierre Bellemare of Saint Paul University.

4   Matteo La Grua, *La preghiera di liberazione*, p. 70. 'Il discernimento è una "luce" particolare che ci fa vedere in Dio come stanno le cose.'

5   Wisdom, knowledge, faith, healing, working of miracles, prophecy, discerning of spirits, speaking in tongues, understanding tongues.

6   Teresa of Avila writes: 'The devil comes with his artful wiles, and, under colour of doing good, sets about undermining [the soul] in trivial ways, and involving it in practices which, so he gives it to understand, are not wrong; little by little he darkens its understanding, and weakens its will, and causes its self-love to increase, until in one way and another he begins to withdraw it from the love of God and to persuade it to indulge its own wishes', *Interior Castle*, 4. 4, 5.

Added to the impulses sent by spirits, theologians say, a person must take into consideration the state of the soul itself, especially because of the imperfections that have resulted from original sin. Concupiscence drives us towards committing 'sins of the flesh', while the higher functions of the soul, such as the intellect, receive graces from God that lead us back to goodness (Rom. 8: 5–8).

7   No. 16 of the Praenotanda, *DESQ*, translated into English by Pierre Bellemare of Saint Paul University.

8   The following information is based on personal interviews with exorcists.

9   Adolf Rodewyk, *Dämonische Besessenheit*, pp. 17–18, as quoted in Gabriele Nanni, *Il dito di Dio e il potere di Satana. L'esorcismo*, p. 272.

10 Gabriele Amorth, *An Exorcist Tells His Story*, p. 70.

11 If the demon does not manifest during the initial diagnosis but the exorcist suspects that he is present, then he will most likely advise the person to return to church, pray daily, receive the Eucharist as often as possible and, above all, go to confession. According to exorcists, if, after two months, the person continues to have problems but the demon has not manifested, then the cause is most likely 'natural'; therefore the person doesn't need an exorcism.

12 Francesco Bamonte, *Possessioni diaboliche ed esorcismo*, pp. 77–8.

13 Barry L. Beyerstein, 'Dissociative States: Possession and Exorcism', *The Encyclopedia of the Paranormal*, Gordon Stein (ed.), Buffalo, NY, Prometheus Books, 1995, pp. 544–52, reprinted on the Web site for Committee for Skeptical Inquiry, http://www.csicop.org/, p. 19.

14 David H. Gleaves, 'The Sociocognitive Model of Dissociative Identity Disorder: A Reexamination of the Evidence', *Psychological Bulletin*, Vol. 120, No. 1, 1996, p. 42. See also 'An Examination of the Diagnostic Validity of Dissociative Identity Disorder' by David H. Gleaves, Mary C. May, and Etzel Cardeña, *Clinical Psychology Review*, Vol. 21, No. 4, 2001, pp. 577–608.

15 Barry L. Beyerstein, 'Dissociative States: Possession and Exorcism', p. 3.

16 Dr Beyerstein was often quoted on the correlation between dissociation and demonic possession, and was interviewed on the History Channel among others. These comments by Beyerstein are taken principally from two sources, an article he wrote for *The Encyclopedia of the Paranormal* (1995), and two interviews conducted over the phone in the autumn of 2006. In the spring of 2007, Dr Beyerstein died unexpectedly of a heart attack.

17 For a summation of this position, read *An Examination of the Diagnostic Validity of Dissociative Identity Disorder* by David H. Gleaves, Mary C. May and Etzel Cardeña, 2001; and *Adult Psychopathology and Diagnosis*, fifth

edition, Chapter 13, 'Dissociative Disorders', by Etzel Cardeña and David H. Gleaves, 2007.

18   For a description of the sociocognitive perspective, read *Multiple Identities & False Memories: A Sociocognitive Perspective* by Nicholas Spanos, 1996.

19   Sociocognitive therapists point to statistics to illustrate that, before the book *Sybil* was published in 1973 and the TV movie staring Sally Field was released in 1976, there were only about 75 documented cases of MPD. Since the film's release there have been about 40,000 cases of MPD diagnosed, for the most part in North America.

The sociocognitive theory of how dissociation works offers the best answer about a number of phenomena associated with possession, including why the victim may not remember what transpired during an exorcism, and feel as if he or she had been taken over by an 'alien' presence. In explaining how this might work, Spanos compares the process to 'A stage actor who becomes immersed in his character [and who] tries to see the world the way his character would see it. The actor attempts to feel what his character would feel and to take on the mind-sets that his character would likely develop in different situations', *Multiple Identities & False Memories: A Sociocognitive Perspective*, p. 217.

20   Nicholas Spanos, ibid., p. 150.
21   Nicholas Spanos, ibid., pp. 150–1.
22   Nicholas Spanos, ibid., p. 171.
23   Nicholas Spanos, ibid., pp. 162–3.
24   Nicholas Spanos, ibid., p. 162.
25   Giuliana A. L. Mazzoni, Elizabeth F. Loftus, Irving Kirsch, 'Changing Beliefs About Implausible Autobiographical Events: A Little Plausibility Goes a Long Way', 2001.

Chapter Ten / Crossing Over
1   The woman's identity has been changed to ensure her anonymity.

Chapter Eleven / The Fall
1   Joseph Cardinal Bernardin, *Gift of Peace*, p. 47.

Chapter Twelve / Suffering of the Soul
1   Thomas Aquinas, *Summa Theologica* I, 52, 1.
2   Francesco Bamonte, *Possessioni diaboliche ed esorcismo*, p. 40.
3   Gabriele Amorth, *An Exorcist Tells His Story*, p. 97.
4   Father José Antonio Fortea, *Interview with an Exorcist*, pp. 66–7.

5   Gabriele Amorth, *An Exorcist: More Stories*, p. 11.
6   Herr name has been changed at her request to protect her anonymity.

Chapter Thirteen / A Pastoral Approach
1   Other exorcists have observed the unusual connection demons have
    with the senses of their victim. 'It is as if the demon, while possessing the
    body, feels whatever the bodily senses feel at a given moment. Whatever
    upsets the body also upsets the demon', José Antonio Fortea, *Interview
    with an Exorcist*, p. 69. In this way, however, the demon will also unwit-
    tingly reveal his presence, by reacting to the prayers of the exorcism.
2   Joshua Trachtenberg, *Jewish Magic and Superstition: A Study in Folk
    Religion*, p. 91. For more on names, see: Gabriele Nanni, *Il ditto di Dio e
    il potere di Satana. L'esorcismo*, p. 186; and S. Vernon McCasland's *By the
    Finger of God: Demon Possession and Exorcism in Early Christianity in the
    Light of Modern Views of Mental Illness*, pp. 96–109.
3   No. 14 in the guidelines of 1952 *Roman Ritual*.
4   Gabriele Amorth, *An Exorcist Tells His Story*, p. 112.

Chapter Fourteen / Windows to the Soul
1   Gabriele Amorth, *An Exorcist Tells His Story*, pp. 83–4.
2   Antonin-Gilbert Sertillanges OP, Catéchisme des incroyants I, 186, from
    Who Is the Devil? by Nicolas Corte, *The Twentieth Century Encyclopedia of
    Catholicism*, p. 88.
3   Pie-Raymond Régamey, OP, *What Is an Angel?* Translated from the
    French by Dom Mark Pontifex, p. 75.
4   Gabriele Amorth, *An Exorcist Tells His Story*, p. 194.
5   Teresa of Avila, *The Book of Her Life*, Chapter 25, p. 19, as quoted in
    Gabriele Amorth, *An Exorcist Tells His Story*, pp. 64–5.
6   *Catechism of the Catholic Church* 149, p. 46.
7   Father José Antonio Fortea, *Interview with an Exorcist*, p. 42.
8   Many people accuse the Catholic Church of practising idolatry in its
    veneration of Mary. The dogma of the Church is quite clear. Mary should
    be honoured for her service to God, but never worshipped. To establish
    a relationship with Mary, theologians say, is to be better united with Jesus
    Christ, who chose Mary as a partner to his earthly ministry. Pope Paul VI
    confirmed this when he said, in an address on 24 April 1970, 'If we want
    to call ourselves Christians we must be Marian, that is, we must recognize
    the essential, vital and providential relationship that unites Our Lady to
    Jesus, and that opens up a pathway to us that leads to him.'
         In one exorcism Father Bamonte recorded the demonic voice saying:

'Under the cross, she gathered with her hands the flooding blood [of Christ] and with those hands she prayed to God, she praised and thanked the Father, she forgave and loved the ones who nailed her son [to the cross] and said that she wanted to feel that pain to alleviate the pain of her son but she knew she couldn't and I suffered, I've never suffered that much.' Another time: 'We wanted to rejoice [at Christ being crucified] but instead she killed us with her crying; her tears are like fire that kills us.'

9   Giovanna is a pseudonym.

10 The name Pseudo-Dionysius denotes an unknown theologian who wrote in the late fifth or early sixth century CE. As a neo-Platonist, Dionysius synthesized elements of Greek philosophy, most notably the teachings of Plotinus and Proclus into a Christian worldview. The breadth of his knowledge suggests that he was a learned man (possibly a student of Proclus) who probably lived in Syria. Dionysius completed four major works, including *Divine Names*, *Celestial Hierarchies*, *Ecclesiastical Hierarchies* and *Mystical Theology*. Though rejected by some within the Church, the writings were later used during the Lateran Council (649) to defend certain tenets of the faith, and in the Middle Ages influenced important Scholastic writers like Peter Lombard and Thomas Aquinas.

11 Dionysius the Areopagite, *Celestial Hierarchies*, p. 3

12 Pie-Raymond Régamey, OP, *What is an Angel?* Translated from the French by Dom Mark Pontifex, p. 48.

13 While Satan is the leader of all the fallen angels, it is very rare for him to physically be present in a demonic possession. Most times, explain exorcists, he pulls the strings from afar, sending lesser demons to do his bidding. But occasionally Satan himself is present. Father Daniel believes he was in this instance because of the length and ferocity of the case.

Chapter Fifteen / Liberation

1   Any identifying traits have been changed to protect the victim's anonymity.

2   Father Matteo La Grua, *La preghiera di liberazione*, p. 105. 'Liberazion è un dono di Dio, e Dio può liberare quando vuole e come vuole, anche senza l'intervento dell'uomo e di intermediari umani.'

3   In Italy, a country that is predominantly Catholic, it may be difficult for non-Catholics to find an exorcist belonging to their particular religion. It is also true that many of the individuals who come to see an exorcist are generally people who don't practise their faith, and as such have no qualms about a Catholic priest praying over them. Since the Catholic

Church believes that the power of Jesus Christ can overcome all demons, the prayers are said to work regardless of the faith of the individual being prayed over.

All major religions believe in evil spirits and in some form of exorcism to cast them out. Islam specifies that people can become possessed by jinns, spirits that can be either good or bad. In order to cast out an evil jinn, the exorcist performs an official ceremony in which he reads passages from the Qur'an to the possessed person. In the Hindu tradition, numerous holy books contain ceremonies for casting out spirits, which is accomplished by reciting names of the Narasimha and reading from the *Bhagavata Purana* (scriptures) aloud. In Judaism, a dybbuk is a wandering soul said to have been turned away from Gehenna (hell), or to be too evil to be allowed to enter, which has the ability to attach itself to a living person. Erich Bischoff documents a Jewish possession and exorcism in the Middle Ages: 'The spirit was the soul of a drunken Jew, who died without prayer and impenitent. Having wandered for a long time it was permitted to him to enter into a woman as she was in the act of blaspheming, and since that moment the woman (an epileptic-hysteric) suffered terribly. Lurja speaks to the tormenting spirit and treats him as Christian exorcists treat the devil; he reprimands him, makes him tell his story, etc. By means of the "Name" he at length obliges him to come forth by the little toe of the possessed, which the spirit thus handled does with his habitual vehemence', from *Die Kabbalah, Einfuhrung in die jüdische Mystik und Geheimwissenschaft*, Leipzig, 1903, p. 87, as quoted in T. K. Oesterreich, *Possession Demonical and Other Among Primitive Races, in Antiquity, the Middle Ages, and Modern Times*, p. 185.

For more on Islamic and Jewish demonology, see T. Witton Davies's *Magic, Divination, and Demonology among the Hebrews and Their Neighbors*, pp. 95–130.

4 Father José Antonio Fortea, *Interview with an Exorcist*, p. 70.

5 Gabriele Amorth, *An Exorcist Tells His Story*, p. 113.

6 All details have been changed to protect the identity of the individual.

7 Father Bamonte believes that Beatrice's involvement in the occult opened her up to a curse placed on her while she was on vacation. During the exorcisms, her face would contort, with her lips turning black and sometimes curling inwards, seeming to disappear.

8 On p. 367 of their book *Varieties of Anomalous Experience: Examining the Scientific Evidence*, Stanley Krippner and Jeanne Achterberg cite a study done by Achterberg in 1985, titled 'Imagery and Healing', Boston: Shambhala.

9 In a documented case, a Filipino American woman whose lupus (a chronic autoimmune disease that can be fatal) had not responded to traditional medical treatment went into remission after visiting a Filipino healer, who claimed to have removed a curse put on her by a jealous lover. R. A. Kirkpatrick, 'Witchcraft and Lupus Erythematosus', *Journal of the American Medical Association*, 245, 1981, as cited in *Varieties of Anomalous Experience: Examining the Scientific Evidence*, Stanley Krippner and Jeanne Achterberg, p. 359.

Likewise, scores of studies have been done on people reporting cures being affected at the shrine of Lourdes, France: R. Cranston, *The Miracle of Lourdes*, New York: Popular Library, as cited by Stanley Krippner and Jeanne Achterberg, ibid., p. 363.

10 Stanley Krippner and Jeanne Achterberg, ibid., p. 359.

11 Steve Mizrach writes: 'It might also allow a person to integrate parts of his personality otherwise jeopardized by narrow social roles – a man's possession by *Erzulie* might allow him to "get in touch" with his "feminine side", so to speak. A quiet mousey woman who was told she had become Ogoun might find her "inner fierceness" after the experience'. 'Neurophysiological and Psychological Approaches to Spirit Possession in Haiti', http://www.fiu.edu/~mizrachs/spiritpos.html

12 I. M. Lewis, *Ecstatic Religion, A Study of Shamanism and Spirit Possession*, third edition, p. 47.

13 Schwartz and Begley, *The Mind and the Brain*, p. 84, as quoted in *The Spiritual Brain*, Mario Beauregard and Denyse O'Leary, p. 130.

14 E. Rodin, 'A neurobiological model for near-death experiences', 1989, as quoted by Bruce Greyson in *Varieties of Anomalous Experience: Examining the Scientific Evidence*, pp. 335–6.

15 As seen on the *Horizon* programme 'God on the Brain', aired on 17 April 2003 on BBC Two.

16 Bruce Greyson, *Varieties of Anomalous Experience: Examining the Scientific Evidence*, p. 337.

17 R. Strassman, 'Endogenous Ketamine-like Compounds and the NDE: If So, So What?' *Journal of Near-Death Studies*, 1997, p. 38; as quoted in *Varieties of Anomalous Experience*, p. 338.

18 John Haught, *Is Nature Enough? Meaning and Truth in the Age of Science*, Cambridge University Press, New York, 31 May 2006.

19 Mario Beauregard and Denyse O'Leary, *The Spiritual Brain*, p. 346.

20 Mario Beauregard and Denyse O'Leary, ibid., pp. 274–6.

21 From a forthcoming book by Dr Craig Isaacs, *Revelations and Possession: Distinguishing the Spiritual Experience from the Psychological*, pp. 67–8.

22 Dr Isaacs references the theories of John Weir Perry, as documented in
    Trials of the Visionary Mind, State University of New York Press, 1999, in
    which Perry evaluates five contending approaches to psychosis. Dr Isaacs
    summarizes them as 'a fear and mistrust of the disorder; viewing brain dis-
    orders as primarily causing psychosis; viewing psychosis as a disorganized
    and unnecessary emotional response to stimuli; a complete negation of
    existence of an inner life; and finally as a desire for quick fixes which
    leads to faulty theory'. In Perry's opinion, the first approach usually wins
    out and, as such, he claims that most theories are designed to 'suppress'
    the behaviour rather than to heal it. Dr Craig Isaacs, ibid., pp. 79–80.
23 Dr Craig Isaacs, ibid., p. 114.
24 Dr Craig Isaacs, ibid., p. 114

Chapter Sixteen / Organizing the Ministry
1   This number is based on estimates taken as of April 2006.
2   Up until the fourth century, when Christianity was officially recognized,
    secret Christians worshipped privately. Wealthy Roman citizens often
    turned their private residences into places of worship. Later these houses
    became known as 'titular churches', and each took the name of its owner.
    Paul mentions the *Titulus Priscae* in his letter to the Romans (Rom.
    16: 3–5).
3   Father Daniel continued his graduate studies in Rome. In 2006 he per-
    formed exorcisms for two years at a church in Rome before finally being
    relocated out of the country in 2008. He and Father Gary met once more
    in Rome in the autumn of 2007 as Father Daniel was preparing to leave
    for his new post.

Chapter Seventeen / The Exorcist
1   Any identifying traits have been changed to protect the couple's
    anonymity.
2   Any translation for the revised rite of exorcism must be officially approved
    by the Congregation for Divine Worship and the Discipline of the Sacra-
    ments. So far the only versions that have been approved are Latin and
    Italian. It would also fall to the American Bishops' Conference to request
    that such a translation be undertaken, which hasn't yet happened.
3   I have purposely kept the location of the exorcism vague.
4   This is one of the miracles that has been associated with Medjugorje, in
    Bosnia-Herzegovina.
5   The Charismatic Renewal is the name commonly given to Pentecostal-
    style groups, both Catholic and Protestant, that promote the belief that

special 'charismatic' gifts, such as speaking in tongues, prophecy, discernment of spirits, and healing, are imparted directly on to those believers who are baptized in the Holy Spirit. Chief among these gifts is the power to cast out evil spirits, a power held by all baptized individuals according to early Christians. Adherents practise a watered-down form of exorcism known as 'deliverance'. By the 1980s the movement had come to dominate the deliverance scene in America.

For more on the charismatic approach to deliverance see: Francis MacNutt, *Deliverance from Evil Spirits*, Chosen Books, twelfth printing, 2005; and Michael Scanlan, TOR, and Randall Cirner's *Deliverance from Evil Spirits*, Servant Books, 1980.

In the 1980s the Catholic hierarchy took steps to rein in the practice of deliverance. Most notably, in 1983, Cardinal Léon-Joseph Suenens of Belgium, a charismatic himself, wrote a report entitled *Renewal and the Powers of Darkness* in which he decried, among other things, the tendency he said of some charismatics to ascribe a majority of everyday problems to a demon – demon of impulsivity, demon of depression, demon of anxiety, and so on. In 1985, the Congregation for the Doctrine of the Faith, at that time headed by Cardinal Ratzinger, issued 'Instruction on Prayers for Healing', reminding bishops and lay people alike that solemn exorcism should be left to those priests nominated by the bishop.

6   I have removed identifying details in these cases to protect the identity of the individuals.

Author's Note

1   For more on spirit releasement, see William J. Baldwin, DDS, Ph.D., *Spirit Releasement Therapy: A Technique Manual*, 1992.

2   Numerous misguided individuals have turned the concept of casting out demons into murder. Among the most recent, in 1997, a five-year-old girl from the Bronx was killed when forced to drink a mixture of ammonia, pepper, olive oil, and vinegar by her mother and grandmother who then bound and gagged her with duct tape in an attempt, they said, to 'poison' the demon out of her. Michael Cooper, 'Mother and Grandmother Charged with Fatally Poisoning Girl', *New York Times*, 19 May 1997.

Then in November 2007, in a ceremony involving nearly forty people, a woman in New Zealand was drowned during an Anglican exorcism ceremony when a member of her 'healing group' held her under water in an attempt to drive out an evil spirit. Simon Winter, 'Exorcism Death Shocks Archdeacon', *New Zealand Herald*, 12 November 2007.

SELECTED BIBLIOGRAPHY

Books

Allen, John L., *All the Pope's Men: The Inside Story of How the Vatican Really Thinks*, New York, NY, Doubleday, 2004.

Allen, Thomas, *Possessed: The True Story of an Exorcism*, New York, NY, Doubleday, 1993.

Amorth, Gabriele, *An Exorcist Tells His Story*, N. MacKenzie (trans.), San Francisco, CA, Ignatius Press, 1999.

——, *An Exorcist: More Stories*, N. MacKenzie (trans.), San Francisco, CA, Ignatius Press, 2002.

Aquinas, Thomas, *Summa Theologiae*, J. Cunningham (trans.), Blackfriars series, vol. 57, London, Eyre & Spottiswoode, 1975.

——, *Summa Theologiae*, T. Gilby (trans.), Blackfriars series, vol. 59, London, Eyre & Spottiswoode, 1975.

Ashe, Geoffrey, *The Hell-Fire Clubs*, Gloucestershire, Sutton Publishing Ltd, 2005.

Athanasius: The Life of Antony and the Letter to Marcellinus, R. Gregg (trans.), New York, NY, Paulist Press, 1980.

Balducci, Corrado, *The Devil: Alive and Active in Our World*, J. Auman (trans.), Staten Island, NY, Alba House, 1990.

Baldwin, William, *Spirit Releasement Therapy: A Technique Manual*, second edition, Terra Alta, WV, Headline Books, Inc., 1992.

Bamonte, Francesco, *Cosa fare con questi maghi? Come liberarsi dalla superstizione e difendersi dai truffatori*, Milan, Ancora, 2000.

——, *Possessioni diaboliche ed esorcismo*, Milan, Figlie di San Paolo, 2006.

Bangley, Bernard, *Butler's Lives of the Saints*, Orleans, MA, Paraclete Press, 2005.

Baumeister, Roy, Ph.D., *Evil, Inside Human Violence and Cruelty*, New York, NY, Henry Hold and Company LLC, 1997.

Benigno, Fra, *Dalla filosofia all'esorcismo*, Associazione Rinnovamento nello Spirito Santo, Roma, 2006

Bernardin, Joseph Cardinal, *The Gift of Peace*, New York, NY, Doubleday, 1997.

Bultmann, Rudolf, *New Testament & Mythology, and Other Basic Writings*, Minneapolis, MN, Augsburg Fortress Publishers, 1984.

Buonaiuto, Aldo, *Le mani occulte: viaggio nel mondo del satanismo*, Rome, Italy, Città Nuova Editrice, 2005.

Cardeña, Etzel, Stephen Jay Lynn, Stanley Krippner, *Varieties of Anomalous Experience: Examining the Scientific Evidence*, Washington, DC, American Psychological Association, 2000.

Catechism of the Catholic Church, With Modifications from the Editio Typica, English translation, New York, NY, Doubleday, 1994.

Chadwick, Henry, *The Early Church*, revised edition, New York, NY, Penguin Books, 1993.

Chilton, Bruce, *Mary Magdalene*, New York, NY, Doubleday, 2005.

Clifton, Charles S., *Her Hidden Children, The Rise of Wicca and Paganism in America*, Landham, MD, AltaMira Press, 2006.

Codex Iuris Canonici, Auctoritate Ioannis Pauli PP. II promulgatus fontium annotatione et indice analytico-alphabetico auctus, Libreria editrice Vaticana, 1989. English translation Code of Canon Law, Latin-English Edition, New English Translation, prepared under the auspices of the Canon Law Society of America, Washington, DC, Canon Law Society of America, 1999.

Cole, Basil OP, *The Hidden Enemies of the Priesthood: The Contributions of St Thomas Aquinas*, Staten Island, NY, The Society of St Paul, Alba House, 2007.

Corte, Nicholas, *Who Is the Devil?* D. Pryce (trans.), *The Twentieth Century Encyclopedia of Catholicism*, Henri Daniel-Rops (ed.), New York, NY, Hawthorn Books, 1958.

Cozzens, Donald B., *The Changing Face of the Priesthood, A Reflection on the Priest's Crisis of Soul*, Collegeville, MN, The Liturgical Press, 2000.

Cristiani, Léon, *Evidence of Satan in the Modern World*, Tan Books and Publishers, Rockford, IL, 1977.

Cuneo, Michael, *American Exorcism: Expelling Demons in the Land of Plenty*, New York, NY, Doubleday, 2001.

Dante, *The Inferno*, translation by Robert Pinsky, New York, NY, Farrar, Straus and Giroux, 1994.

Davies, Stevan L., *Jesus the Healer: Possession, Trance, and the Origins of Christianity*, New York, NY, Continuum, 1995.

Davies, Thomas Witton, *Magic, Divination, and Demonology among the Hebrews and their Neighbors*, reprint of 1898 edition, Kessinger Publishing, Whitefish, Montana, 1997.

Davis, Winston, *Dojo: Magic and Exorcism in Modern Japan*, Stanford, CA, Stanford University Press, 1980.

Delbanco, Andrew, *The Death of Satan: How Americans Have Lost the Sense of Evil*, New York, NY, Farrar, Straus and Giroux, 1995.

Diagnostic and Statistical Manual of Mental Disorders, fourth edition, Michael B. First (editor), Washington, DC, American Psychiatric Association, 2000.

Dickason, Fred C., *Angels, Elect & Evil*, Chicago, IL, Moody Press, 1975.

Dolan, Monsignor Timothy M., *Priests for the Third Millennium*, Huntington, IN, Our Sunday Visitor Publishing Division, 2000.

Drane, John, *What Is the New Age Still Saying to the Church?* London, Marshall Pickering, 1999.

Eberle, Paul and Shirley, *The Abuse of Innocence: The McMartin Preschool Trial*, Amherst, NY, Prometheus Books, 2003.

Esorcismo e preghiera di liberazione, edited by the Instituto Sacerdos of the Ateneo Pontificio Regina Apostolorum in collaboration with the Gruppo di Ricerca e Informazione Socio-religiosa (GRIS), Rome, Italy, Edizioni Art, 2005.

Ferber, Sarah, *Demonic Possession and Exorcism in Early Modern France*, New York, NY, Routledge, 2004.

Ferguson, Everett, *Demonology of the Early Christian World*, symposium series, vol. 12, New York, NY, Edwin Mellen Press, 1984.

Fortea, Fr. José Antonio, *Interview with an Exorcist: An Insider's Look at the Devil, Demonic Possession, and the Path to Deliverance*, West Chester, PA, Ascension Press, 2006.

Gibson, David, *The Coming Catholic Church: How the Faithful Are Shaping a New American Catholicism*, New York, NY, Harper Collins, 2003.

Goodman, Felicitas D., *The Exorcism of Anneliese Michel*, Eugene, OR, Wipf and Stock Publishers, 1981.

Graf, Arturo, *The Story of the Devil*, translated from the Italian by Edward Noble Stone, New York, NY, MacMillan Company, 1931, Kessinger Publishing reprint.

Haddock, Deborah Bray, M.Ed., MA, LP, *The Dissociative Identity Disorder Sourcebook*, New York, NY, McGraw-Hill Books, 2001.

Hersen, Michael, Samuel M. Turner, Deborah C. Beidel, *Adult Psychopathology and Diagnosis*, fifth edition, Hoboken, NJ, John Wiley & Sons, Inc., 2007.

Huxley, Aldous, *The Devils of Loudun*, New York, NY, Harper Collins, 1952.

Josephus, Thackeray, H. St. John, Ralph Marcus (trans.), Vol. 5, Cambridge, MA, Harvard University Press, 1988.

Kaplan, Harold I. and Benjamin J. Sadock, *Synopsis of Psychiatry, Behavioral Sciences/Clinical Psychiatry*, tenth edition, Maryland, MD, Lippincott Williams & Wilkins, 2007.

Kelly, Henry Ansgar, *The Devil, Demonology and Witchcraft: The Development of Christian Beliefs in Evil Spirits*, Garden City, NY, Doubleday & Company, Inc., 1968.

——, *The Devil at Baptism: Ritual, Theology, and Drama*, Ithaca, NY, Cornell University Press, 1985.

Klass, Morton, *Mind over Mind: The Anthropology and Psychology of Spirit Possession*, Lanham, MD, Rowman & Littlefield Publishers, Inc., 2003.

La Grua, Matteo, *La preghiera di liberazione*, Palermo, Italy, Herbita editrice, 1985.

Lane, Anthony N. S., *The Unseen World, Christian Reflections on Angels, Demons and the Heavenly Realm*, Grand Rapids, MI, Paternoster Press and Backer Book House, 1996.

Langton, Edward, *Essentials of Demonology: A Study of Jewish and Christian Doctrine, Its Origin and Development*, London, Epworth Press, 1949.

——, *Satan, A Portrait: A Study of the Character of Satan through All the Ages*, Folcroft, PA, Folcroft Library Editions, 1974.

LeBar, Revd James J., *Cults, Sects, and the New Age*, Huntington, IN, Our Sunday Visitor Publishing Division, 1989.

Lecky, W. E. H., *History of the Rise and Influence of the Spirit of Rationalism in Europe, Part 1*, New York, NY, D. Appleton and Company, 1882, reprint, Kessinger Publishing, 2003.

Lewis, C. S., *The Screwtape Letters*, New York, NY, Harper Collins, 1942.

Lewis, I. M., *Ecstatic Religion: A Study of Shamanism and Spirit Possession*, third edition, New York, NY, Routledge, 2003.

Lynn, Steven Jay and Irving Kirsch, *Essentials of Clinical Hypnosis: An Evidence-Based Approach*, Washington, DC, American Psychological Association, first edition 2005.

MacNutt, Francis, *Deliverance from Evil Spirits: A Practical Manual*, Grand Rapids, MI, Chosen Books, 1995.

——, *Healing*, rev. and expanded, Notre Dame, IN, Ave Maria Press, 1999.

Martin, Malachi, *Hostage to the Devil: The Possession and Exorcism of Five Living Americans*, San Francisco, CA, Harper, 1992.

Mastronardi, Vincenzo M., Ruben de Luca, Moreno Fiori, *Sette sataniche*, Roma, Newton Compton editori, 2006.

McCasland, S. Vernon, *By the Finger of God: Demon Possession and Exorcism in Early Christianity in the Light of Modern Views of Mental Illness*, New York, NY, Macmillan Co., 1951.

Menghi, Girolamo, *The Devil's Scourge: Exorcism during the Italian Renaissance*, Gaetano Paxia (trans., intro. and ed.), York Beach, ME, Weiser Books, 2002.

Métraux, Alfred, *Voodoo in Haiti*, translation by Hugo Charteris, New York, NY, Schocken Books, 1959.

Michela, *Fuggita da Satana*, Casale Monferrato, Edizioni Piemme, 2007.

Morabito, Simone, *Psichiatra all'inferno*, Tavagnacco, UD, Italy, Edizioni Segno, 1995.

Nanni, Gabriele, *Il Dito di Dio e il Potere di Satana. L'esorcismo*, Città del Vaticano, Libreria Editrice Vaticana, 2004.

Nathan, Debbie and Michael R. Snedeker, *Satan's Silence: Ritual Abuse and the Making of a Modern American Witch Hunt*, New York, NY, Basic Books 1995.

Nicola, John, *Diabolical Possession and Exorcism*, Rockford, IL, Tan Books and Publishers, Inc., 1974.

Origen: Contra Celsum, H. Chadwick (trans.), Cambridge, University Press, 1953.

Osterreich, T. K., *Possession: Demonical and Other Among Primitive Races in Antiquity, the Middle Ages, and Modern Times*, D. Ibberson (trans.), New Hyde Park, NY, University Books, 1966.

Oxford Dictionary of the Christian Church, F. L. Cross and E. A. Livingstone (editors), New York, NY, Oxford University Press, 2005.

Parente, Fr. Pascal P., *The Angels*, Rockford, IL, Tan Books and Publishers, Inc., 1961.

Peck, Scott, *People of the Lie: The Hope for Healing Human Evil*, New York, NY, Simon & Schuster, 1983.

Pseudo-Dionysius: The Complete Works, Froehlich, Karlfried, Leclercq (trans.), Mahwah, NJ, Paulist Press, 1987.

Régamey, Pie-Raymond OP, *What Is an Angel? The Twentieth Century Encyclopedia of Catholicism*, New York, NY, Hawthorn Books, 1960.

Rodewyk, Adolf, *Possessed by Satan: The Church's Teaching on the Devil, Possession, and Exorcism*, M. Ebon (trans.), Garden City, NY, Doubleday, 1975.

Roman Ritual: Complete Edition, P. Weller (trans.), Milwaukee, WI, Bruce Publishing Company, 1964.

Russell, Jeffrey Burton, *Witchcraft in the Middle Ages*, Ithaca, NY, Cornell University Press, 1972.

——, *The Devil: Perceptions of Evil from Antiquity to Primitive Christianity*, Ithaca, NY, Cornell University Press, 1977.

——, *Satan: The Early Christian Tradition*, Ithaca, NY, Cornell University Press, 1981.

——, *Lucifer: The Devil in the Middle Ages*, Ithaca, NY, Cornell University Press, 1984.

——, *Mephistopheles: The Devil in the Modern World*, Ithaca, NY, Cornell University Press, 1986.

——, *The Prince of Darkness: Radical Evil and the Power of Good in History*, Ithaca, NY, Cornell University Press, 1988.

Russell, Jeffrey Burton, and Alexander Brooks, *A History of Witchcraft, Sorcerers, Heretics and Pagans*, second edition, London, UK, Thames & Hudson, 2007.

Salvucci, Raul, *Cosa Fare Con Questi Diavoli? Indicazioni pastorali di un esorcista*, Milan, Italy, Ancora Editrice, 1992.

Satan, Bruno de Jesus-Marie (ed.), New York, NY, Sheed & Ward, 1952.

Scanlan, Michael, TOR, and Randall Cirner, *Deliverance from Evil Spirits: A Weapon for Spiritual Warfare*, Cincinnati, OH, St Anthony Messenger Press, 1980.

Shapiro, Francine, Margot Silk Forrest, *EMDR: The Breakthrough 'Eye Movement' Therapy for Overcoming Anxiety, Stress, and Trauma*, New York, NY, Basic Books, 1997.

Sharp, Lesley A., *The Possessed and the Dispossessed: Spirits, Identity, and Power in a Madagascar Migrant Town*, Berkeley, CA, University of California Press, 1993.

Spanos, Nicholas, *Multiple Identities & False Memories: A Sociocognitive Perspective*, Washington, DC, American Psychological Association, 1996.

St Augustine, *City of God*, Vernon J. Bourke (editor), Gerald C. Walsh, Demetrius B. Zema, Grace Monahan, and Daniel J. Honan (trans.), Garden City, NY, Image Books/Doubleday, 1958.

St Justin Martyr: The First and Second Apologies, L. Barnard (trans.), Ancient Christian Writers, no. 56, Mahwah, NJ, Paulist Press, 1997.

Suenes, Léon-Joseph, *Renewal and the Powers of Darkness*, O. Prendergast (trans.), Ann Arbor, MI, Servant Books, 1983.

Synan, Vinson, *The Century of the Holy Spirit: 100 Years of Pentecostal and Charismatic Renewal*, Nashville, TN, Thomas Nelson Publishers, 2001.

Tertullian: Apologetical Works and Minucius Felix: Octavius, R. Arbesmann, E. Daly, and E. Quain (trans.), *The Fathers of the Church*, vol. 10, New York, NY, Fathers of the Church, Inc., 1950.

Turch, Michael E. M., *Considering a Career in Mortuary Science*, West Hartford, CT, Graduate Group, 1995.

Victor, Jeffrey S., *Satanic Panic, the Creation of a Contemporary Legend*, Chicago, IL, Open Court Publishing, 1993.

Vogl, Carl, *Begone Satan! A Soul-Stirring Account of Diabolical Possession*, C. Kapsner (trans.), Rockford, IL, Tan Books and Publishers, Inc., 1973.

Walker, Daniel P., *Unclean Spirits: Possession and Exorcism in France and England in the Late Sixteenth and Early Seventeenth Centuries*, London, Scolar Press, 1981.

Articles and Other Sources

Allison, Ralph B., 'The Possession Syndrome on Trial', *American Journal of Forensic Psychiatry*, Vol. VI, No. 1, 1985, pp. 46–56.

——, 'If in Doubt, Cast It Out? The Evolution of a Belief System Regarding Possession and Exorcism', submitted to the *Journal of Psychology and Christianity*, April 1999.

Beck, J. and G. Lewis, 'Counseling and the Demonic: A Reaction to Page', *Journal of Psychology and Theology*, 17 (1989), pp. 132–4.

Beyerstein, Barry L., 'Dissociative States: Possession and Exorcism', *The Encyclopedia of the Paranormal*, Gordon Stein (ed.), Buffalo, NY, Prometheus Books, 1995, pp. 544–52.

Collins, James, MA, 'The Thomistic Philosophy of the Angels', Washington, DC, *The Catholic University of America Philosophical Studies*, Vol. 89, 1947.

Congregation for Divine Worship and the Discipline of the Sacraments, Decree *Inter sacramentalia*, in *Notitiae*, 35 (1999), p. 137.

——, Notification, *De ritu exorcismi*, 27 January 1999, in *Notitiae*, 35, 1999, p. 156.

——, *De exorcismis et supplicationibus quibusdam*, editio typica, Vatican City, Typis Vaticanis, 1999.

——, *De exorcismis et supplicationibus quibusdam*, editio typica emendata, Vatican City, Typis Vaticanis, 2004.

Congregation for the Doctrine of the Faith, Instruction on Prayers for Healing *Instructio de orationibus*, 14 September 2000, in *Notitiae*, 37 (2001), pp. 20–34; English translation ibid., pp. 51–65.

Congregation for the Doctrine of the Faith, Letter, *Inde ab aliquot annis* [On the Current Norms Governing Exorcisms], 29 September 1985, in *Acta Apostolicae Sedis*, 77 (1985), pp. 1169–70, English translation in *Canon Law Digest*, vol. 11, pp. 276–7.

Ferrari, Giuseppe, 'Phenomenon of Satanism in Contemporary Society', *L'Osservatore Romano*, 29 January 1997.

Gleaves, David H., 'The Sociocognitive Model of Dissociative

Identity Disorder: A Reexamination of the Evidence', *Psychological Bulletin*, Vol. 120, No. 1, 1996, pp. 42–59.

Gleaves, David H., Mary C. May, Etzel Cardeña, 'An Examination of the Diagnostic Validity of Dissociative Identity Disorder', *Clinical Psychology Review*, Vol. 21, No. 4, 2001, pp. 577–608.

Grob, Jeffrey S., 'A Major Revision of the Discipline on Exorcism: A Comparative Study of the Liturgical Laws in the 1614 and 1998 Rites of Exorcism', Ontario, Canada, Saint Paul University, 2006.

Halligan, Revd Nicholas, OP, 'What the Devil!' *This Rock*, November 1995.

Hauke, Manfred, 'The Theological Battle over the Rite of Exorcism: "Cinderella" of the New *Rituale Romanum*', in *Antiphon*, 10, no. 1 (2006), pp. 32–69.

Henneberger, Melinda, 'A Priest Not Intimidated by Satan or by Harry Potter', *New York Times*, Art's Abroad, 1 January 2002.

Hyland, Michael E., Ben Whalley, Adam W. A. Geraghty, 'Dispositional Predictors of Placebo Responding: A Motivational Interpretation of Flower Essence and Gratitude Therapy', *Journal of Psychosomatic Research* 62, 2007, pp. 331–40.

'Interview with Carlo Climati: When Young People Fool with Satanism', Rome, *Zenit*, 11 September 2001.

James, Susan Donaldson, 'People Need Both Drugs and Faith to Get Rid of Pain', ABC News, 1 August 2007, ABC News Internet Ventures.

John Paul II, general audience, 'La caduta degli angeli ribelli, August 13, 1986', in *Insegnamenti di Giovanni Paolo II*, vol. 9, Vatican City, Libreria editrice Vaticana, 1986, pp. 361–6, English translation in *L'Osservatore Romano*, 19, No. 33, 1986, pp. 1–2.

John Paul II, general audience, 'La vitttoria di cristo sullo spirito del male, 20 August 1986', in *Insegnamenti di Giovanni Paolo II*, vol. 9, Vatican City, Libreria editrice Vaticana, 1986, pp. 395–8, English translation in *L'Osservatore Romano*, 19, No. 34, 1986, pp. 1–2.

Langley, M., 'Spirit-Possession, Exorcism and Social Context: An Anthropological Perspective with Theological Implications', *Churchman*, 94 (1980), pp. 226–45.

Lilienfeld, Scott O. et al., 'Dissociative Identity Disorder and the Sociocognitive Model: Recalling the Lessons of the Past', *Psychological Bulletin*, 125, 5, 1999, pp. 507–23.

Macchitella, Sara, 'Italy Rocked by Satanic, Drug-Induced Sexual Abuse in Kindergarten', *Malta Star*, 28 April 2007.

Mayaram, Shail, 'Recent Anthropological Works on Spirit Possession', *Religious Studies Review*, 27 (2001), pp. 213–22.

Mazzoni, Giuliana A. L., Elizabeth F. Loftus, Irving Kirsch, 'Changing Beliefs about Implausible Autobiographical Events: A Little Plausibility Goes a Long Way', *Journal of Experimental Psychology*, Vol. 7, No. 1, 51–9, March 2001.

Medina Estévez, J., 'Il Rito degli Esorcismi, 26 January 1999', *Notitiae*, 35, 1999, pp. 151–5, English translation in *L'Osservatore Romano*, 32, No. 5, 1999, p. 12.

National Conference of Catholic Bishops, 'New Rite of Exorcism', *Committee on the Liturgy Newsletter*, 35 1999, pp. 58–60. National Conference of Catholic Bishops.

New Advent Catholic Encyclopedia (online version), Kevin Knight, 2008, http://www.newadvent.org/

Nicola, John J., 'Is Solemn Public Exorcism a Viable Rite in the Modern Western World? A Theological Response', exerpta ex dissertatione ad Doctoratum in Facultate Theologiae Pontificiae Universitatis Gregorianae, Washington, DC, 1976.

Paci, Stefano, 'The Smoke of Satan in the House of the Lord: An Interview with Rome's Exorcist, Father Gabriele Amorth', in *30 Days*, 19, no. 6, 2000, pp. 52–9.

Paul VI, address, *Liberaci dal male*, 15 November 1972, in *Insegnamenti di Paolo VI*, vol. 10, Vatican City, Tipografia poliglotta Vaticana, 1972, pp. 1168–73, English translation in *The Pope Speaks*, 17, 1973, pp. 315–19.

Penney, Douglas L. and Michael O. Wise, 'By the Power of Beelzebub: An Aramaic Incantation Formula from Qumran (4Q560)', *Journal of Biblical Literature*, Vol. 113, No. 4 (Winter 1994), pp. 627–50.

Pisa, Nick, 'Hitler and Stalin Were Possessed by the Devil, says Vatican Exorcist', *Daily Mail*, London, 28 August 2006.

——, 'Italian Priests Join the War on Satanic Crime', *Sunday Telegraph*, 8 January 2007.

——, 'Pope's Exorcist Squads Will Wage War on the Devil', *Daily Mail*, London, 29 December 2007.

Sacred Congregation for the Doctrine of the Faith, 'Christian Faith and Demonology', 10 July 1975, *L'Osservatore Romano*, pp. 6–9.

Taylor, A., 'Possession or Dispossession?' in *Expository Times*, 86, 1974–5, pp. 359–63.

Van Slyke, D., 'The Ancestry and Theology of the Rite of Major Exorcism, 1999/2004', in *Antiphon*, 10, No. 1, 2006, pp. 70–116.

'Why Another Course on Exorcism and Satanism', Rome, *Zenit*, 9 September 2005.

INDEX

Matt Baglio is a freelance writer and journalist living in Rome. Over the years he has worked for a variety of magazines and news organizations including the Associated Press, the *International Herald Tribune*, the *American Magazine* and *Colors*. *The Rite* is his first book.